# Good Homemaking

Melita Neal
Jean James

BLACKIE

© Melita Neal and Jean James 1983
First published 1983

ISBN 0 216 91377 2

BLACKIE & SON LTD
Bishopbriggs, Glasgow G64 2NZ
Furnival House
14–18 High Holborn, London WC1V 6BX

Printed in Great Britain by
Bell and Bain Ltd, Glasgow

# Contents

**1 Somewhere to Live** ——————————————— 1

Types of accommodation — Finance and mortgages —
Technical terms — Moving house — FURTHER STUDY

**2 House into Home** ——————————————— 11

Furniture and upholstery — Floor coverings — Treatment
of walls — Curtains — Blinds — Cushions — FURTHER
STUDY

**3 Heating and Lighting your Home** ——————— 41

Heating — Insulation — Cookers — Ventilation —
Lighting — FURTHER STUDY

**4 Running a Home** ——————————————— 69

Organization — Methods of cleaning — Labour-saving
equipment — Home maintenance — FURTHER STUDY

**5 People at Home** ——————————————— 89

Members of the family — Government services: the National
Health Service, the education service — Social and welfare
services — Leisure services — Voluntary organizations —
Pets in the home — Flowers and plants in the home —
FURTHER STUDY

**6 Catering for the Family** ——————————— 109

Kitchen planning and equipment — Nutrition —Entertaining — Buying food — FURTHER STUDY

**7 Budgeting and Spending** ——————————— 141

Money management — Effects of advertising — Consumer
rights — Methods of shopping — FURTHER STUDY

**8 Finance** ——————————————————— 154

Banking — Saving — Credit — FURTHER STUDY

## 9 The Family Wash — 164

Methods — Detergents — Laundering procedure — Dry cleaning — Stain removal — FURTHER STUDY

## 10 Safety in the Home — 190

Government legislation — Safeguards — Accidents — First aid — Home nursing — FURTHER STUDY

## 11 Services to the Home — 209

Gas — Electricity — The telephone — Water — Sewage disposal — Waste water disposal — Dry refuse disposal — The Post Office — Special services — FURTHER STUDY

## 12 Healthy Living — 234

Hygiene — Looking good and feeling good — Social habits — Health foods — General economies — FURTHER STUDY

## Useful Information — 252

Metric weights and measures — Oven temperature scales

## Index — 254

# Somewhere to Live 1

'A place of my own'—once a rosy dream for those hoping to be married or a customary perquisite of the rich; now, owing to the rapid and extreme changes in our social structure, a real possibility for young people who are developing a keen desire and, indeed, a need, to become independent. Even the latter stages of school life are coloured by the possibility, not to say the inevitability, of having to make decisions about, cope with and be happy in a home of your own making. A fairly common pattern is now emerging of the fledgling teenagers leaving a family home in which they have been perfectly content, in order to spread their wings freely in rented accommodation initially shared with their friends and later with their chosen partners, usually with home *ownership* as an ultimate goal. As always, however, freedom is accompanied by its own responsibilities and much thought has to be given to the choice and considerations which must be faced before making decisions which could result in the difference between happiness and disaster. Let us, then, consider these questions:

1 How much can you afford?
This is *the* most important factor in deciding the type of accommodation you can consider, and will naturally depend upon your wages or salary, your savings and whatever help you are able to count on from your family or the recognized financial-aid societies. Remember that the basic rent or mortgage is not the extent of your out-going expenses— you still have to pay rates, keep warm, feed yourself and be adequately clothed!

2 What types of accommodation are available?
a) Should you be entering a university, a polytechnic or similar educational establishment, non-financial advice will undoubtedly be available from the respective accommodation officers, who will be prepared to recommend suitable rooms. The quality of these will be a very important factor in your student life so be careful to check the heating, lighting, storage space, laundry and cooking facilities available, as well as the comfort and adequacy of the furniture. It is wise, too, to verify the financial arrangements involved, particularly if rooms are to be shared. Economic disagreements have ended many beautiful friendships!

b) Young people travelling to London in search of work and with no immediate prospect of lodging *may* be accommodated in one of the limited number of hostels allocated solely for the unemployed, although these must be regarded as temporary shelters only.

c) Certain types of employment, such as nursing, farming, the Armed Forces, the restaurant and hotel services supply 'live-in' facilities either as part of the respective remuneration or at a nominal fee automatically deducted from it. Although this is often a short-term arrangement it will still be 'your' temporary home and must be cared for as such. At a later stage, a career as a teacher, a publican or a bank manager can mean having to move to different areas with the job and often help is available in procuring accommodation on a 'tiding-over' basis until more permanent arrangements are made.

d) The most modest independent dwelling place must go with the lowest income and may be merely a lodging in a household in which you are almost one of the family, but with your own bedroom, and no responsibilities other than your rent and board to pay. Privately rented accommodation such as this is usually found through advertisements in newspapers or by word of mouth and is often difficult to obtain.

It might be possible to rent a furnished or unfurnished room or two in a house (rents are obviously higher for furnished rooms). The landlord must supply you with a rent book to record payment or lapses in payment. Also, check your obligations for rates, insurance and maintenance arising from such a tenancy. In their offices, local authorities keep a register of fair rents which is available to the public. Before agreeing to rent accommodation always view the premises, make sure that everything is in order and ask the landlord to have any repairs carried out. Tenancy is legal without a written contract but if you are asked to sign an agreement outlining your obligations as a tenant, read it carefully before signing. If in doubt, see a solicitor or consult the Citizens' Advice Bureau.

e) Should you or a group of friends be able to afford self-contained accommodation, you have the choice of a flat, a maisonette (one floor of a two-storey building), a house or a bungalow (either of which may be terraced, semi-detached or detached). Any of these may be owned privately or by the Local Authority, the former either rented or purchased outright, the latter usually being rented. When two or more people decide to share rented accommodation they should establish a joint tenancy to ensure protection under the Rent Act.

Before considering the relative advantages of buying or renting your property it is well to remember:

> *Freehold* is a term used to define the status of a property, the owner possessing both the land and the building on it. (This term is no longer used in Scotland, *feu* being the nearest equivalent.) Both exterior and interior maintenance is the responsibility of the owner.

*Leasehold* is a form of tenancy under which ground rent is paid to the owner of the land or buildings for a specified number of years (often 99). At the end of the period the ownership of the property reverts back to the landlord. Mortgages are more difficult to obtain on leasehold than on freehold property. Exterior decoration and maintenance is the responsibility of the landlord but a maintenance charge is included in the conditions of tenancy. Interior matters are in the hands of the tenant.

3 What are the advantages and disadvantages of moving into a flat?

| Advantages | Disadvantages |
|---|---|
| a) Usually cheaper to buy than a house. | a) Sometimes difficult to obtain a mortgage. |
| b) Smaller, easier to clean than a house. | b) Less spacious than a house. |
| c) Other people within easy reach. | c) Neighbours (above and below) may be noisy. |
| d) No private garden to maintain. | d) May be a service charge to cover communal areas, maintenance, gardens, etc. |
| c) Heating often installed. | e) No choice of heating. |
| f) Heating bills usually lower than for a house. | f) Lack of garage or position of garage space may affect insurance premiums. |
| | g) Lifts may present problems. |
| | h) May be restrictions on keeping pets. |

You should note that most flats are leasehold and the resale value depreciates towards the end of the lease.

In leasehold property there is a clear and binding agreement as to who is responsible for repairs and maintenance. Responsibility for the care and maintenance of, for example, communal stairs and landings in freehold property is not always stated in the legal documents and this information is required by the mortgage lender.

4 What is a council house?

All local authority councils have certain housing responsibilities. Estates of council houses or flats are usually easily recognizable by their uniformity and these dwellings are available to those who choose to rent such accommodation or have difficulty in obtaining a home by any other means. The council is obliged to provide housing for the genuinely homeless but this may be on a 'bed and breakfast' basis or in old empty properties. Otherwise, names go on a waiting list (at 17 years of age, although they are not considered until the applicants reach the age of 18) and often a points system is used to qualify applicants for council accommodation. Points are awarded according to such factors as length of residence in the area, number of children and degree of present overcrowding. Rents are normally lower than for private accommodation and usually an inclusive charge for rent, rates and possibly heating is levied. Essential repairs and maintenance are the responsibility of the local authority. Enquiries should always be made initially with the Housing Department of this authority.

5 Is it worth while to buy a house or flat?

The purchase of your own property will almost certainly be the largest financial outlay of your life and needs much consideration. Providing that you expect to stay in the same locality for several years it is money well spent, being a transferable asset which normally will appreciate in value. Moreover, it is a comforting thought that at some stage in your life you will be the owner of property. So go carefully into the following factors:

a) *Finance:*
   How much can you afford and how much can you borrow? (See Chapter 8.)
b) *Size:*
   Is there the possibility of the family enlarging? Do you need a garage?
c) *Area:*
   Do you like the district and is it sufficiently close to open spaces to please you?
d) *Transport:*
   Are there convenient bus and train services to enable you to reach your work if you do not possess or may be without a car?
e) *Services:*
   Are there desirable schools, shops and facilities for social life within a convenient distance?

   First-time buyers will almost certainly require a loan in order to buy a property and usually this can be obtained by taking out a mortgage through:
a building society;
the local authority;
a bank;
an insurance company.

6 How much can you borrow?

a) Mortgages are based mainly on:
your age;
your income;
the type and age of the property you wish to buy.
b) Most lenders base the loan on your gross basic pay so overtime and bonuses are disregarded.

c) Loans to couples are based on the higher of the two incomes, although it is possible for an allowance to be made for the second income under some circumstances.

d) You can borrow multiples of $2-2\frac{1}{2}$ times your yearly income (before tax) on a mortgage to be repaid over 25 years. Some lenders will offer 95%–100% of the price of a new home. Local authorities will allow 100% mortgages and some larger building societies and banks will do so if the loan required is under £20,000.

7 What types of mortgage are available?
See Table 1 on page 6.

The Government offers a special scheme for first-time buyers. Providing that you have been saving for at least two years and have at least £600 in your savings account with a recognized savings institute that is taking part in the Government scheme (these include building societies, banks, Trustee Savings Banks, Friendly Societies, the National Girobank, the National Savings Bank and the Ulster Bank), there are two benefits available:
a cash bonus of up to £110 (depending on the amount you have saved);
a loan of £600 which can be put towards your mortgage loan.

Here is an example of the second benefit:
> You are buying a home priced at £15,000 and are offered a mortgage of £13,000. You would normally have to find the difference of £2,000, but with the extra loan you have only to find £1,400. Moreover, you will not normally have to pay any interest on that £600 for five years.

Some building societies have schemes which guarantee you a mortgage after saving with them for at least two years. (Information is available from your local Citizens' Advice Bureau or in *Building Societies and House Purchase* published by the Building Societies Association.)

Most banks, insurance companies and building societies allow their employees to take out mortgages at reduced rates after having been in their employ for a specified number of years.

8 What people do you need to know?
a) *Estate agents:*
> In buying, selling or letting property an agent is not essential but can be helpful. Their commission rates vary and some will be more enterprising than others in arranging photographs and advertisements. VAT is always added to the stated fees. It is advisable to go to accredited agents (i.e. those belonging to professional associations, indicated by the letters following their names—RICS, ISVA, NAEA).

b) *Surveyors:*
> Building societies will send their own surveyor to inspect the property for which you want to borrow money, to ensure that their

TABLE 1: TYPES OF MORTGAGE AVAILABLE

| Type | Availability | Advantages | Disadvantages | Tax Relief? |
|---|---|---|---|---|
| 1 Repayment | From building societies, local authorities, banks. Good for first-time buyers. | Cheapest type in early years. Paid off in monthly instalments which include the interest. During the first few years the monthly premiums mainly pay off the interest. | Interest fluctuates with economic pressures but steep rises can be offset with extended repayment period. A cheap protection insurance should be taken out to safeguard the home in the event of the mortgagee dying before the mortgage is paid off. | Yes, on the interest only, which decreases year by year as the original loan is paid off. |
| 2 Endowment | From building societies, insurance companies, banks. Not recommended for first-time buyers. | Advantageous to high taxpayer: tax rebate is constant, as is the interest. An endowment policy is linked in. 'With profits' mortgage is available in which the lender accrues profits from investing your money. Gives you a little 'nest egg' when the mortgage is paid off. | Expensive. Interest is paid on full amount borrowed for full period of repayment. Premiums on life assurance policy have also to be paid. Rate of interest is sometimes higher than for 1. | Yes. Constant amount of tax relief over whole period of loan since principal is not repaid. |
| 3 Low cost endowment | From building societies, insurance companies, banks. | Endowment policy linked in which gives a small 'nest egg' at maturity. | Marginally more expensive than 1. Interest paid on full amount. | Yes, on life policy premium and interest. |
| 4 Option | Government sponsored. From building societies, insurance companies. For people on low incomes, paying little or no tax. | Low rate of interest. Repayment rate remains the same throughout, apart from changes in interest rate. Can be changed to repayment type if desired after one year. | Interest rate may fluctuate. | No. |

loan can be recovered if necessary. Although you will have to pay the fee you need not necessarily be informed of the findings and it is always advisable to have your own survey done as well. A new house with a National Home Builders' Registration Council certificate need not be surveyed for structural defects as it holds a ten-year guarantee, but it is always wise to have a professional opinion on such matters as wiring, drainage, plumbing, woodwork and dampness.

c) *Solicitors:*
Contracts of sale must be legal and a solicitor is usually employed to draw them up. He is also in a position to make what is called a 'search', to ascertain the stability of the ground, future building plans and road developments which may affect the pleasure and the value of your new home. You can consult the Land Registry at your local council offices for your own satisfaction.

When engaging a solicitor to act on your behalf, discuss at the preliminary interview the scale of fees charged. There is always the possibility that your first attempt to buy might not be successful and that he might have to repeat the legal processes more than once.

It should be noted that verbal agreements between vendor and purchaser regarding house sale are not legally binding in England and Wales. In Scotland such agreements are binding.

If you have no family solicitor, the Citizens Advice Bureau will give you a list of those practising in your area, or you can consult the Yellow Pages of the Telephone Directory. Banks and building societies will also advise.

9 What do some of these legal terms mean?
a) *Stamp duty:*
This is a tax paid to the Government calculated on the price of the house and paid by the purchaser. The amount of the tax is on a sliding scale according to the price of any property over £25,000, so the higher the price the higher the duty. This is often a bill which is not taken into account and if carpets and curtains are to be included in the price of a house some saving can be made by deducting their value from the overall cost and making a separate sale of them.
b) *Grants:*
Your local authority is empowered to pay the cost of improving old property (e.g. the installation of a bathroom) and its decision can affect your eligibility for a mortgage. The Department of the Environment has issued a Housing Booklet No. 14 called *Home Improvement Grants* and this should be studied and your requirements discussed with a council official before further steps are taken.
c) *Rates:*
These are taxes paid to the local council and supported by the Government, to pay for the services which we tend to take for

granted, such as education, the police force, transport, highways, local authority housing, social services, refuse collection, etc. Accompanying your rates demand you will find a list of these services and the share of the money allocated to each. The amount demanded depends on the value of your property (see 9e) and is actually the amount that could be charged for rent if the property were to be let on the open market. It is due in 2 half-yearly instalments (April and October) but can be paid in total in one instalment or by monthly debit through your bank account.

d) *Water rates:*
These used to be included in the general rates (and still are in Scotland) but are now levied by the relevant Water Authority, not by the local council. Domestic rates are calculated as a percentage of the rateable value of the property (see 9e) and may be paid half-yearly or in instalments. It is now possible to pay for the water you use, which is calculated by means of a meter which is officially installed. For a rough estimate of the advantage or otherwise that this would be to you, it is normally assumed that each person uses 40 gallons of water per day.

e) *Rateable value:*
This is calculated by the Inland Revenue authority, taking into account the number of rooms within the property, the presence of a garage, central heating, garden area, insurance, maintenance costs, etc. When this figure is ascertained the local authority levies its general rate as so much due for every pound of rateable value. If the rateable value of a property is £520 and the rate levied in the pound is £1.05, the rates demand will be for £1.05 × 520, i.e. £520 + £26 = £546.

10 How would you plan to move house?
Assuming that the legal requirements have been dealt with, the following points will ease what could otherwise be a very traumatic experience:
a) The cheapest way to move if you have only a few possessions is to hire or borrow a van and move them yourself.
b) If you decide to employ a removal firm, 'shop around':
Be guided by friends who have had personal experience of moving.
Consult the Yellow Pages for reputable firms.
Ask for several different estimates before choosing, and give the firm as much notice as possible.
Find out:
  if it is going to be cheaper to pack your own goods;
  whether the firm supplies packing cases;
  whether the removal men unpack the cases in your new home and if so, whether they unpack the cases immediately;
  whether the firm accepts responsibility for breakages.

c) Have any newly purchased goods delivered straight to your new home.

d) Make sure that floors are clean *before* moving furniture in.

e) Label all boxes, cases, bags and cartons to show their contents.

f) Prepare a packed meal and plenty of thermos flasks of hot or cold drinks so that you can eat between periods of working.

g) Carry by hand, or transport by car, any specially valuable ornaments, clocks, lamps and plants.

h) Leave your old dwelling in the state in which you would hope to find it if you were moving *in*.

i) Arrange to have your mail re-directed. The Post Office makes a charge and you can pay for this service to continue for three, six or twelve months. Ask for the appropriate form at your local post office.

j) Inform as many people as possible of your new address, particularly your local council, your insurance company, British Telecom (if necessary), any savings organizations (building society, National Savings, etc.), your bank, your doctor.

———————————————— FURTHER STUDY ————————————————

**Things to Do**

1 Find out what these initials mean: NHBC, CAB, RICS, ISVA, NAEA.
2 Find pictures or draw examples to show the differences between: a terraced house, a semi-detached house, a detached house, a bungalow, a chalet bungalow, a block of flats, a town house.
3 Visit estate agents' windows and note the prices of various types of accommodation. Discuss the reasons for these differences.
4 Find or draw examples of the following windows: bay, sash, casement, picture, bow, dormer, fan-light, hopper, louvred.
5 Discover and discuss the differences in appearance between the following styles of building: Georgian, Victorian, mock Georgian, timbered, half-timbered, thatched.
6 A *bridging loan* is something which may be required when you are moving house later in life. Find out what it is.
7 Find out the rateable value of your own home and your local general rate in the pound.
8 Find out the advantages and disadvantages of a loan obtained from the Index Linked Mortgage and Investment Company Ltd.
9 Find out if industrial premises are rated on the same basis as those of a private householder. How do they compare?
10 Discuss the possibility of dispensing with the services of a solicitor when buying or selling property. Consult magazines such as *Which?* and report on your findings.

## Questions to Answer

1 Write out and complete each of the following statements with the correct term chosen from the list in the right-hand column.

a) A self-contained apartment consisting of four rooms on one floor of a two-storey building is called a ⎯⎯⎯⎯⎯.

mortgage

b) A loan from a building society or a bank which has to be repaid with interest over a number of years is a ⎯⎯⎯⎯⎯.

landlord

c) The person occupying rooms in a house belonging to someone else is called a ⎯⎯⎯⎯⎯.

tax relief

d) The person owning accommodation which is let to other people is called a ⎯⎯⎯⎯⎯.

rateable value

e) The tax paid to the Government when a property is purchased is called ⎯⎯⎯⎯⎯.

surveyor

f) The part of your income which is used to pay a mortgage is shown on your income tax return as being eligible for ⎯⎯⎯⎯⎯.

stamp duty

g) A person who examines property to assess its suitability for mortgage allowance is called a ⎯⎯⎯⎯⎯.

grant

h) Notification of ownership of a property is registered in the ⎯⎯⎯⎯⎯.

maisonette

i) Money which is *given* by a local authority to be used to improve property is called a ⎯⎯⎯⎯⎯.

Land Registry

j) General rates and water rates are based on the ⎯⎯⎯⎯⎯ of a property.

tenant

2 Discuss the advantages and disadvantages of high-rise flats.

3 If you were applying for a mortgage and were refused, what reasons might there be for the decision?

4 Look at the table on page 3 and further develop five of the advantages and disadvantages listed.

5 What do you understand by the following terms which could appear in advertisements? Illustrate your answers:
gable; porch; extension; integral garage; double glazed; vacuum sealed; basement; loft

6 Living in the most delightful dwelling can be spoiled by inconsiderate or thoughtless neighbours. What steps would you take to make yourself a good neighbour if you were living in *either* a semi-detached house *or* a flat?

7 How do you account for the social change in domiciliary habits of young people referred to in the first sentence of this chapter?

Your 'house' becomes your 'home' when it begins to reflect your personality; when it provides for your individual needs; when it is comfortable; when it becomes a place in which you are relaxed and happy—in short, somewhere 'nice to come home to'. Much of the fun in creating a home is in doing it little by little, fitting the pieces together like a jigsaw puzzle to make a complete picture.

When you embark upon this adventure, remember:

1 Take your time in buying—mistakes can be expensive.

2 Be certain of how much money you have to spend—avoid too much hire purchase.

3 Spend as much time as you can 'shopping around'; wait for sales; compare prices of similar articles in different shops—these can vary considerably.

4 Collect leaflets, brochures and good magazine features on the item you wish to purchase and compare them critically.

5 Ask advice from specialist shops, your family and your friends.

6 Read labels carefully; if none is available ask for information from the retailer.

7 Plan for short-term and long-term purchases.

8 Don't expect to begin with the same degree of comfort to which you may have been accustomed in your parents' home. It has taken them all their lives together to achieve this, and it is only by having to work for something that you really appreciate it.

Children also need to be comfortable in their home environment, so:

1 Remember that flecked and patterned carpets show marks less than plain ones.

2 Use vinyl wall coverings or washable wallpapers so that little finger marks can be easily removed.

3 Allow children to choose their own bedroom décor as soon as they are old enough. (This is an important point to bear in mind, also, if you have an elderly person living with you—personal choice of colours and fabrics will help towards a feeling of being at ease and 'wanted'.)

Finally, bear in mind that sufficient storage facilities are absolutely essential to ordered, efficient and comfortable living. Shelving is a cheap and flexible form of storage and can be purchased in many forms, not the least satisfactory being merely planks (stained, painted or covered in adhesive plastic) resting on painted bricks (see Figure 2.1). Children and

*Modern storage units in a young person's room (Schreiber Furniture Ltd)*

*Figure 2.1 A fitment improvised from bricks and planks*

young people require quite as much storage space as adults need and, often, a door frame fitted into a shelved alcove can make all the difference between a safe, restful and tidy room and a cluttered, irritating and difficult-to-clean one.

## FURNITURE

1 Take your time! Families can often help with an odd piece of unwanted furniture and you may obtain others quite cheaply through the 'Second-Hand' advertisements in your local paper or at auctions. These can be painted or renovated to satisfy your colour schemes and will keep you comfortable while you are deciding, and saving up for, exactly what you want.

2 Draw a sketch of your room, with measurements, and plan the positions of the pieces you wish to buy. Remember that a few good items will look better and last longer than a clutter of cheap ones.

3 If you are going to buy on credit (see page 148) look for stores which offer interest-free credit on large purchases.

4 Shop around for the best prices or wait for sales.

## Basic Furniture for Dining/Living Room

TABLES
1 Gate-legged, drop-leaf or extension types take up less room than conventional round or oblong ones.
2 Suitable standard height is 70–76 cm. (28″–30″).
3 They may be made of wood, plastic or metal with a glass top.

CHAIRS
1 These should be sturdy, with straight backs and comfortable seats.
2 Look for simple shapes which are easy to clean.
3 Check that the seat height is correct for the table. (Sit in the chair at the table to be sure, and at the same time tilt it gently on to its back legs. If it creaks it probably won't stand up to much wear!)

CHAIRS FOR RELAXING
1 Choice depends a good deal upon the age of the user—elderly people prefer a high-backed, winged armchair which keeps off draughts; young people like to curl up in a low, wide-seated chair; others like to put their feet up and hope for a recliner chair with adjustable positions— and a high cost!
2 The Office of Fair Trading now encourages manufacturers to supply relevant information about the composition, care and cleaning of their furniture, so read the labels and ask questions before you buy. Deaths caused by the poisonous gases given off by burning acrylic upholstery (even when only smouldering) have made the public very aware of latent danger. From October 1980 onwards the Upholstered Furniture Safety Regulations apply to all new upholstered furniture. Red warning labels must be displayed on all pieces which have not passed the British Standards tests for safety in the event of a lighted match or cigarette coming into contact with the upholstery. Since the end of 1982 no furniture which has not passed the smouldering cigarette test may be sold. However, furniture which has failed the match test can continue to be sold as long as it carries the warning triangle. New furniture which has passed both tests now carries a square label with a green border.

*Furniture safety labels (Department of Trade)*

## SETTEES/SOFAS

1 If you have no spare bed or even a spare bedroom it is worth considering one of the large range of attractive bed-settees now available; check this for comfort in both sitting and sleeping positions.
2 High backs are more comfortable than low ones as they provide support for the neck.
3 'Three-piece suites' are *not* essential; several armchairs of different sizes may be more convenient.
4 Some manufacturers sell directly to the public, cutting out the retailer and so making their furniture cheaper than that in the shops. Famous names nearly always mean high prices.
5 If you wish to make fitted loose covers for a settee or for chairs, some manufacturers will supply paper patterns to fit their models.

## MATERIALS USED IN UPHOLSTERY

1 *Leather*
   Luxurious but expensive; can be cleaned by hand.
2 *Velvet*
   May be all cotton but is more likely to be a mixture of cotton and man-made fibres; may be professionally cleaned at home.
3 *Moquette*
   Looped pile fabric, often of wool or wool/man-made fibre mixture; soft, warm and hard wearing; may be sponged or professionally cleaned at home.
4 *Cotton and linen*
   Usually used for loose covers; may be washed by machine.
5 *Brocade*
   Luxurious effect; usually a blend of viscose and acetate; expensive; must be dry-cleaned.
6 *Tweed*
   Mostly wool, mixed with some synthetic fibre; hard-wearing and attractive; may be sponged at home.
7 *Plastic*
   Usually vinyl; often made to imitate leather; tends to split; cigarette burns cause complete holes; textured surfaces can be scrubbed.

## FILLINGS USED IN UPHOLSTERY

Natural
{
1 *Animal hair, e.g. horse*
   Firm but expensive; safe.
2 *Sisal*
   A leaf fibre, also used for tablemats.
3 *Coir*
   Coarse brown fibre obtained from coconut husks.
4 *Kapok*
   Seed fibre; soft; light in weight; loses buoyancy.
5 *Flock*
   Odd pieces of clean material and wool, finely shredded.

Man-made ⎰ 6 *Latex foam*
           Used for padding and cushions.
      7 *Polyether*
           Used for firmer types of upholstery.
      8 *Polystyrene*
           Used for soft padding and cushions, e.g. sag-bags.
      9 *Polyurethene*
           Used for any type of above.

## Beds

APPROXIMATE SIZES
Double bed (standard):  150 cm. × 200 cm.
                      5' 0" × 6' 6"
Double bed (small):    135 cm. × 190 cm.
                      4' 6" × 6' 3"
Single bed (standard):  100 cm. × 200 cm.
                      3' 3" × 6' 6"
Single bed (small):     90 cm. × 190 cm.
                      3' 0" × 6' 3"

1 Choose your bed with care! About one-third of your life will be spent in it, so make sure that it is long enough—the general rule is 15 cm. (6") longer than the user's height.

2 Nowadays most beds are of the divan type, i.e. an oblong, fabric-covered base standing on legs or castors (which make it easy to move). This base may be:
a) *Solid*
   The springs are enclosed within the wooden frame.
b) *Sprung*
   The springs extend to the edge of the base, with either a sprung or a firm edge (wooden). (A sprung bed is advisable if you like sitting on it; this type will not sag under your weight.)

3 Headboards are an optional extra, attractive but not essential.

4 Storage drawers may be fitted underneath the bed, either as an integral part of the divan or independently situated. These are useful for extra storage space, but the bed must be moved for cleaning underneath it.

5 A bed should always be tested by lying on it before buying it.

*A bed with fitted drawers*
*(Price Bros & Co. Ltd)*

MATTRESSES

When buying these, make certain that they fit the base correctly, particularly if a new mattress is to be used on an old base. Buy the best mattress you can afford and try to change it every ten years. There are two types you can buy:

1 *Interior sprung*
   a) Open springing: figure-of-eight shaped springs held from top to bottom by strong wiring.
   b) Continuous springing: sometimes called 'posture springing'; springs are made from one continuous piece of coiled wire.
   c) Pocket springing: more expensive than either of the above but gives better support; each spring is set in its own individual pocket.

2 *Foam filled*
   Most of these mattresses are made from two layers of foam of different densities. As comfortable as sprung mattresses, they do not need turning. They do not harbour dust (important to those suffering from allergies to house dust) and prices are similar to those of sprung mattresses.

As with other items to be purchased, shop around. Collect leaflets and brochures, read the labels and ask questions.

If you wish to economize, make your own bed base and spend your money on a good mattress. 'Dunlopillo' will supply D.I.Y. instructions.

## Bedding

The choice of this depends upon personal taste and money available.

PILLOWS

1 *Natural fillings*
   a) Down: soft and durable, but expensive.
   b) Feathers: less soft but less expensive. A mixture is usually a good compromise.

2 *Synthetic fillings*
   Terylene or foam: light and comfortable. These are good for allergy sufferers.

The degree of softness and firmness of a pillow is a matter of personal preference, but it should be sufficient to support the head and neck without sinking too deeply into it.

DUVETS (CONTINENTAL QUILTS, SLEEPING QUILTS)

1 Cheaper to buy than a combination of sheets, blankets and an eiderdown.

2 Equally as warm as conventional bedding.

3 Make bed-making much easier.

4 British Standards (BS 2005) sets the quality of sleeping quilts, including a definition of the fillings:

a) *Down*
   Warmest and lightest; must not contain more than 15% by weight of feathers; must be professionally cleaned.
b) *Down and feather*
   Must contain not less than 51% by weight of down; must be professionally cleaned.
c) *Feather and down*
   Must contain at least 15% by weight of down; must be professionally cleaned.
   British Standards also requires that *new* down and feathers be used.
d) *Polyester*
   A synthetic which is light but also a good insulator; suitable for allergy sufferers and for children; cheaper than any of the fillings a–c; may be washed.

5 Warmth is measured in 'tog' ratings, the lowest 8.5, the highest around 13.5; the higher the tog rating the warmer the quilt. In centrally heated homes a tog rating of 11.5 would be sufficient.

6 The filling should be firmly and evenly distributed throughout the duvet—this will be indicated by the method and amount of stitching used in manufacture.

7 The duvet should overhang the sides of the bed all round by 22 cm. (9″).

8 They are available in single, double and king sizes, but it is possible to make your own. Many colleges and adult education centres hold classes for instruction and assistance in doing so.

BLANKETS
1 Their warmth depends on how well they trap air, so acting as an insulator between the warmth from your body and the cool air outside.
2 They can be made of cotton, wool, wool mixtures or man-made fibres. Pure wool is the lightest and warmest but also the most expensive.
3 Cellular blankets are particularly light and, apart from cotton ones, warm.
4 Labels should tell you the fibre content and cleaning instructions.

SHEETS AND PILLOWCASES
1 Now mainly made of cotton and polyester, they need little laundering.
2 Nylon is hard wearing and cheaper, but some people do not like its slippery, non-absorbent surface. Brushed nylon is not slippery but can make the sleeper even hotter than the smooth type does.
3 Flannelette sheets, made of brushed cotton, are warm and soft initially but the nap tends to be lost after several washings.
4 Fitted sheets, i.e. sheets made to fit the mattress, are more difficult to iron than flat ones and cannot be transposed, but they do make for a tidy bed.
   Queries about bedding can be made to:

a) *The National Bedding Federation*
   251 Brompton Road
   London SW3
b) *Space Saving Bed Centre*
   13 Golden Square
   London W1

## Woods Used in Furniture (see also Fitted Furniture)

There are two classes of wood used for making furniture:
a) *Hardwoods*
   Woods such as oak, walnut, teak, beech, mahogany.
b) *Softwoods (from conifers)*
   Woods such as pine, larch, yew, cedar.

Originally all furniture was made of solid woods but nowadays, due to their high cost, the framework is often made of wood and the panels filling it made of chipboard (a man-made material consisting of sawdust and small chips of wood bonded together with resin). *Veneer* is used to cover these panels and is made by sticking very thin slices of real wood extremely carefully to the chipboard or to cheaper woods. Plastic is now often used to imitate wood veneers. (See Table 2 opposite.)

*Some examples of woods*

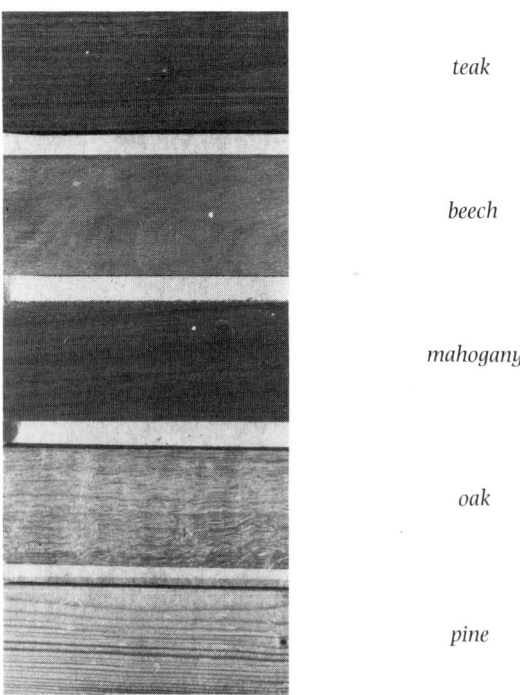

teak

beech

mahogany

oak

pine

TABLE 2: WOODS USED IN FURNITURE

| Wood | Grain | Colour | Characteristics | Uses |
|---|---|---|---|---|
| 1 Oak | Knotty | Deep straw to dark straw | May be 100 years old when felled. Very slow 'seasoning' but when completed is a very hard, strong wood. Expensive. | Furniture, flooring, house construction |
| 2 Walnut | Highly figured | Grey to warm brown | Hard wood. Very popular wood early this century. | Veneers, furniture |
| 3 Teak | Fine | Deep red brown | Very strong, hard wood. Fire and acid resistant. Oiled rather than polished. | Furniture, outside use |
| 4 Beech | Close | Pale to darker brown with golden fleck | Stronger than oak. Takes stain very well. | Furniture frames, e.g. chair legs, flooring |
| 5 Mahogany | Close, decorative | Golden to reddish brown | Much used in the 18th century. Often simulated in cheaper woods. | Furniture |
| 6 Pine<br>7 Larch<br>8 Yew<br>9 Cedar | Undistinctive | Light | Soft woods. Cheaper than hardwoods. Red cedar is resistant to fungi, decay, insect attack, therefore often untreated. | Flooring, joists, rafters, door and window frames, kitchen furniture, exterior work, e.g. garden sheds |
| 10 Cane, Bamboo | Smooth with characteristic nodes | Pale cream to yellow | Attractive but not strong. Can be bought in self-assembly packs. Wide range of prices. | Occasional furniture, garden furniture |

## Fitted Furniture

These are units of furniture made to customers' specifications, to fit on to or into walls. Finishes are available in a wide range of colours, decoration and styles. Advice on measurements is normally given by the staff of the shop supplying the fitments. Fitted furniture is space-saving and attractive, but expensive. The surface is usually a plasticized coating on chipboard or cheap wood.

### Self-Assembly Furniture

Parts of units are supplied in a package and you assemble it yourself. An extensive range of items, makes, styles and sizes is available; you must do your own measuring, which *must* be accurate. There are many large warehouses where this D.I.Y. furniture can be viewed in its assembled form.

● It is important that when any type of furniture is delivered to your home, you check it carefully for faults before signing the delivery note. Damage discovered later may not be accepted as the responsibility of the retailer or delivery firm.

### LIGHTING

Daylight is always preferable to artificial light but often has to be boosted by it. If you are able to start from scratch, give yourself flexibility to experiment by installing additional electric points. This will also prevent overloading of a single outlet point with the use of adapters, and the additional danger of trailing flexes.

Lighting is dealt with in more detail in Chapter 3.

### FLOOR COVERINGS

Remember that floors receive the greatest amount of wear, tear and dirt of any other area of the home. Heavy furniture is placed upon them, much is spilled on them and many feet walk over them—yet we still want them to be decorative.

Before deciding on the type, texture and colour of the floor covering you will choose, consider:
how much wear each room is going to receive;
how easy it will be to clean (especially in kitchens and children's rooms);
how much warmth it will provide;
how much it will cost.

Having decided upon the type of covering you are going to buy (see Table 3 on pages 22–3), careful preparation of the floor is essential for a successful result.

*Parquet flooring*

*Brick flooring*

*Quarry tile flooring*

TABLE 3: TYPES OF FLOOR COVERING

| Type of flooring | Special points | Advantages | Disadvantages |
|---|---|---|---|
| 1 Boards | If sound, sand them down (a machine can be hired) and give two coats of polyurethane seal. | Available in a variety of colours. Warm, resilient. Show off rugs well. | Initial labour of sanding. Can show dusty footmarks. |
| 2 Tiles | The solid concrete floor laid on the ground floor of most modern houses is an excellent base. Floor must be flat and clean. A rubberized screed 18 mm. ($\frac{3}{4}$') thick should be laid first to give resilience. Available as glazed, unglazed, ceramic or vitrified (glass-like) types. | Available in a large range of colours, designs and shapes which can be adapted to your own pattern. Can be laid without professional help. Very long-lasting. Resistant to spillage. | Expensive. Tiring to stand on for long periods if non-resilient. Cold, noisy. |
| 3 Cork sheets or tiles | Available with vinyl layer painted on to the surface. Can be laid by D.I.Y. enthusiasts, fixed with special adhesive to a wooden or concrete floor. If sealed, surface does not need to be polished. | Non-porous. Softer and warmer than 2. Hard wearing, resilient, quiet. | Mainly brown, (but some coloured ones are available if sought for). Heavy furniture may cause dents. |
| 4 Linoleum sheets or tiles | Not now easily available but can be found. Pattern may be printed on the surface or go right through the depth (inlaid). Can be laid as D.I.Y. job (cuts easily for fitting). | Printed type cheaper than inlaid. Warm, quiet, resilient, comfortable. Easy to sweep. | Pattern on printed type may wear off. Reacts badly to water so not wholly suitable for bathrooms and kitchens. |
| 5 Vinyl sheets or tiles | Easy to fit but sheet type shrinks slightly after laying, so should not be trimmed exactly. Available with cushioned backing. | Warm and quiet if cushion backed. Large range of colours and designs available. | Slippery if surface is wet—care needed for elderly people. |
| 6 Wood block (parquet or mosaic) | More than one type of wood may be used. Bought as tiles and set in mastic. | May be laid to own design. Attractive and hard wearing. | Great care required in laying. |

| Type of flooring | Special points | Advantages | Disadvantages |
|---|---|---|---|
| 7 Carpets (see also page 25) | Very large and bewildering range of types and colours available in both natural and man-made fibre. Many shops give cut-price and occasional free-fitting promotion offers. | Comfortable, warm, quiet. Add degree of luxury. | Expensive |
| a) Wool | Wholly natural fibre. | High resilience. Warm, luxurious to walk on. Anti-static. Soil resistant, non-inflammable. | Expensive |
| b) Cotton | 100% natural fibre. | Wears well, easy to clean. | Pile flattens quickly. |
| c) Acrylic, Modacrylic | Looks and feels similar to wool but is a thermo-plastic. 100% man-made fibre. | Modacrylic is less inflammable than acrylic. | Stains easily. Acrylic is inflammable. |
| d) Nylon | 100% man-made fibre. | Hard wearing | Pile tends to flatten. May cause problems with static electricity though this problem is being researched. |
| e) Polyester | 100% man-made fibre. | Soft texture, waterproof, hard wearing. | |
| f) Viscose | 100% man-made fibre. | Cheap, soft, warm. | Shows dirt easily. Pile flattens quickly. Inflammable. |
| g) Modified viscose | Similar in appearance to viscose. 100% man-made fibre. | Better resistance to dirt than f and flattens less easily. | |
| h) Polypropylene | 100% man-made fibre. | Easy to clean, resists dirt and stains. Impervious to liquids—good in bathrooms and kitchens. | |
| 8 Underlays | Solid floors have no resilience and carpet laid directly on to them will quickly become shabby and lifeless. Buy the best underlay you can afford. | For economy, carpets may be bought with a foam backing (beware of underfloor heating). Lay this over brown or purpose-made paper to prevent dust rising and carpet from sticking. Underlays help to insulate the room and increase the warmth and quietness of the carpet. | |

*Parquet and brick tile flooring*

*Cork tile flooring*

*Ceramic tile flooring*

*Ceramic and brick tile flooring*

1 Empty the room of furniture as far as possible.
2 Ensure that the floor is clean and free from dust.
3 Check that the floorboards are secure and that there are no protruding nails.
4 Plane down any knots in the floorboards and fill in any cracks.
5 Complete all decorating before laying new flooring.
6 Read manufacturers' instructions carefully.

## Buying a Carpet

1 As a rough guide, the more wool the carpet contains the better the buy, providing that the price is within the limits you have set yourself. Wool can be blended with nylon to give an extremely hard wearing, attractive and well-textured carpet.
2 Try not to economize by buying cheap synthetic-fibre carpets which will compact badly and quickly lose their looks.
3 There is no written guarantee given for any carpet, the onus being on you, as the buyer, to choose the quality best suited to your requirements.
4 Decide upon the fibre you wish to purchase and then examine the density of the pile. The closer it is the longer the carpet will last.
5 Remember that patterns on carpets always appear smaller in a large showroom than they will when laid in a smaller space.
6 Different grades of carpet are needed for different rooms, since a hall and staircase carpet will receive much more wear than one in a bedroom.
7 Fitted carpets give added warmth and luxury and make rooms look larger, but they cannot be turned to spread the wear. A carpet square is more versatile and can be moved to another house with you!
8 Colour is of the utmost importance and the wrong choice is an expensive mistake which you may have to live with for a long time. Decide on the overall colour scheme of the room before you look for a carpet. If in doubt it may be advisable to buy an inexpensive floor covering, like rush matting, to be laid on stained boards while you decide upon and save for what you really want.
9 Seek advice from specialist shops, read books and consumer leaflets, read labels, ask questions and consider all the options before purchasing what is bound to be a very expensive item.
10 Look out for shops offering free fitting as an incentive to purchase carpets from them. This service can considerably reduce your outlay and/or may allow you to buy a more expensive, better quality carpet.

CLASSES OF CARPET (SEE FIGURE 2.2)
1 *Woven*
   These are pile fabrics, woven in one operation with the backing. Axminster and Wilton carpets are made in this way, the different

names indicating only different methods of weaving. Both are made in varying grades.

2 *Tufted*

The backing is woven first and the pile then inserted in much the same way as hand-made rugs are made. The backing is then coated with an adhesive to hold the tufts securely, and often a second backing is attached.

3 *Corded*

This is woven on a Wilton-type loom and looks similar to a Wilton carpet but is cheaper because it has no pile and is usually made from hair or sisal. It is extremely hard wearing but not very comfortable to walk on, particularly on stairs, where its rather shiny surface makes it dangerously slippery.

4 *Bonded*

Here the pile is glued to the backing in varying degrees of density. It is available in many colours and is relatively cheap, but does not wear or clean as well as other types.

5 *Carpet tiles*

These are available in a large range of fibres and colours and are easily laid, either loosely or stuck down. Loose-laid ones can be moved around to spread the wear but care must be taken not to allow the edges to curl. They can be laid to your own design and many can be hand washed.

*Figure 2.2  Classes of carpet*

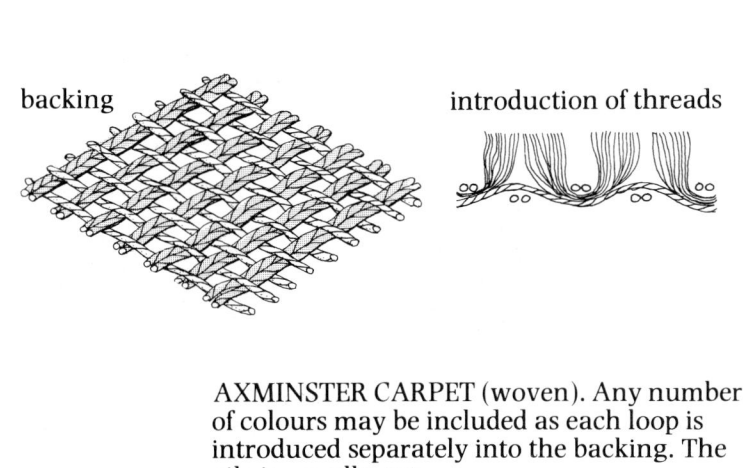

backing

introduction of threads

AXMINSTER CARPET (woven). Any number of colours may be included as each loop is introduced separately into the backing. The pile is usually cut.

## — WILTON CARPET (woven). —————————————

backing

introduction of threads

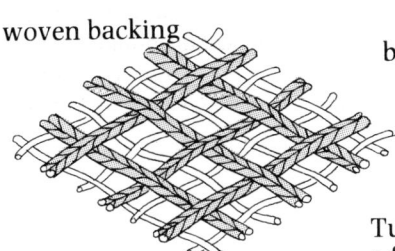

In patterned Wilton carpets, the different coloured threads are carried across the backing, making a very thick, durable carpet. However the colours are limited, usually to five. The pile may be cut or uncut.

## — TUFTED CARPET. ————————————————

woven backing

introduction of tufts
(with foam layer
between two backing fabrics)

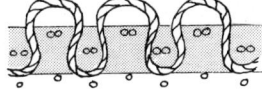

Tufts are introduced into a fabric backing, fixed with a thin layer of latex adhesive and then a foam layer is placed underneath it. A secondary backing is added. The pile may be looped or cut.

## — BONDED CARPETS. ————————————————

introduction of tufts

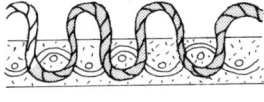

woven backing

Fibres may be heat fused to a backing or punched through a backing fabric impregnated with resin.

CARPET CLASSIFICATION SCHEMES
*British Carpet Classification Scheme (BCCS)*
This is based on test results and subjective assessment of:
a) weight of pile in a given area;
b) density of pile in a given area;
c) dynamic loading;
d) static loading;
e) tendency to soil;
f) durability.
● Weight and density of pile along with durability are the factors with the most weight in grading.

| Category | Suggested Suitability |
|---|---|
| BCCS 1: Light Domestic | Spare bedrooms; light traffic only. |
| BCCS 2: Medium Domestic | Main bedrooms; occasional rooms. |
| BCCS 3: General Domestic | Areas not subjected to heavy wear. |
| BCCS 4: Heavy Domestic | Frequently used rooms, stairs, halls. |
| BCCS 5: Heavy | Not normally sold for domestic use. |
| BCCS 6: Luxury | Carpets with an aesthetic value, e.g. Chinese, Persian, Turkish. Not suitable for all areas of the home. |

Information given on the BCCS label includes:
size;
fibre content;
construction;
method of cleaning;
special laying instructions.
*British Carpet Performance Rating Scheme (BCPRS)*
This scheme is now often used instead of the BCCS and is modified for international use by the ICCO.

| Category | Suggested Suitability |
|---|---|
| A: Extra Heavy Wear | Locations where good durability etc. is required, e.g. in public buildings. |
| B: Very Heavy Wear | Heaviest domestic use and most contract areas, e.g. offices, foyers. |
| C: Heavy Wear | Busy domestic areas and medium contract areas, e.g. restaurants, corridors. |
| D: General Wear | Most domestic areas and light contract usage, e.g. hotel bedrooms. |
| E: Medium Wear | Domestic areas not subject to concentrated usage, e.g. sitting rooms. |
| F: Light Wear | For occasional domestic use, e.g. spare bedrooms. |

*International Carpet Classification Organization (ICCO)*
On the continent of Europe some countries use the BCCS ratings preceded by 'T' (e.g. T2).

*Symbol Scheme—International Co-ordinating Committee (ICC)*
In West Germany, Austria and Switzerland 3 symbols are used without language:
1 A bed—indicating suitability for bedrooms.
2 An easy chair—indicating suitability for general domestic use.
3 A desk and chair—indicating suitability for contract use.

MEASURING FOR CARPET
Measurements must be accurate. If fitted, measure into *all* the corners of the room, allowing for inclusion of window bays and fireplace recesses. It is advisable to have these fitted professionally, but ask for an estimate first (see page 25 point 10).

## TREATMENT OF WALLS

When dampness is present it may be brought to your notice by:
brown water-marks on walls;
the growth of fungi;
crumbling plaster;
peeling wallpaper;
a distinctive odour.

*Figure 2.3 The effects of interior dampness*

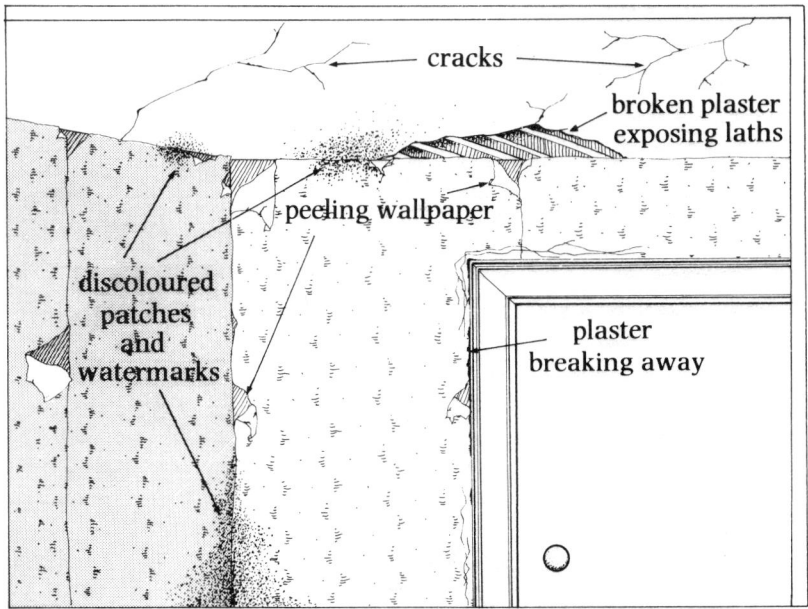

B

The usual causes are:
1 Rising damp due to
a) lack of a damp course;
b) a defective damp course;
c) damaged brickwork.
2 Seeping pipes.
3 Defective roofing/pointing.
4 Blocked guttering.
5 Obstructed air-bricks.
6 Condensation—modern houses with concrete floors are particularly vulnerable.

To safeguard against dampness:
1 Make sure that a damp course exists (a surveyor's report should indicate this). If you find it does not, consult a reputable damp-proofing specialist.
2 Check that all water pipes are sound. If water pressure at the taps is low, seek advice from a plumber.
3 Keep a regular check on all outside maintenance and have worn or damaged pointing, etc., repaired as quickly as possible.
4 Keep all gutters clear and pay particular attention to these in the early winter after the autumnal fall of leaves.
5 Make sure that there is a clear passage of air through every air-brick. These are installed to ventilate walls and can be blocked outside by the natural growth of plants, etc., and inside by furniture.
6 Keep the whole premises well ventilated (see page 60).

## Decoration

The decoration chosen for your walls can give the background mood to your room, e.g. calm, elegant, bold, romantic, sophisticated. Every room has a different function and this can be emphasized by the décor chosen. This will obviously be renewed or changed more often than carpets or curtains are, so it is a very good field for experiment; it can also be as cheap or as expensive as you wish.

Wall treatment is the most common and the most popular of D.I.Y. jobs and, providing that you
a) prepare the walls carefully, making sure that they are smooth and dry and
b) follow the instructions exactly for the use of paint and wallpaper, results should be very satisfactory.

PREPARATION
1 *Dampness*
This can spoil decoration very quickly.
a) Treat *inside* walls with a proprietary primer/sealer to prevent damp stains from spreading.

b) If dampness is severe, plaster may have to be removed and replaced, although it is also possible to cover the offending areas with plasterboard, which is an easier method of dealing with it.

c) Line *outside* walls, which also require insulating, with thermal plasterboard sheets now on the market.

2 *Cracked/uneven walls and ceilings*

a) Rub down and fill with proprietary filler if the faults are slight.

b) If the faults are severe, cover with grained paper such as woodchip wallpaper and paint over it if required.

## PAINT

1 This is easy to use with a good brush of the right size, or a roller.

2 There is a wide selection of colours and several varieties of finish (e.g. eggshell, gloss; water-based, oil-based) to choose from, and some retailers will blend colours for you with a special mixing machine. If the paint is to match a specific fabric, take a piece of it with you to ensure the nearest match possible. Do this in daylight as fluorescent lighting can distort colours dramatically. Remember that a plain painted wall makes an excellent background for pictures, plates, etc., but more adventurous effects may be achieved by incorporating murals or wallpaper borders.

3 An interesting idea now on the market is an embossed rubber roller with which you can roll a pattern on to a wall with paint or superimpose a differently coloured pattern on to a plain background.

4 Different colours produce different overall effects:

blues —cool and restful
reds —warm and bright
yellows—cheerful and soothing
greens —cool and restful
greys —cool and sombre
gold —luxurious
white —pure and clean, clinical

## WALLPAPER

Prices vary considerably so decide your overall price bracket, ascertain roughly how many rolls you need (see overleaf), divide the number of rolls into your budget figure and look for papers within the range of the resulting amount. Remember, however, that cheap papers are often difficult to hang. Some papers may be purchased ready-pasted, but these are more expensive than unpasted ones.

1 *Choice*

a) Choose papers suitable for the use of the room to be decorated, e.g. a bedroom paper may be less heavy and 'important' than that for a dining room; kitchens and bathrooms need non-absorbent, washable or vinyl papers.

b) Lincrusta, anaglypta and woodchip papers help to disguise rough, uneven surfaces on walls.

*Matching bedroom accessories (Dorma)*

c) Some department stores stock matching wallpapers, curtains and duvets. These sets are attractive but may present problems when the wallpaper needs renewing.

d) The decoration of each room should relate to the others to give a feeling of continuity throughout. Shades of a single colour on the walls or in the carpet, or both, will achieve this effect.

e) Wallpaper can be taken over shabby wardrobe or cupboard doors to give an impression of space.

f) Patterns and colours flatter or disenchant rooms the same way as clothes do for a figure:

Pale colours make walls appear to be further apart than they actually are; bright ones and large patterns have the effect of bringing them closer together.

Vertical lines make walls seem taller.

Horizontal lines make ceilings appear lower.

Dark coloured ceilings appear lower.

A 'busy', colourful paper requires balancing with neutral or plain colours in the rest of the furnishings.

2 *Estimating the number of rolls required to paper a room*

a) Measure the height of the room from the top of the skirting board to the ceiling.

b) Divide this into the length of the roll of paper (i.e. 10 m. or 33′) to see how many lengths each roll will provide, e.g. 1 roll will allow 4 lengths for a wall 2.4 m. (8′) high.

c) Measure round the room, including all doors and windows (to allow for wastage in matching patterns).

d) Divide the total distance by the width of the roll, i.e. 52 cm. (21″).

e) Divide the figure arrived at in d by that in b. This will be the number of rolls required.

If in doubt, consult the wallpaper retailer or buy an extra roll which can be returned to the shop within a reasonable time, providing that it is unopened.

3 *Some useful hints for hanging wallpaper*
    a) Use a lining paper (plain, thin, cheap) on walls which have previously been painted. Hang it horizontally.
    b) Begin work at the window end of a wall if possible, to distract light from joins. However, if there is any conspicuous feature of the walls, e.g. chimney breast, the centre of this should be the starting point, with the pattern centralized exactly in the middle of the wall section. (This *may* not be the edge of the roll, particularly of striped paper.) Designs are then continued from either side, making a continuous pattern round the room towards the door or window.
    c) Use two rolls of paper concurrently if the pattern has a large repeat. This can reduce wastage.
    d) Make sure to hang plain-grained paper all one way to prevent shading (think of napped fabrics).
    e) Allow 12.5 cm. (5″) surplus on lengths of paper, matching patterns at the top end. Trim at the skirting board after positioning paper exactly and brushing out all creases and bubbles.
    f) Fold wet or pasted paper concertina-wise for lifting to the wall.
    g) Use an adhesive suitable for the weight of the paper. (Ask advice from the retailer.)
    h) To make a neat finish round switches, FIRST TURN OFF THE ELECTRICITY. Loosen the screws of the switch plate and pull it forward. Tuck the cut edges of the paper behind it and replace it.

A PLUMBLINE
A plumbline is used to identify and guarantee vertical lines on walls where upright units are to be fixed or paper is to be hung. It is basically a weight at the end of a line (see Figure 2.4) and, although a commercial one is a well-shaped purpose-made 'bob' fixed to fine twine, a satisfactory substitute may be improvised by tying any small heavy object (such as a thick washer or a tiny tool) to a length of smooth string.

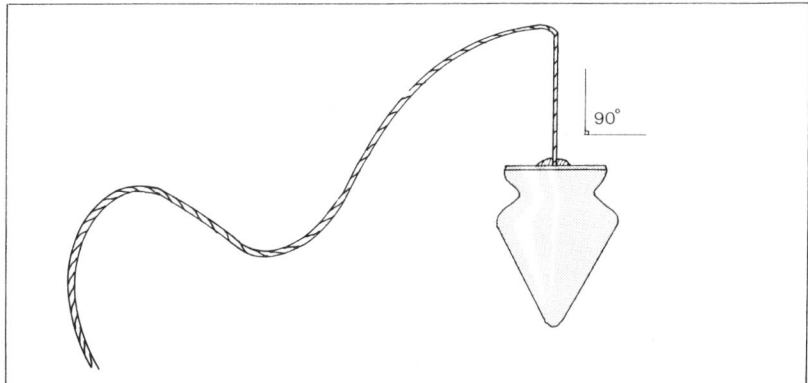

*Figure 2.4  A plumbline*

*Use—either*

> 1 Dust the line with French chalk (talcum powder or even flour will do as a substitute).
>
> 2 Support the line at the required height and let the weight come to rest.
>
> 3 'Ping' the line gently against the wall, leaving a fine white line.

*or*

> 1 Suspend the line and fix it at the top or have someone else hold it.
>
> 2. Allow the 'bob' to come to rest.
>
> 3 Make vertical 'dashes' down the length of the line on the wall with a soft pencil.

MIRRORS

1 The use of plain mirrors or mirror tiles will give the impression of added space and light by means of reflection, particularly in narrow hallways or in alcoves.

2 Walls must be quite flat if mirror tiles are to be used.

WOOD

1 This is an excellent disguise for poor walls (or ceilings).

2 It can be used horizontally, vertically or diagonally to give decorative effects, and can be stained in light and/or dark colours.

3 Tongued-and-grooved or lapped boarding is available from wood-yards or from D.I.Y. centres.

4 This finish acts as a good insulator.

5 To reduce the danger of fire, a special intumescent finish may be used, the base coat giving fire protection and the sealer providing a decorative, easy-clean surface. New extensions which require building permission and are fitted with wood-clad ceilings *must* now be treated in this way.

BRICK

If desired, plaster may be stripped from brick walls to expose the natural surface, which may then be sealed or painted.

FABRICS

Hessian-like fabrics may be hung in the same way as wallpapers.

## CURTAINS

### Fittings

The type of fitting you use will affect the amount and type of curtaining you require, so choose first between:

Rails or tracks

1 These must be flexible if they are to follow the curve or angle of a bay window.

2 They may be made from plastic or aluminium, with runners or gliders slotted into a channel in the track. The curtain hooks fit into the gliders.

3 There are several types on the market and it is advisable to compare details from leaflets before deciding which best suits your purpose and pocket.

Poles

1 These may be of solid wood, bamboo or brass (the poles on which carpets are rolled for delivery make excellent curtain supports) and are usually used with large rings attached to the curtain, either directly or with dependent hooks.

2 Imitation poles are hollowed at the back and the rings are on gliders which run in this groove; the curtains need separate hooks.

## Headings

1 These are the types of finish given to the top edge of your curtains and variations are achieved by the use of different kinds of 'Rufflette'-type tapes and hooks (see Figure 2.5).

2 The heading chosen varies according to whether or not a pelmet is used, whether the rail is to be visible or covered and whether the pole is to be seen or hidden.

3 Curtain shops will supply leaflets and advice.

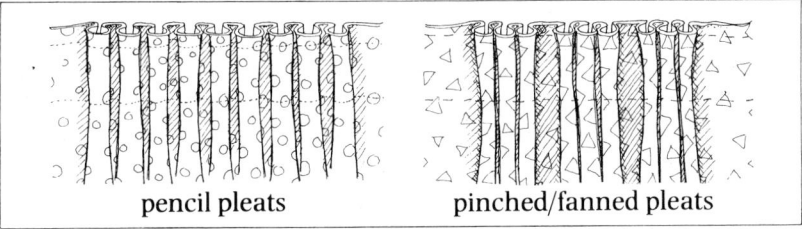

pencil pleats          pinched/fanned pleats

*Figure 2.5 Curtain headings*

## Fabrics

When considering the type of material to choose for your curtains remember that:

1 Department stores and specialist shops will offer you the widest choice.

2 Curtain fabrics rarely have a 'care' label attached, so enquire as to the fibre content, washing or cleaning requirements and flame resistance.

3 Heavy fabrics hang better than thin ones.

4 Thin fabrics hang better if they are lined; the lining also increases their insulating quality.

5 Interlining increases insulation even more. Milium, i.e. fabric impregnated with aluminium, is particularly effective.

6 Ready-made curtains are available from most department stores.

7 Most specialist shops offer a curtain-making service, if you are not able to make your own. Be sure to obtain a quotation before placing an order and look out for special 'free making' offers.

8 The following are the most commonly used fabrics for domestic curtains (do *not* under-rate the flame-resistant qualities).

| *Fabric* | *Characteristics* | *Reaction to Flame* |
|---|---|---|
| 1 Acrilan | Light and strong. Mothproof. Washable, unshrinkable. | Does not burn readily. |
| 2 Bonded fabric | Hangs well, no linings required. Mothproof. | Burns, possibly with pungent fumes. |
| 3 Brocade | Luxurious effect; figured fabric. Mothproof. | Burns readily. |
| 4 Cotton | Inexpensive. Often treated to have drip-dry properties. May shrink. Mothproof. | Burns readily. |
| 5 Glass filament/fibre | Suitable for kitchens. Hangs stiffly; difficult to press, difficult to sew. Unshrinkable. Mothproof. Limited range. Liable to crack. | Fireproof. |
| 6 Hessian | Available in natural or dyed forms. Hard wearing. Stiff— suitable for long curtains. Mothproof. | Burns. |
| 7 Linen | Strong. Creases unless mixed with other finishes. Mothproof. | Burns. |
| 8 Nylon | Hard wearing. Mothproof. Available in large range of weights and finishes. | Melts. |
| 9 Plastic | Useful for shower curtains; water resistant. Can become brittle when cold. Mothproof. | Melts. |
| 10 Rayon | Available in matt or shiny finishes. Mothproof. | Burns. |
| 11 Repp (cotton or wool) | Strong. Hangs well. Guaranteed not to fade. | Burns if made of cotton; does not burn if wool. |
| 12 Terylene | Usually fine fabrics. Mothproof. Easy to wash; needs no ironing. | Melts. |
| 13 Towelling | Washes well. Hard wearing. Absorbent. Mothproof. | Burns readily; no fumes. |
| 14 Velvet | Luxurious effect. Expensive. | Burns; no fumes. |

## Measuring

1 Measure carefully (and check again before cutting) according to the length you require (sill, apron or floor length), making sure that hem and heading allowances are added (see Figure 2.6).

2 Allow extra fabric for pattern repeats in both length and width.

3 Allow for shrinkage unless fabric is stated to be shrink-proof.

4 Allow sufficient fullness in width for curtains to hang gracefully when drawn back *and* together. Buy rather more reasonably priced fabric which will hang well instead of skimping on expensive material. Thin fabrics need three times the width of the curtain rail to appear at their best; thicker or lined curtains require one-and-a-half times to twice the width.

5 Allow 5 cm. (2″) at each side for hems, and 15 cm. (6″) for overlap. Allowance for headings depends upon the style used and the depth of hem turnings depends upon the weight of the fabric (for example, very thin fabrics require double turnings).

### BLINDS

#### Venetian

These are horizontal slats made of plastic, adjustable to give simultaneous control of sun, air, light and privacy. They can be made to order and are available in a variety of colours and widths. May be washed with a special pronged sponge.

#### Roller

These are popular alternatives to curtains. They are available in a wide variety of plain colours or patterns; may be made to order from your own material. Particularly suitable for kitchens and bathrooms.

#### Vertical

These are made on the same principle as Venetian blinds but the slats are vertical and wider. They hang from a carriage incorporating a

*Figure 2.6 Measuring for curtains*

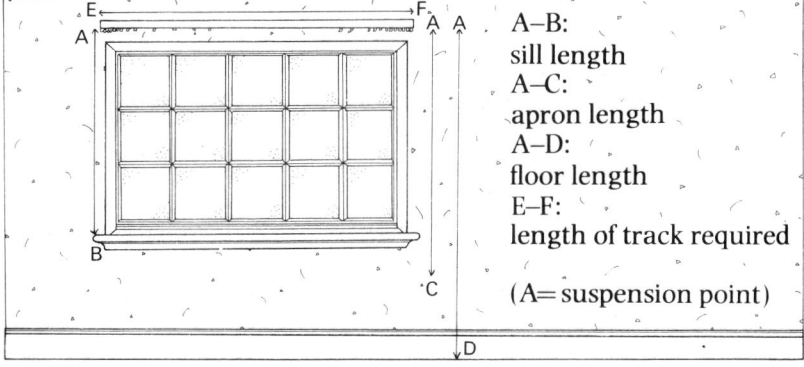

A–B:
sill length
A–C:
apron length
A–D:
floor length
E–F:
length of track required

(A= suspension point)

mechanism which pulls or retracts the slats and also rotates them through 180 degrees. Good for controlling the amount of sun passing through large windows.

All blinds are easy to instal.

## CUSHIONS

Cushions supply physical comfort by supporting parts of your body, and aesthetic enhancement by contributing touches of colour, pattern or texture to the room's background. They may be made in any shape you choose and are an easy and satisfactory item to make for yourself; good cushions are expensive to buy.

### Fillings

The filling of a cushion should be enclosed in a separate cover so that the outer decorative one can be removed for washing or cleaning. Adequate amounts should be used, to ensure comfort and retention of shape. Materials used include down, Terylene, kapok, feathers, foam rubber pads, foam chips and old nylon tights (washed and cut small).

### Fastenings

These should be easily handled if used at all; otherwise fastenings may be omitted and the opening slip-stitched.

SUITABLE FASTENINGS
1 *'Velcro'*
   Consists of two $2\frac{1}{2}$ cm. (1″) wide nylon strips, one covered in tiny hooks, one furry, which adhere to each other.
2 *Zip fasteners*
   These should be 5 cm. (2″) shorter than the seam in which they are inserted.
3 *Popper tape*
   A tape fitted with fixed press fasteners.

──────────────── **FURTHER STUDY** ────────────────

### Things to Do

1   Make a list of the furniture you consider absolutely essential for
    a)   your living room;
    b)   your bedroom;
    c)   your kitchen.

Collect illustrations of the items you would like and cost them. Add the small items of equipment and soft furnishings you want and work out the basic cost of each of these rooms.

2 Describe ways of improvising: a set of bookshelves, a bedside cabinet and a shoe cupboard, as cheaply as possible.

3 Collect samples, with prices, of:
carpet, tiles, upholstery fabric, curtain materials and plastic coverings.

4 Draw a plan of *either* a living room *or* a bedroom, showing doors and windows. Insert outlines of furniture required and show where lights and electric plugs would be fitted. Work out a colour scheme and supply patterns of suggested fabrics.

5 Collect brochures for six different mattresses, with prices. Decide which you would choose for yourself and why you have made this choice.

6 Find out what the principle of a plumbline is. Discover exactly how it is used as an aid to interior decorating.

7 Visit a retail wallpaper shop and observe the commercial aids there are available for the wallpaperer. Sketch the items you find, name them and say exactly what they are used for.

8 Measure a window for curtains which you would like to make. Estimate the amount of fabric you require for curtains
a) of a plain colour
b) of a repeated pattern
and compare the cost.

9 Measure a room to which you have access and estimate the number of rolls of wallpaper you would require to decorate it.

10 Find out the meanings of the following terms used in D.I.Y. processes:
architrave, lintel, return, riser, tread, curved coving, dado, sander, runner, borrowed light.

## Questions to Answer

1 Write out and complete each of the following statements with the correct term chosen from the list in the right-hand column.

a) Dangerous fumes can be given off from smouldering upholstered furniture, particularly if stuffed with _____ fibre.

screed

b) A thin slice of good wood covering cheaper board to give the appearance of solid wood is called a _____ .

parquet

c) A popular hard-wearing covering for upholstered fabric is a looped-pile fabric called _____ .

Wilton

moquette

d) _____ is a wood often used for garden sheds because it is fungi and decay resistant.

e) A layer of impervious material inserted just above the base of a house wall to prevent the rise of moisture from the earth is called a _____ .

f) _____ is a vegetable fibre which is often used as an upholstery filling but can also be made into mats for floors and tables.

g) _____ flooring consists of small rectangular pieces of wood arranged in a pattern.

h) In order to make them less tiring to stand on, tiles should be laid on a rubberized _____ .

i) The name _____ refers to the way in which the carpet named after it is woven.

j) The curtain heading tape which determines the type of pleating achieved is called _____ .

'Rufflette'

cedar

acrylic

sisal

veneer

damp course

2 How do you account for the rise in price of
   a) natural fibres for household furnishings;
   b) solid wood furniture?

3 What is 'seasoning' of wood? Why is it necessary?

4 What type of pillow would you choose for
   a) a small child;
   b) an elderly person who has to spend much time in bed?

5 Give detailed instructions to a friend as to how to
   a) prepare the living room
   b) cut the paper
   for repapering.

6 Describe how you would make a small, dark attic with a dormer window into a light and attractive study bedroom.

7 How would you decorate, light and furnish a steep staircase leading out of a long narrow hallway? Pay special attention to safety aspects.

8 Discuss the relative merits of
   a) papered;
   b) gloss painted;
   c) emulsion covered walls.

9 Describe three different headings for curtains. Say what fittings you would use and suggest suitable fabrics for each.

10 What differences can you suggest have taken place in the decoration and furnishings of kitchens between the beginning of the century and today?

## HEATING

Since the earliest days of Man's awareness of his own needs he has sought warmth, and a manufactured heat is probably one of civilization's first luxuries. It has become, nowadays, an expensive necessity, taken for granted by too many of us; but it is, nonetheless, a worthwhile investment. So, think carefully about how you are going to warm your home before you spend money on expensive furnishings.

### Sources of Heating

SOLID FUEL

1 *Wood*

The burning of logs of varying sizes was undoubtedly the first method of obtaining heat by Man's enterprise and is still used to the exclusion of all other sources in many parts of the world. In this country it is an attractive but inconvenient and extravagant way of producing warmth and a great grief to conservationists. On an open fireplace, however, the occasional log fire is a useful and productive procedure for disposing of diseased timbers and dead trees. Not all woods burn well and a good deal of smoke is produced; the ash must be cleared before further fires can be lit.

2 *Coal (and products)*

Reserves of coal, although not inexhaustible, are larger than those of either gas or oil, and the long-term prospect is that, because of this, the price of coal may be lower than that of any alternative fuel. It is, however, an inconvenient form, being bulky, heavy, dirty to handle and smoke-producing.

In 'smokeless zones', operating in most urban areas, coal is normally burned in a modified form, such as coke, anthracite and other branded fuels. These vary considerably in the amount of heat they produce (e.g. anthracite provides much more than coke), according to their density. Ash and clinker produced by their combustion have to be removed daily (unless the fireplace is of the open convector type) which is often an unacceptable chore to the flat-dweller, the infirm and the elderly. Modern solid fuel boilers are automatically refilled from built-in hoppers.

*Examples of solid fuel fires (left photo Solid Fuel Advisory Service)*

*A gas radiant convector heater*

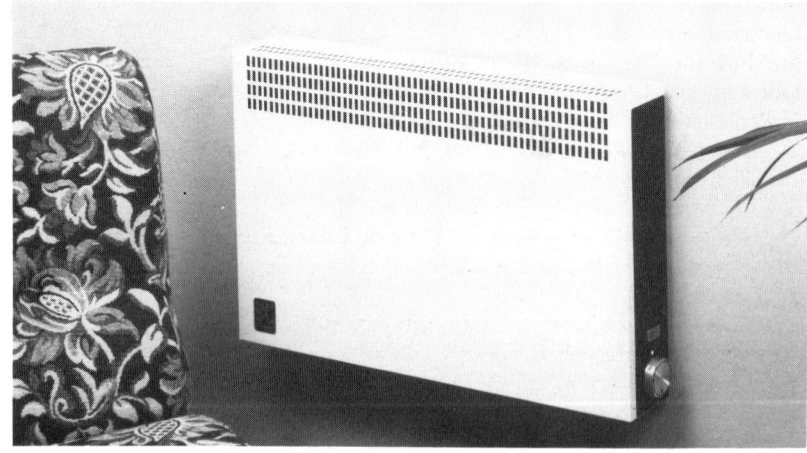

*A wall mounted electric convector heater (Dimplex Heating Ltd)*

An open fire is a cheerful and attractive focal point of a room but at least 85% of the heat goes up the chimney and the rest of the room is not warmed. In very cold weather the fire can, in fact, produce chill draughts as the air which the fuel requires for burning is drawn in under the door and through window frame cracks to replace what has been used. The most efficient solid fuel room heater is that which stands away from but is sealed into the grate aperture and consists of a fire-box encased in steel (e.g. 'Parkray'). The fire is visible behind a tightly fitting glazed door and the whole unit radiates heat.

GAS

Gas fires can be fitted into an existing fireplace so long as it has a chimney or flue. The types available are:

1 *Radiant*

Cheapest type but the least efficient—40% efficiency only.

2 *'Log'*

Gives very attractive appearance of an open fire, flames being produced by burning gas. Uneconomical; certain degree of safety hazard.

3 *Radiant convectors*

Heating elements (can resemble coal or logs) are behind glass. Efficiency is greater than either of the above.

CENTRAL HEATING BY GAS—SEE PAGE 47.

● Note that if mains gas is not supplied to your home it is possible to use Calor gas cylinders ('bottled' gas) which are delivered by a supplier, stored outside the building and piped to special appliances. (This method of obtaining warmth is safer than paraffin heaters.)

ELECTRICITY

Electric fires have the advantage of being portable and easily switched on, but they do present certain safety hazards—see page 194. The following are the types available:

1 *Radiant fires*

Because heat travels in straight lines, these models warm what is in direct line with them and it takes a long time for the whole room to become warm. Cheap to buy. Must have a guard to protect children and old people from being burned if they should stumble against the fire. See page 194.

2 *Convectors*

Much safer than 1 as elements are not exposed. Can be thermostatically controlled.

3 *Fan heaters*

Can be used to heat part of a room only, therefore particularly suitable for invalids. Can be thermostatically controlled. Cheap to buy. Inclined to be noisy.

CENTRAL HEATING BY ELECTRICITY—SEE PAGE 47.

## Central Heating

WHAT IS IT?
Central heating is a system whereby the home (whole or part) is warmed from one main source.

1  *Full central heating*
   Guaranteed provision of a temperature of 18°C (70°F) in living rooms and 13°C (55°F) in the rest of the rooms.

2  *Partial central heating*
   The heating of certain rooms from one source, other rooms heated by independent means.

3  *Background heating*
   The heating of all rooms to about 12°C (50°F), with individual rooms 'topped up' as required by other means.

'WET' SYSTEM
This system can be successfully installed into older property as well as into the building of a new house. It is the most popular of central heating systems and may depend upon a gas, oil or solid fuel boiler, or upon the back boiler of a gas or solid fuel fire. Having been heated, water is forced through $1\frac{1}{4}$ cm. ($\frac{1}{2}''$) copper pipes (small bore) in conjunction with slim panel radiators. This circulation is usually assisted by an electrically driven pump, but in some older systems a less successful result is obtained (without a pump, by means of 'gravity feed') by the use of larger pipes.

Domestic hot water is provided by an indirect system coincidentally with room heating. If hot water only is required (e.g. during hot weather) this system can be isolated by switching off the central heating pump. The water system required for heating is kept separate from that used at the taps and passes continuously through the coiled pipe (see Figure 3.1), any sediment (dirt or rust) picked up being retained within the system.

*Boilers*
These are the sources of heat for the water system and may be situated at the back of a gas or solid fuel fire, floor standing or wall hung. They may be powered by gas, oil or solid fuel and must be of the correct size for the amount of work required. Heating engineers will give advice about this but if you wish to perform a D.I.Y. operation you must consider:
the number of rooms to be heated;
the amount of insulation existing (see page 50);
the number of windows involved;
the position of the house.
(*WHICH?* Report 1981 gives a boiler-size calculator.)

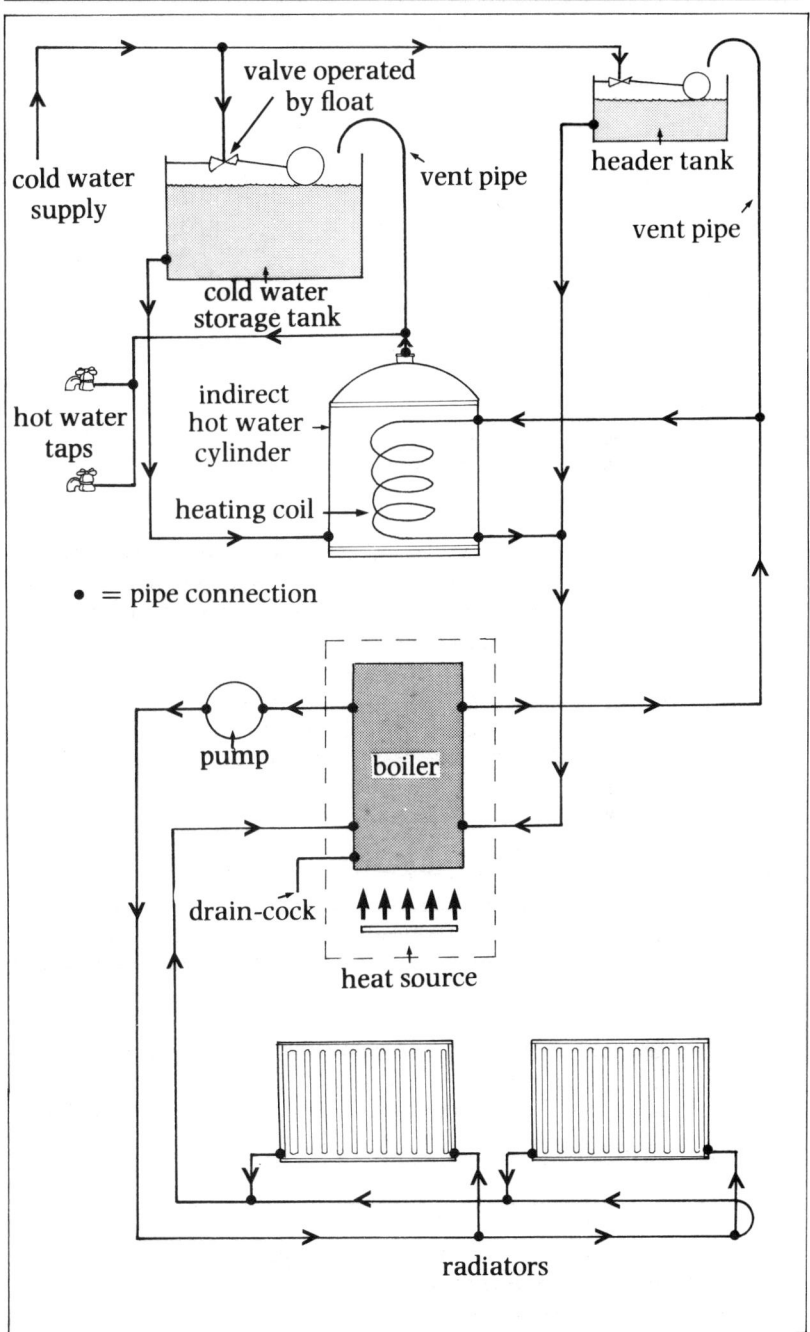

*Figure 3.1 Domestic heating and hot water supply*

*A room thermostat*                    *A thermostatic radiator valve*

Back boilers may be:
a) gas powered—These are conventionally flued boilers combined with fires; each can conveniently be used separately.
b) solid fuelled—These can only operate when the fire is alight and can therefore present problems when hot water is required during the summer.

*Controls*

These allow you to select the temperature required for rooms and tap water, making the system as efficient and economical as you wish.

1 Boiler thermostat—This measures the temperature of the water in the boiler and switches off/on the fuel source, together with the pump, as it rises and falls.

2 Time clock—This can be programmed (by means of lugs and dials) to switch the heating on and off at selected times; it will also switch off the pump if hot tap water only is required.

3 Room thermostat—This is a dial which you can set to the temperature of rooms which you require. When this is reached the pump is automatically switched off, switching on again as the temperature falls.

4 Thermostatic radiator valves—These are expensive to instal but may be an economical measure over a long period. By using these, each radiator is individually controlled and room heating can be used as required.

'DRY' SYSTEM

This method of house-warming must be installed when the house is being built, depending as it does upon the ducting of warm air through grilles into the various rooms. If this warm current is produced by gas a flue is necessary; if by electricity no flue is required and it is usually run at off-peak periods.

ELECTRIC STORAGE SYSTEM

By this system solid masses of concrete (either complete floors or blocks encased in metal containers) are heated by electric elements. Being good non-conductors these blocks retain the heat for a long time, absorbing it during cheap off-peak periods and releasing it gradually into the room atmosphere during the day and evening. Although it can be called 'central heating' this method is really only effective as background warmth and cannot supply hot water. Night storage heaters run on a 'white meter' system charged at below half of the standard rate.

| Choice of fuel | Advantages | Disadvantages |
|---|---|---|
| 1 Electricity | Two tariffs are available:<br>a) standard—all units are priced at the same cost regardless of when they are used;<br>b) off-peak—'white meter' can be installed; all electricity used during night hours is then charged at a cheaper rate. (See storage heaters above.)<br>Electricity can be generated by means of nuclear energy and, because other energy resources are diminishing, electric central heating *may* become more common and less expensive in the future. | Very expensive. |
| 2 Natural gas | Cheaper than other fuels at present.<br>Provision of service pipes and meters are the responsibility of the Regional Gas Board. A one, two or three-star service insurance can be contracted with the Board for annual servicing and repairs to the central heating system.<br>During the summer months there are often special offers of reduced costs of installation. | Costs may increase as the expenses involved in obtaining gas from below the North Sea rise and the supply diminishes. All problems concerned with gas supply and heating systems must be attended to by a Gas Board specialist or by a CORGI representative. |
| 3 Oil | Choice of two oils, depending on the type of burner in the boiler. Convenient method. | More expensive than gas or solid fuel. Oil has to be stored in a tank—siting is important. Filters in boilers must be cleaned regularly, at 6–12 monthly intervals. |
| 4 Solid fuel—<br>see page 41 | | |

FLUES

All combustion requires air and produces fumes.

*Solid fuel boilers*

These must be provided with a draught to burn efficiently and the waste products are carried up the chimney (which should be lined to prevent bricks from absorbing fumes).

*Gas/oil boilers*
These require a flue ('balanced flue') to allow the passage of air in to assist combustion and the dispersal of fumes out of the room. They may also be installed to a conventional chimney if it is lined.

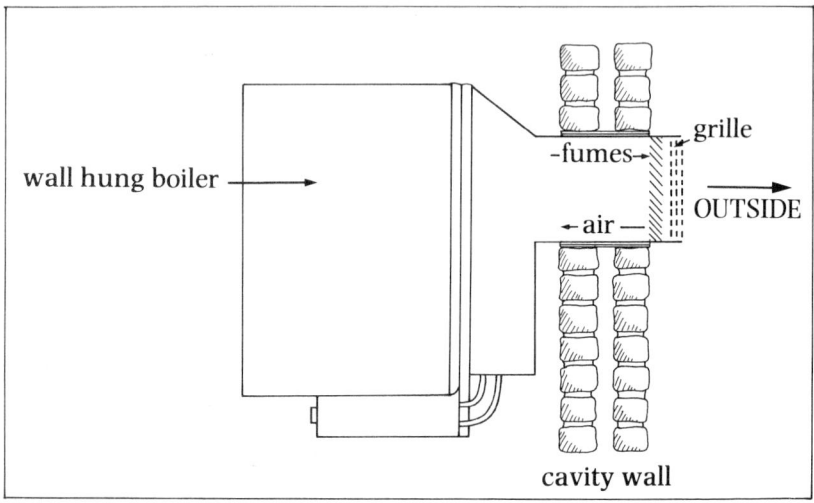

*Figure 3.2  A balanced flue*

## Methods of Heating

Room heat is provided by either radiation or convection.

RADIATORS
The most commonly used method of emitting heat and available in various shapes and sizes. Hot water circulates through channels inside the metal 'skin' of the radiator, and the radiated heat warms the surrounding air. Radiators are usually placed under windows to catch the cold air which falls from the glass.

NATURAL CONVECTORS
Hot water flows through piping inside a metal box, warming cold air entering from the bottom. As the air becomes warm it rises and filters out into the room through a grille or slot at the top.

FAN CONVECTORS
Similar principle to natural convectors but more efficient, as the convection currents are accelerated by an electric fan.

SKIRTING HEATING
A convector strip is fixed to the bottom of a wall, often where it is not convenient to instal a radiator (e.g. under low windows), instead of a skirting board. A good method of preventing floor draughts.

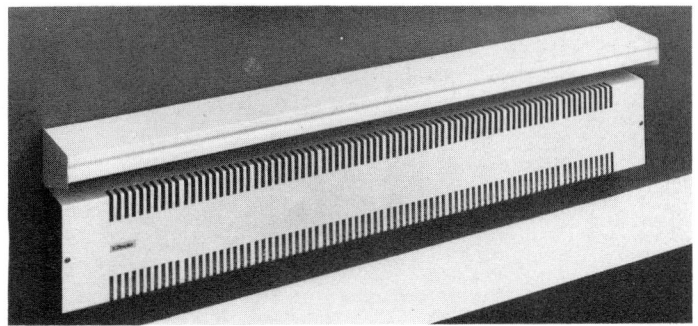

*A skirting board convector heater (Dimplex Heating Ltd)*

## Independent Hot Water Supply

HEATED BY ELECTRICITY

1 *Immersion heater*

An electrical heating element similar to that in an electric kettle can be fitted (immersed) into almost any existing hot water tank or cylinder which is in good condition. This method of heating water is expensive, but costs can be reduced slightly by using two elements:

a short one at the top of the tank to provide small quantities of domestic hot water;

a larger one at the bottom to provide bulk hot water for baths, etc.

2 *Over-sink storage heater*

Provides instant hot water from an insulated storage heater (heated by an electric element) fixed over sinks, baths or basins. Capacities range from 7 l. ($1\frac{1}{2}$ gal.) to 68 l. (15 gal.).

3 *Under-sink storage heater*

Similar to 2, but fitted under a work surface or draining board where it is not possible to fit an over-sink unit.

HEATED BY GAS

1 *Over-sink heater*

An insulated cylinder is fitted over the sink, basin or bath and supplies hot water to one or more taps. Cold water from the mains passes through pipes which are heated by gas jets as taps are turned on.

2 *Storage heater*

A self-contained floor-standing system consisting of an insulated tank which will hold sufficient hot water for your daily needs.

3 *Circulators*

Miniature gas boilers which are used with a conventional hot water storage cylinder and can be thermostatically controlled.

● Note that it is important that any hot water storage tank or cylinder is properly lagged. Failure to do this will mean that a high proportion of the heat will be lost. Insulating jackets should be 75 mm. (3″) thick and can be purchased from a number of sources including D.I.Y. specialists.

# INSULATION

Efficient insulation prevents heat penetration in the summer and heat loss in the winter, so any heating system will function most efficiently and economically in a well insulated house. Hot air rises, so the insulation of the roof cavity is a most important consideration. Whatever form this takes the insulating material is placed between the ceiling joists and can easily be done by the D.I.Y. enthusiast.

## Insulating Materials

SHEET
1 *Glass fibre*
   A good insulator; available in rolls 100 mm. (4″) thick and 400 mm. (16″) wide. Users should always wear a mask and gloves as tiny loose fibres scratch and irritate.
2 *Mineral fibre 'wool'*
   Slightly less effective than glass fibre, but slightly cheaper.
3 *Aluminium foil*
   Quite effective either laid *across* the joints, or crumpled and laid *between* them. (Note that if the first method is used, the loft space cannot be used for storage.)
4 *Fibre board*
   Laid either *across* or *between* the joists. (Note if the first method is used, a good 'floor' is obtained.)

LOOSE FILL
Mineral fibre granules are emptied from sacks into the spaces between the joists; not expensive.

POLYSTYRENE TILES
Fixed to ceilings underneath the loft, these will afford a small amount of insulation. Really good heat retention requires a thickness of 100 mm. (4″) of material.

An efficiently insulated loft will preclude warm air from rising into it and will therefore become very cold during the winter. Water tanks situated in the loft are then in danger of freezing and these must be separately insulated. Blankets or commercial glass fibre 'jackets' (75 mm. (3″) thick in either case) should be tied round the tank; the floor below the tank should be left uninsulated so that warm air can rise beneath it; all pipes should be well wrapped with fabric or foam sheeting strips.

GRANTS AVAILABLE

1 Assistance towards the cost of loft insulation may be obtained by house owners, occupiers, landlords, private tenants or council tenants under the Government's Home Insulation Scheme. At present this is 66% of the cost but if such assistance is required, a council representative will have to inspect the loft and advise on the type of insulation to be used *before* the work is begun.

2 Elderly people receiving supplementary benefit *or* qualifying for a rent/rate rebate may receive a grant of 90% of the cost.

## Cavity Wall Insulation

As shown in Figure 3.3 on page 52, more heat is lost through the external walls of an uninsulated house than through any other part. Most modern houses are built with cavity walls, that is, two separate courses of brickwork with a gap between. This space in itself provides a certain degree of insulation. The efficiency of this can be increased, however, by filling the cavity with

loose pellets;

mineral wool;

foam plastic. (This process *must* be carried out by expert contractors. In some cases considerable difficulties have been experienced from the production of fumes which have seeped through walls, sometimes forcing occupants to leave their homes. These fumes are caused by inefficient mixing of the formaldehyde compound, often practised by 'cowboy' operators.)

All of these are blown through holes produced by *either* drilling through the external wall and making good afterwards *or* removing a complete brick and replacing it with new cement after the insulating material has been injected.

These are expensive procedures but over a few years there will be an appreciable saving in fuel bills. If you are an owner-occupier a grant may be available, providing that

a) the property was built before 1961;

b) the rateable value of the property is less than £225.

If you are the landlord this does not apply. You may, of course, put in an application and hope.

Before committing yourself to a large financial outlay, check that:

1 The contractor you choose undertakes to work to British Standard specifications or is approved by the Building Research Establishment. (A list of approved contractors is available.)

2 The type of insulation you have chosen is approved for the area.

3 The contractor agrees that your property is in a fit condition to be treated.

4 Local authority approval is/is not required.

After work has been carried out, check that all external wall drill-holes or missing bricks have been made good.

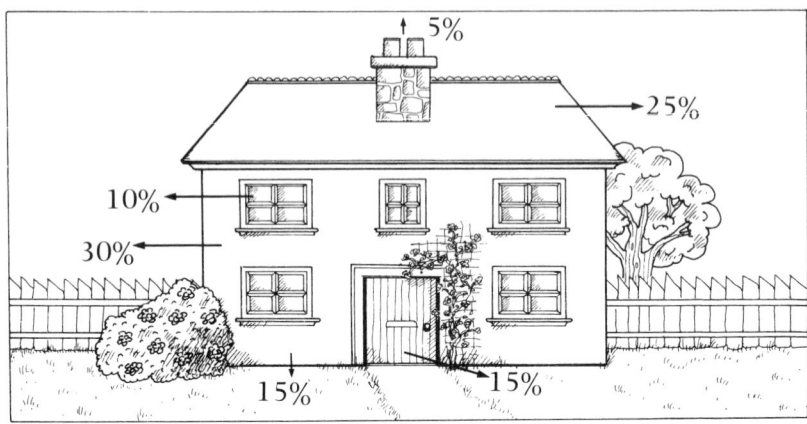

*Figure 3.3  Heat loss from an uninsulated house*

*Installing cavity wall insulation*

## Wall Insulation

Cork/polystyrene tiles and wood panels offer a small degree of insulation of internal walls. (See also pages 35–6.)

## Window Insulation

The large windows built into modern houses certainly make rooms light and attractive but they do also allow a considerable amount of heat to escape. The most expensive method of counteracting this is double glazing—a very expensive procedure to have carried out professionally but one which can be accomplished at a much reduced financial outlay by doing it yourself. Time and effort, however, are required in large amounts!

Savings on fuel bills are not high (about 15%) but draughts from windows are eliminated; outside noise is reduced; a certain amount of condensation is prevented; there is a degree of burglar deterrent; and investment in this form of insulation is worth considering in conjunction with that in the rest of your home.

TYPES OF DOUBLE GLAZING
The space between panes should be:
20 mm. ($\frac{3}{4}''$) for heat retention;
100 mm. (4'') for noise exclusion.
1 *Replacement windows*
    Existing windows and frames are removed entirely and replaced by mounted double panes.
2 *Secondary windows*
    An additional pane is fitted either inside or outside the existing window; this is the method most easily carried out by non-professionals.
3 *Sealed windows*
    The single panes of the original windows are removed and replaced by double panes sealed after air has been vacuum evacuated from between them. (Ensure that a guarantee is given.)
● Note that fully glazed doors must be fitted with safety glass.
A satisfactory D.I.Y. method can be achieved by using plastic sheeting. This is available in various thicknesses and qualities and advice on your choice may be obtained from reputable stockists.
Before embarking upon any work of this kind yourself:
1 Read as much as you can about the various types of double glazing available.
2 Look at the samples in shops and discuss them with the specialist retailers.
3 Be certain that your measurements are absolutely accurate.
4 Read the instructions carefully and do not begin until you have understood them completely.
5 Have the glass you require cut by a glazier; the cost is small and well worth the outlay.
If, for any reason, double glazing cannot be considered and there is an excessive amount of cold draught from your windows, look to your curtains for insulation. Long, thick, lined curtains will help considerably, particularly when pulled at night. Interlining of thin sheet metal or metallized fabric will increase their effectiveness.

## Floor Insulation

Most newly-built homes today have solid floors which seldom present draught problems. Older buildings, however, are usually floored with tongued-and-grooved boards which may have worn or shrunk, allowing cold air to creep up in between them. These draughts can most conveniently be reduced by fitting wall-to-wall floor covering—tiles, linoleum, parquet or carpet (see pages 22–3).

## Draught Excluders

About 15% of the heat in your home escapes through badly fitting door and window frames. Very effective draught excluders are available from hardware stores, builders' merchants and D.I.Y. shops, and are a most cost effective form of insulation.

● Remember that however valuable insulation is in the home, rooms must still be adequately ventilated.

## COOKERS

Before following common practice and considering the purchase of a conventional cooking stove, assess your own needs and eating habits and ask yourself whether you need an oven *and* a hob *and* a grill. Each of these can now be obtained separately and fitted independently to either the gas or the electricity supply; so purchase only what you are likely to use, possibly supplemented by one of the many specialized cooking appliances available, e.g. slow cooker, contact grill (infra-red), pressure cooker, microwave cooker.

### Choosing your Cooker

Consider first which fuel you wish to use:
a) electricity;
b) mains gas;
c) a combination of gas and electricity as indicated above;
d) solid fuel, e.g. Rayburn, Aga;
e) 'bottled' gas.
   Remember the following points:
1 The old-fashioned kitchen range is now updated to a combined cooker/heater.
2 Second-hand cookers can be 'good buys' when families are moving house.
3 Reconditioned cookers are available from both the Gas and the Electricity Board Showrooms. These are reasonably priced and of good value.
4 Split-level combinations of oven and hob are possible, the hob built, as and where convenient, into a worktop and the oven separately, usually at waist level. This arrangement is a good opportunity to enjoy the cleanliness of electricity on the one hand with the flexibility of gas on the other.

Ask yourself the following questions:

1 How much space can you allow in your kitchen for your cooking equipment? (Measure carefully and take your tape measure with you when you go to choose it.)

2 How much do you want to spend? (Fix your price limit and consider items within this cost range only.)

3 How many automatic devices do you want? (These all raise the price of the cooker and are wasted unless used regularly, e.g. a rotisserie.)

4 Do you prefer an eye-level or a waist-high grill? (Consider the respective safety hazards, particularly if young children are about.)

5 Do you want a self-cleaning oven? (See page 56.)

6 Will a left-handed, right-handed or pull-down oven door fit most conveniently into your kitchen plan?

7 What height is most convenient for you?

Gather and study all the leaflets you can, ask questions of friends and consult qualified staff of Gas and Electricity Board Showrooms.

## Electric Cookers

HOB FITTINGS

1 *Radiant rings*
Metal-covered coiled elements which glow red when hot; some have a dual circuit allowing the central part to heat alone.

2 *Disc rings*
Solid metal plates with a shallow depression in the middle; slower to heat than radiant rings.

3 *Griddle*
Non-stick rectangular metal plate on which foods (normally grilled or fried) can be cooked by direct surface heat.

4 *Ceramic hobs*
These do not behave in the same way as gas or electric hobs.
a) Vitreous ceramic is positioned over the heating elements in one continuous surface.
b) Although some hobs have a warning light which glows after the hob has been switched off, most do not, so the heat areas can appear cool while actually still being dangerously hot.
c) Special care has to be taken to ensure that the surface is not scratched by moving saucepans *across* it; they must be lifted.
d) Heat centres respond slowly to being turned up and down.
e) Although easy to clean, *only* the type of cleaner recommended by the manufacturers should be used.
f) Three colours are available—white, black and brown, but there is no difference in performance.

5 *Magnetic induction*
An advancement on the ceramic hob. When a ferrous (iron or steel) metal pan is placed on the hob, the hob automatically heats

up. Normal heat settings are used and as soon as the pan is removed the heat supply is switched off. At present these models are not readily available.

GRILLS

These are usually at waist or eye level. In split-level unit arrangements they may be above, below or inside the main or the second oven, or completely separate, wall-mounted. They may be combined with a rotisserie (motor-driven spit).

OVENS

*Conventional ovens*

Electrical elements are set at both sides of the oven behind removable enamelled panels. Since hot air rises the oven is slightly hotter at the top than at the lower levels.

*Fan assisted ovens*

A fan (electrically operated) is situated in the back panel of the cooker, circulating the hot air more efficiently than in a conventional oven, providing an even temperature throughout.

*Ducted fan ovens*

The fan directs heat through ducts on to individual shelves.

Both fan assisted and ducted fan ovens reduce cooking time, so saving fuel, in comparison with the conventional oven.

*Desirable extras*

1 Easy-clean oven linings—Most ovens (both gas and electric) have catalytic (self-cleaning) linings; the chemical coating, combined with the oven heat, continuously decomposes any fat or grease deposited on to the linings into harmless gases. More expensive electric cookers may have pyrolytic linings; the self-locking oven door is closed and the temperature turned up as high as possible; fat and grease are decomposed and deposited as a fine powder which you are able to wipe away. It is important to follow manufacturers' instructions and not to expect a sparkling-clean oven interior. The surface, being dull-textured, will only be 'presentable', but if you have shining shelf rails (cleaned manually) these will offset the possible disappointment of a non-gleaming interior surface.

2 Inner glass door/partially glazed door—These allow cooking progress to be monitored without actually opening the oven door, particularly if assisted by an interior oven light.

3 Electronic touch-control panels—These are available on very up-to-date cookers; information is fed into the cooker by pressing buttons in a manner similar to that used when employing a calculator.

4 Automatic controls—These are features of both gas and electric cookers and will switch the oven on and off at times prescribed by you.

MICROWAVE COOKERS

To call these cookers 'ovens' is misleading, as they will undertake the operations normally carried out by both the hob and the oven of the conventional cooker.

Microwaves are high-frequency electro-magnetic waves (produced by a magnetron) similar to radio waves, which are dispelled in different directions by a fan. They bounce off and across the metal walls of the cabinet in a regular pattern, thus ensuring that the food is evenly heated. The waves will pass through air, glass, china, plastic and paper without heating them, but when they strike food or liquid they are absorbed. This causes the molecules in the structure of the food to vibrate, causing friction which generates heat. Any food to be cooked in a microwave cabinet must contain moisture, to enable it to cook in its own juice.

This cooker does not completely replace the conventional one but it is particularly useful for those who batch-bake, freeze-store and have limited time for starting-from-scratch cooking.

*Advantages*

1  Defrosts deep-frozen foods rapidly.

2  Can be connected to any 13 amp socket outlet.

3  Portable—can be taken to temporary lodgings, etc.

4  Fast, clean, safe and simple to use—refer to the handbook.

5  No cooking smells to dispel.

6  Turntables are available for use in the cabinet—desirable but not essential.

7  Built-in device ensures that the current is automatically cut out when the door is opened.

8  Very versatile—consult specialized microwave cookery books.

*An electric cooker*
*(TI Creda Ltd)*

*A microwave cooker*
*(Toshiba UK Ltd)*

*A gas cooker*
*(British Gas)*

*Disadvantages*

1 Food does not normally become browned (but *some* models now include a browning or searing dish).

2 Grilling cannot normally be carried out (but a few models include a conventional grill in the roof of the cabinet).

3 Deep-fat frying is not possible.

4 No metal containers, or gilt-edged crockery, should be used— these cause 'arcing', manifested by audible and visible sparking.

● When choosing a microwave cooker make sure that it has a BEAB approval tag.

TABLE-TOP OVENS

These are small, free-standing ovens which can be plugged into a 13 amp socket. They are, in fact, miniature ovens and some have automatic timers. The oven grill is not very adequate and for best results it would be advisable to purchase a separate grill.

PORTABLE HOB

There is an electric hob on the market which has two ring sizes, needs no special fitting and can even be carried to the table. It can be stood on a working surface in use and plugged into a socket using a 13 amp fused plug.

TABLE-TOP COOKER/MULTI-COOKER

This is a free-standing cooking unit running off a 13 amp fused plug inserted into a convenient socket. It is shaped like a large, deep, square frying pan and can be used with or without the lid, so acting as a baking, steaming, frying or stewing cooker. It is thermostatically controlled.

## Gas Cookers

A piped gas supply is not as widely available as mains electricity is, but bottled Calor gas can be used for most cookers and is particularly useful for mobile-home dwellers. As a fuel it is convenient and versatile; the flames can be seen and controlled, which makes economy easier to practise than with electricity.

● It is important to note that although flames are *usually* clearly visible, it has been found that they virtually 'disappear' when the sun is shining upon them, and great care must then be taken to notice whether or not the tap is turned on before reaching across the hot plate.

Most domestic gas is 'natural' nowadays and therefore non-toxic, but the characteristic artificially-introduced smell has been preserved so that leaking gas is apparent. It must be remembered that, even if it is no longer possible to 'gas' oneself, a mixture of gas and air is still explosive and leakage must not be ignored.

HOB FITTINGS

These may be parts of complete cookers, *either* placed above the oven *or* separate from the oven set into a work surface in a convenient position. The hob may consist of one, two, three or four burners.

*Special features*

1 Control knobs which have to be pressed in to release the gas flow—this is a safety measure, particularly for old people (who may not smell unlit gas) and children, who could turn on the gas accidentally.

2 A simmering control which will keep flames burning very low, for long, slow cooking.

3 Thermostatically controlled burners which will keep the contents of pans at constant temperatures.

4 Removable shallow troughs fitting round the burners to catch overflowing liquids and facilitate cleaning.

GRILLS

These may be

a) part of a complete cooker, sited above the hob at eye level, under it at waist level or inside the oven (as in most continental cookers);

b) independent of the main cooker, fixed to the wall in a convenient position.

They may be heated

a) from rear or central jets which heat the grill frets, with the radiant heat reflected downwards by a cover;

b) (less commonly, but more efficiently) by a grill burner which radiates heat over its entire surface.

*Special features*

1 An electrically rotated spit ('rotisserie').

2 An adjustable wire-mesh tray for use in the grill pan, taking the food to be cooked nearer to or further from the flames.

OVENS

The conventional oven is an insulated steel box heated by rows of gas jets which are able to burn in the current of air drawn in through an aperture at the bottom. Normally, because hot air rises, the hottest part of the oven is at the top, lower temperatures corresponding with lower positions.

*Special features*

1 Automatic control which will cause the oven to switch itself on and off at pre-selected times. This model must be attached to the electricity supply as well as to the gas main and is particularly useful for those people who are at work all day, enabling them to return to a cooked meal.

2 A fan, which distributes heat evenly throughout the oven. Again, this requires access to an electricity supply.

3 Siting at the same height as the hob, requiring no bending.

4  An electrically-operated spit in the roof.
5  A glass panel in the door to allow cooking progress to be checked.
6  An interior light which makes it easier to see what is happening.
7  A lining which cleans itself as it is heated.

IGNITION
Grill, hob and oven jets may be ignited
a)  by separate, continually-burning pilot lights;
b)  semi-automatically, when the gas flow is turned on and an ignition switch is pressed to light the jet;
c)  automatically, a flame being produced as soon as the gas flow control is switched on.

Automatic re-ignition will re-light burners and, sometimes, ovens if they have inadvertently gone out.

Ignition is normally activated by electricity, either by means of a battery or by a Piezo system (sparking device).

Gas jets should always burn with a blue flame. If the flame shows any yellowing, have the burners checked by a Gas Board official.

The 'marriage' between gas and electricity as sources of domestic fuel is now familiar and, as has been shown, electric power is frequently used to boost the efficiency of a gas cooker. If a split-level cooker is preferred, the different units may well be fired by either fuel.

**Solid Fuel Cookers**

The modern version of the old-fashioned kitchen range (which can also be fired by gas or oil) requires a large kitchen, as it is a bulky piece of equipment. It provides constant hot water and some models can be used as sources of central heating as well.

These items are expensive to buy and are really only economical in use if a great deal of cooking is carried out. However, they are available in beautiful colours and look attractive. Unfortunately, when the cooker is in use heat is produced, whether it be winter or summer weather.

VENTILATION

The principle of ventilation is that stale, hot air should be removed, to be replaced with fresh, cooler air. Open windows give satisfactory ventilation but some means of fixed ventilation is essential in rooms subjected to fumes from the products of combustion (e.g. gas cookers, oil stoves), steam or dampness.

AIR ACTIVATED
These are revolving plastic discs, available in various sizes, which fit into window panes and help to clear condensation without opening the

window. They are activated by natural draughts and convection currents and are only moderately efficient.

ELECTRIC EXTRACTOR FANS
These can be fitted into windows or walls and are legally a 'must' in a bathroom without windows; the most effective method of fan ventilation available. Running costs are low but the fans tend to be noisy.

COOKER HOODS
Alternatives to extractor fans.
*Exhaust hood*
    Has a duct leading into an air vent in the wall.
*Re-cycling hood*
    Filters the air and returns it to the room; less efficient than exhaust type; has no air duct.
    Both of these are noisy in use.

## LIGHTING

Inside the home artificial lighting is easier to control than daylight, and careful planning will ensure that you have exactly what you need. Consider:

1 How many wall-mounted power points do you need?
Look to the future as well as to your present circumstances. There are usually far too few of these sockets available in both old and new buildings. The cost of installation of additional points is well worth the convenience afforded and also safeguards the possibility of overloading sockets by using multi-adapters and precludes the danger of trailing flexes.

2 Where should new power points be sited?
The conventional position at the skirting-board level is not always the most convenient. In the kitchen, particularly, sockets at worktop level are very desirable and waist-height points also do not attract inquisitive tiny fingers as do those at just-above-floor level.

3 Do you need static or flexible lighting?
In bathrooms and kitchens static lighting is probably the best, good light being required in the bathroom on the hands and face, in the kitchen on the work surfaces. In living-room areas more flexible lighting is required. An even all-over light from a fixed central fitting is usually insufficient and rather depressing in effect; areas of light and shade provide interest and localize illumination as required. The use of a diffuser will soften the glare of fluorescent lighting tubes, or they may be partially concealed behind cornices or frames. Dimmer switches allow you to control the amount of light a lamp gives out; a bright overhead

C

*A dimmer switch (MK Electric Ltd)*

light may be dimmed to provide a softer glow for watching television, entertaining, etc.

4  Is it worth inserting an automatic lighting switch?
The automatic switching-on of one or more lights at dusk may be a valuable burglar-deterrent if you are out or away. This may be achieved by setting a time-clock which will cause the lamps to come on and go off at the normal times and give the impression of occupation to an empty house. Your local Crime Prevention Officer will give you useful advice.

## Types of Lighting

GENERAL
An overall light, usually from a ceiling pendant. Some fittings throw light downwards, some upwards, so the distribution of light desired must be considered. Variations in intensity may be achieved by the use of a dimmer switch and by fixing an adjustable pendant light, e.g. over the dining table.

EFFECT
Highlighting of certain areas. Table lamps, standard lamps and/or spotlights are used.

SPECIFIC
Localized light for specific tasks. Reading, writing, sewing, etc., require a light from the left side or from behind to prevent the worker from performing in his/her own light.

Most lamps used in the home have a coiled or even double-coiled tungsten filament which glows brightly and is protected by an inert gas inside the bulb. The glass bulbs can be of various shapes—pear, mushroom, candle, short tube (as perhaps concealed under a bedhead), etc. and in general, pearl or opal glass is better than clear to avoid glare and shadows. These filament lamps give off only about 4% of their output in light, the rest in heat, so they are wasteful of energy and you have to be careful how powerful a lamp you use in certain fittings or you might scorch or melt the shade.

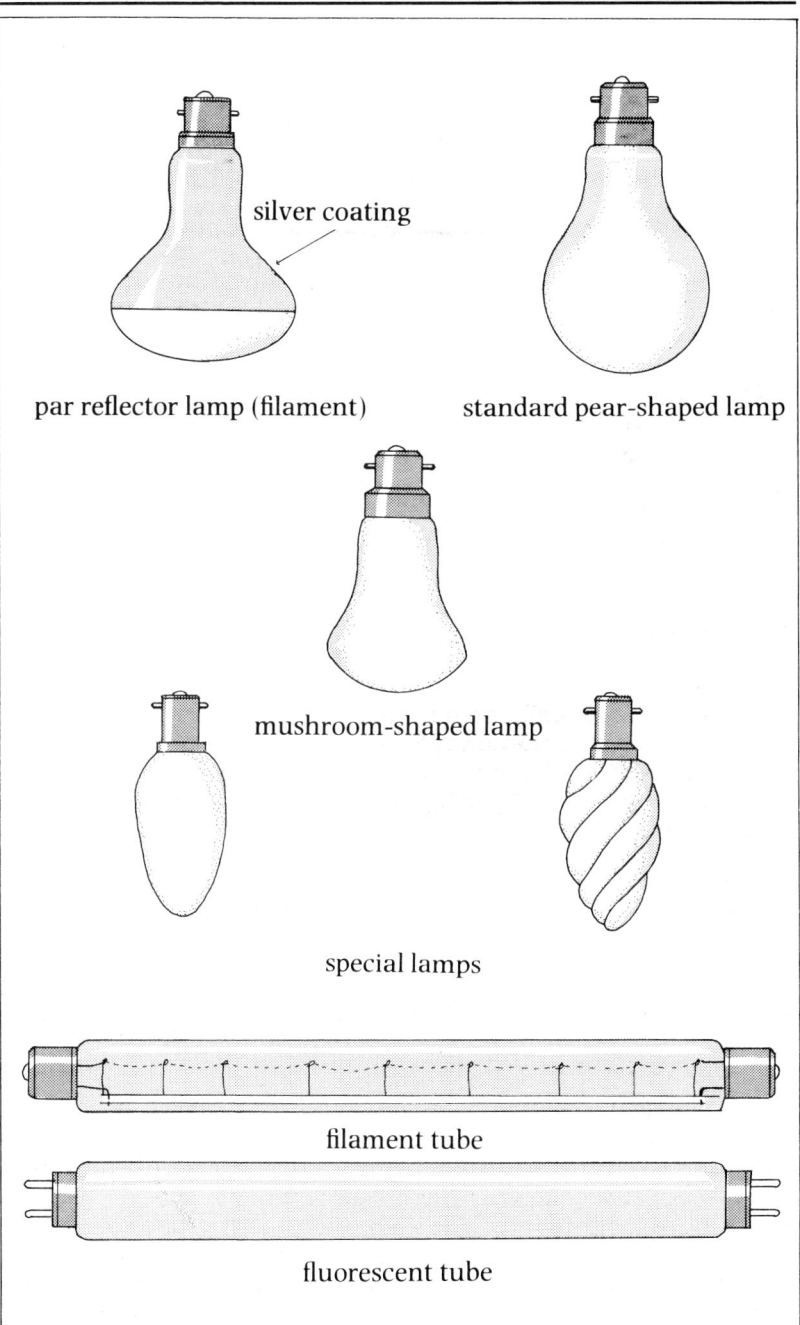

silver coating

par reflector lamp (filament)     standard pear-shaped lamp

mushroom-shaped lamp

special lamps

filament tube

fluorescent tube

*Figure 3.4  Lamps*

Fluorescent tubes, on the other hand, have no filament but have two electrodes, one at each end, which are activated by a starter, and are filled with a gas which glows. They are shadowless and give off about 12% of their energy in light so will run for about 7,500 hours (compared with the filament lamp's 1,000 hours or a 'long-life' one's 2,000 hours) and therefore are more economical to run after the higher initial outlay.

## Special Lighting

IN THE KITCHEN
Fluorescent lighting is particularly suitable, fixed over the sink and the work surfaces (*under* wall cupboards) to avoid shadows.

IN THE BEDROOM
Adjustable spotlights are required for reading in bed; lights over mirrors are desirable.

IN THE HALL
Light should be warm and welcoming.

ON THE STAIRCASE
A good, strong light is essential, worked by switches at the top and the bottom of the stairs.

OVER FRONT/BACK DOORS
Usually needs to be left on for long periods.

## Switches

If a turned-on switch becomes hot to the touch it almost certainly requires replacing; if broken it should be replaced at once. The safest course of action is to consult a qualified electrician, but in any case the switch plate should *never* be unscrewed unless the main supply is switched off. Note that this also applies when stripping and replacing wallpaper—see page 33.

## Sockets

Ideally, every electrical appliance should have its own socket, but if adapters have to be used these should be as few as possible. *Never* use an adapter which does not accept all the pins of the plugs used. For the protection of children, whose inquisitive fingers may explore socket holes, it is possible to obtain shuttered sockets of 5 and 13 amps, which become inaccessible when the plug is removed. Unshuttered sockets may be safeguarded with a square plug inserted when the point is not in use.

## Plugs

Modern plugs are of the fused type with flat pins designed for use with 13 amp socket outlets. Covers are usually plastic but it is possible to obtain rubber covered plugs which do not crack when dropped. All plugs should conform—and state that they do—to British Standards.

If you are using round-pinned plugs in your home, it is quite likely that the wiring system is out of date and the Electricity Board should be consulted about the advisability of re-wiring the house.

● Make sure that the plug of any appliance which recommends earthing is wired with 3 wires, as shown in the photograph below. For re-wiring, see page 83.

## Fuses

A fuse is a weak link inserted into the stronger chain of the electrical system—i.e. the melting point of its wire is lower than that of the main circuit. Should it become overheated and destroyed the whole current is cut off, and fire resulting from faulty wiring is prevented. This 'blowing' of a fuse may indicate only a worn-out fuse which just needs replacing, but if it 'blows' a second time there is a more serious fault. After checking that the size of the fuse is correct for the appliance which 'blew' the fuse, seek expert advice.

SIZE OF FUSES
These must be suitable for the appliance to which the plug is attached; a rough guide is usually printed on the back of the fuse pack as purchased. The wattage of the appliance will be indicated either on the unit itself or in the handbook and the corresponding size of fuse should be fitted:

*A correctly wired plug, a shuttered socket and a fuse (MK Electric Ltd)*

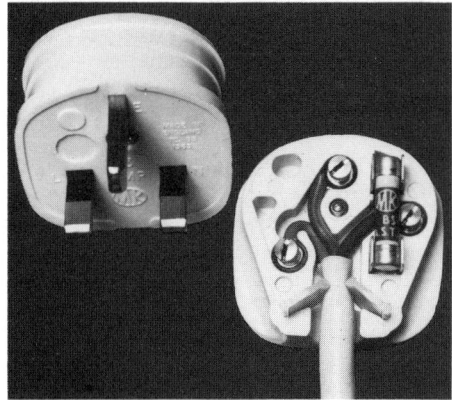

Appliances up to 750 watts      — 3 amp fuse
Appliances from 750 to 1,250 watts   — 5 amp fuse
Appliances from 1,250 to 1,750 watts— 7 amp fuse
Appliances from 1,750 to 3,250 watts—13 amp fuse
Colour television sets may require a fuse higher than 3 amp and manufacturers' instructions should be followed.

## Flexes

Flexes vary like fuses and it is as important to use the correct size of flex for an appliance as it is to fit a suitable fuse. If in doubt, consult your supplier.

| | |
|---|---|
| Lamps and radios | 3 amp |
| Electric irons | 6 amp |
| Electric kettles | 10 amp |
| Washing machines ⎫ Large fires ⎭ | 15 amp |
| Small cookers | 25 amp |

———————————— **FURTHER STUDY** ————————————

## Things to Do

1   Find out the meaning of CORGI and BEAB.
2   Discover how 'underfloor' heating operates. Discuss its advantages and disadvantages.
3   Solar heating is a method which is still being developed. Find out as much as you can about it and consider whether it is a possibility for your own home heating.
4   Discuss the reasons why conservationists do not approve of wood-burning boilers and fires. Find out which are good and which poor woods for burning and why.
5   Find out the connection between coal, coke and old-fashioned gas works.
6   Collect as many brochures as you can for:
     **a)**   gas cookers
     **b)**   electric cookers
     with their prices. Study these, consider what accounts for the differences between their costs and choose what you think is the best value for money. Give your reasons.
7   Visit several lighting specialist centres and examine fittings and shades suitable for: a) a kitchen; b) a sitting room; c) a bedroom.

Draw the ones which most appeal to you, give your reasons and state the price of each.

8 Look at the range of electric light bulbs available in specialist stores or departments; list the types, wattage, colours, shapes and prices and suggest uses for each. Illustrate your list.

9 Discover the source of draughts in your own home. (You can find these by carrying a lighted candle, *in a safe holder*, round the walls of a room, across floors and close to windows. The candle flame will 'bend' against the draught.) Suggest ways in which these could be prevented.

10 Study the text of this chapter carefully and list as many safety measures as you can find.

## Questions to Answer

1 Write out and complete each of the following statements with the correct term chosen from the list in the right-hand column.

a) When _____ double glazing is used the windows cannot be opened even in hot weather.

conduction

b) The third wire in an electric plug is used as a safety measure; it is called the _____ wire.

insulation

c) The percentage of heat lost through an uninsulated roof is _____%.

tungsten filament

d) Water heated by an immersion heater is warmed by _____ from the heated element.

sealed unit

e) In an over-sink gas boiler the water is heated by gas jets underneath it producing _____ currents.

sixty-six

f) Free-standing electric fires warm the rooms by _____ of their heat.

earth

g) The reduction of the passage of warm air from the inside to the outside of a house depends upon the degree of _____ employed.

twenty-five

h) Domestic lamps which use 96% of their energy in producing heat are called _____ lamps.

fluorescent

i) _____ lighting is the cheapest form to run and casts no shadows.

radiation

j) A grant of _____% of the cost may be obtained from the government for an approved installation of roof insulation.

convection

2 Page 51 gives information about the grants obtainable from the Government for insulating your roof. What do you consider to be the reasons for this assistance being offered?

3 Draw *either* an electric cooker *or* a gas stove, labelling all the parts. Give your reasons for preferring one to the other for your own use.

4 A poet refers to 'the benison of hot water'. List the benefits you have found in having access to a domestic hot water system.

5 List the electrical appliances you use in your own home and state the size of the fuse you should be using in each plug.

6 What steps would you take to ensure that your sitting room is as safe as possible for:
   a) an elderly woman;
   b) a very young child?

7 What method of room heating would you recommend for the occupants of:
   a) a third-floor flat;
   b) a country cottage;
   c) a 'town' house?
   Give your reasons.

8 In which ways have methods of lighting and heating developed during the last three centuries? What differences have these developments made to:
   a) the domestic staff situation;
   b) the housewife;
   c) the elderly?

# Running a Home 4

When two people marry their whole lives change—they take on the responsibility of helping each other as husband and wife and of planning their life together so that they have a good marriage in a well-ordered home.

The role of the woman has always been, and probably always will be, essentially the domestic one. Traditionally, the housework, cooking, shopping and care of the children have been tasks carried out by her, while the provision and administration of financial affairs have been in the hands of the man of the house. However, the standard pattern of family life is changing considerably and more and more young mothers are involved in activities outside the home. Most wives continue to bring home a wage packet after they marry, many return to work soon after becoming mothers and others do so after many years at home with their families. If asked why they do this the answer is almost always concerned with money—even if supplementary reasons are given, such as boredom, frustration and the loss of independence, the underlying motive is likely to be financial. Whatever the true reason, the running of the home and the care of the family must continue and a good organizer will delegate her tasks, not only to reduce her own load but to involve other members of the household in the enjoyment and satisfaction of management.

● Note that providing that a woman has worked for her employer for two years, she is entitled to maternity leave. She must give him her expected dates of confinement and return to work; she will then qualify for six weeks' maternity benefit and her job will be kept open for her for up to twenty-nine weeks after the baby's birth. If she resigns from her job, she cannot claim maternity benefit.

A revolutionary situation in housekeeping is the exchange of roles between the male and female partner, where the family income is provided by the woman and domestic affairs are carried out by the man of the house. This may be a matter of choice or of economic necessity; in either case the problems to be coped with are similar.

Both men and women can find themselves having to carry out the responsibilities of the housekeeper *and* the breadwinner, sometimes, unfortunately, with those of looking after children as well.

All these situations bring their own problems but the common ones of running the home remain the same.

The home is the hub of family life and should be a warm, welcoming and relaxing place to return to at the end of each day. Homemaking is a very important job and a satisfying and pleasurable one to those who do it well.

## ORGANIZATION

1 Your day should be managed so that you have sufficient time to do what you *have* to do and still leave enough hours to do what you *want* to do.

2 Housework should not be set to too rigid a pattern—you are going to be looking after a house, part or full-time, for many years, so it should be planned so that you enjoy it!

3 Certain tasks, such as getting up in the morning and getting the children off to school, do have to be kept to an exact timetable, but many others can be carried out when you choose.

4 In the early days of housekeeping it is a good idea to divide the chief tasks into two distinct lists:

| *Daily Tasks* | *Weekly Tasks* |
| --- | --- |
| Attend to children (including 'playing' time) | Carry out general cleaning of living room, bedrooms, kitchen, hall, staircase, bathroom, toilet; vacuum-clean throughout if possible |
| Open windows to air all rooms as necessary | |
| Empty ashtrays (preferably immediately after use, invariably before going to bed) | Do family and household washing, ironing and mending |
| Make beds; tidy bedrooms | Clean windows (inside; outside as often as convenient) |
| Prepare and serve meals | Do shopping after checking reserve stores |
| Wash dishes as required | |
| Tidy and dust as necessary; water flowers | Change bed linen |
| Attend to floors as required, particularly in kitchen | Polish furniture and mirrors |
| Carry out essential washing and ironing | Wipe over inside of oven and refrigerator |
| Wipe over toilet seat and wash-basins | Sweep outside paths |
| Wipe over work surfaces in kitchen, including cooker hob | Disinfect drains |
| Check contents of refrigerator | |
| Empty kitchen refuse bin | |
| Rest and enjoy yourself | |

5 The more physical types of job are best performed in the mornings if possible, when you expect to be at your freshest and most energetic.

6 If you are likely to become bored by repetitive household chores it is advisable to be flexible in your arrangements and to avoid doing the same tasks on the same day every week. To some people the exact opposite is preferable and they welcome the discipline of specified washing days, shopping days, etc.

7 Another list is valuable, noting those 'special' tasks which need doing periodically; you can then fit these in as and when convenient to you:
Tidying and cleaning out cupboards
Washing paintwork and walls
Washing or cleaning curtains
Shampooing carpets or having them professionally cleaned
Airing duvets; professional cleaning/washing as necessary
Washing blankets
De-frosting refrigerator (unless automatic de-frost type)
De-frosting deep-freezer and checking contents

8 A cleaning routine is a very personal piece of planning and depends upon
the type of accommodation;
the size of the accommodation;
the number and ages of the occupants;
how much each member of the household can contribute.

Boys as well as girls should be encouraged to help, certainly by keeping their own rooms tidy and by washing up, as soon as they are old enough. They may take longer and be less efficient than you are, but it is a good start to full participation in household duties.

## Washing Up

a) By machine—see page 116.
b) By hand—this need never be an unpleasant chore, particularly if it is well organized. The essentials are:
a good supply of hot water;
liquid detergent;
a scourer;
a clean tea-towel.

PREPARATION
1 Scrape food scraps on to newspaper or kitchen paper and dispose of them.
2 Empty slops down the sink.
3 Fill dirty saucepans with water, cold if the pan has been used for starchy or milky foods; hot, with a little soda (detergent if pan is aluminium), if greasy. Add salt to the water if there are any burnt areas. Leave to stand.
4 Stack plates and saucers in piles; group cups and glasses separately.
5 Sort knives, forks and spoons separately.

*After the meal!*

*Group and stack the dishes beside the sink*

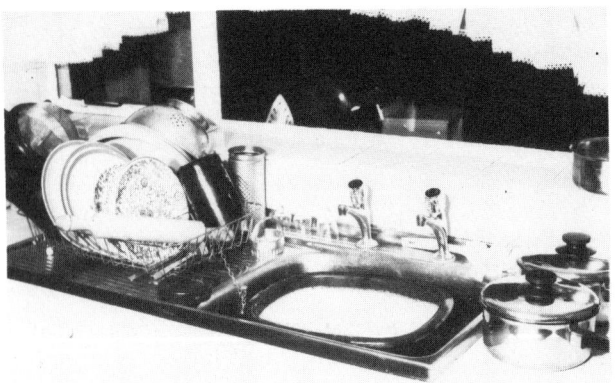

*Leave the dishes to drain*

6 If knives have bone, plastic or other non-metallic handles, stand them in a jug of hot water deep enough to cover the blades.

WASHING
1 Fill the bowl or sink with water as hot as the hands can bear.
2 Add sufficient liquid detergent to make a slight lather.
3 Wash glasses first. Rinse under running hot water if possible. Stand them upside down on the drainer.
4 Wash cups, rinse if possible, stand upside down to drain.
5 Wash the cleanest remaining crockery and continue until all are clean, the dirtiest being the last to be washed. As each item is washed and rinsed, stack it overlapping on drainer supported by cups (not glasses). If a drying rack is available, stand each plate on edge in one of the grooves.
6 If water is dirty, change it for a fresh supply of hot water and washing-up liquid.
7 Wash, rinse and drain cutlery.
8 Wash, rinse and drain any cooking utensils.
9 Wash, rinse and drain saucepans and baking tins, starting with the least soiled.

DRYING UP
1 If a drying rack is used, crockery may be left in it to dry completely before being put away. Glasses must be polished with a dry cloth.
2 If no drying rack is used:
a) dry and polish glasses;
b) dry and polish cutlery;
c) dry plates, saucers, cups;
d) dry cooking utensils;
e) dry saucepans and baking tins.

CLEARING UP
1 Empty dirty water.
2 Clean washing-up bowl and sink. Wipe sink surround.
3 Wash out tea-towel and hang to dry.
4 Wash out washing-up cloth and hang to dry.
5 Rinse sink with clean water. (Once a day, preferably after last washing-up session of the day, add a little disinfectant to the rinsing water.)
6 Put away all washed articles.

## Methods of Cleaning

Every hard surface in the home—wood, metal, plastic, glass—benefits from regular care, many from periodic polishing; the polish (rather than the surface) takes the wear, dirt does not adhere easily and dust is easily removed.

POLISHES

1 *Floor polishes*

Some are water based; when applied to a surface the water evaporates, leaving a hard-film finish. Water can damage wood so it is not advisable to use floor polish on furniture unless it states on the container that it is suitable. Other floor polishes are spirit based.

2 *Furniture polishes*

These are all spirit based.

3 *Silicones*

These act as lubricants and make the polishing agent (wax) easy to apply. They reduce the rubbing required and give a long-lasting shine. They should be avoided on carved or antique furniture where a high gloss is not desirable.

4 *Creams*

Consist of light-coloured waxes, solvents and water, highly emulsified. They are used on highly polished surfaces (which the very small water content cannot permeate).

5 *Dry-bright polishes*

Blends of waxes, solvent and silicone, available in spray or aerosol forms. They require no polishing-off and are suitable for all woods with high gloss, paint, enamel or ceramic surfaces. Not suitable for antique furniture.

6 *Wax*

Hard and soft waxes blended together in a solvent, giving a smooth paste. It requires good rubbing-in. Good for 'feeding' antique and neglected furniture.

7 *Oil*

Oils and resins mixed with a solvent. This only needs to be applied once or twice a year. Suitable for furniture with a matt surface, e.g. teak.

## LABOUR-SAVING EQUIPMENT

There is no doubt that some of the up-to-date appliances available can make life a great deal easier for the busy person looking after a house and family than it used to be. However, these goods are costly and it is very easy to be 'conned' into spending money on items which you will rarely use.

PRESSURE COOKER

1 In an ordinary saucepan the liquid boils and the steam escapes and evaporates. In a pressure cooker the steam cannot escape because the lid is sealed with a rubber ring. Pressure builds up inside the stout pan and the food is cooked quickly.

2 Up to 75% of fuel and time used with conventional saucepans may be saved. High-domed lids add versatility, allowing for bottling processes.

3 Moderately priced.

TABLE 4: CARE OF SURFACES

| Surface | Special Points | Uses | Care |
|---|---|---|---|
| 1 Wood | Porous, therefore has a protective finish applied. Identify the finish on your furniture and treat it accordingly. | | |
| a) French polished | | Furniture; doors; floors; door/window frames; window sills | Liquid silicone furniture polish. Rub well. |
| b) Waxed | | Furniture; doors; floors | Paste wax or furniture cream (avoid silicones—give an undesired sheen). Do not use too much polish—causes stickiness. Wait for polish to dry, buff with clean duster. |
| c) Oiled | | Furniture; doors; floors | Apply teak oil or cream suggested by manufacturer. Use sparingly—excess will cause wood to darken and become sticky. Do *not* use any other polish. |
| d) Varnished/lacquered | | Furniture; doors; floors | Any furniture polish. |
| e) Painted (matt/gloss) | | Door/window frames; window sills; doors | Wash down with mild detergent. Polish with solvent-based polish (aerosol). |
| 2 Laminated plastics | Solvents should be avoided—may dissolve surface. | Kitchen units; work surfaces; kitchen furniture; occasional tables (cantilevered) | Wipe over with damp cloth. Polish with silicone polish and dry, clean duster. |
| 3 Glass | Requires cleaning and polishing without smears. | Windows; table tops; mirrors; wall tiles | Use chamois leather and warm water + 15 ml. vinegar/methylated spirit: $\frac{1}{2}$ l. water or proprietary window cleaner—aerosol spray or opaque liquid. |
| 4 Glass fibre | Scratching of surface must be avoided. | Baths; sinks | Mild detergent (washing-up liquid). No abrasives. Remove stains with bleach if |

| Surface | Special Points | Uses | Care |
|---|---|---|---|
| | | | necessary (on uncoloured surfaces). Finish with dry, soft cloth. Treat coloured finishes with neat liquid detergent applied with a soft cloth. |
| 5 Vitreous enamel | Scratching of surface must be avoided—abrasives *scratch* away offending marks. | Baths; washbasins; sinks; cooking hobs | Use cream cleanser: follow manufacturer's instructions. Do *not* use caustic stain-removers on coloured surfaces. |
| 6 Stoved enamel (paint sprayed on to metal) | Avoid scratching. | Washing machines; cookers; refrigerators; freezers; baths; washbasins; sinks | Wipe over with a damp cloth, rub dry with clean duster. Remove stubborn stains with mild detergent. |
| 7 Glazed/unglazed tiles<br>8 Sheet vinyl | | Floor coverings | Mop over with mild detergent. Unglazed tiles may be scrubbed with proprietary cleanser. |
| 9 Aluminium | Alkalis should be avoided—metal may be damaged; therefore do not treat burnt pans with hot soda water. | Cookware | Wash in mild detergent. Remove solid soiling with nylon scourer. Remove stains by boiling apple peelings. Prevent stains caused by boiling water by adding lemon juice/vinegar. |
| 10 Stainless steel | | Cookware; sinks | Wash in mild detergent. Greasy items should be filled with hot *soda* water and left to soak. Burnt items should be filled with *salt* water and left to soak. |
| 11 Brass<br>12 Pewter<br>13 Copper<br>14 Silverware | | Cookware; cutlery; ornaments; food containers | Follow manufacturer's instructions. Clean with appropriate proprietary polish. Wash cutlery/cookware in mild |

| Surface | Special Points | Uses | Care |
|---|---|---|---|
| | | | detergent, dry and polish on clean cloth after cleaning. |
| 15 Glass ovenware | Avoid placing hot dishes on to cold surfaces or into cold water—causes cracks. Avoid abrasives. | Casseroles; cookware; plates | Wash in mild detergent water as 10. Remove solid debris with nylon scourer or brush. |
| 16 Wallpaper | | | |
| a) Non-washable | | | Dust or sweep with soft vacuum brush or broom. |
| b) Vinyl | | | Wipe over with mild detergent—avoid over rubbing and too much water. |
| 17 Upholstery fabric | Use any proposed cleaning method on a test area first. Avoid ordinary soap or detergent—makes fabric harsh and sticky. | Settees; chairs; stools | On small areas, use grease solvent (working from outside inwards). Weekly care: vacuum clean/brush with soft brush. Shampoo with recommended brand—read instructions carefully. |
| 18 Upholstery vinyl/leather | Make sure of the nature of the upholstery when purchasing—vinyl is a very convincing copy of leather. Price will indicate which it is. | Settees; chairs; stools | Vinyl—wipe over with mild detergent—remove stains with abrasive cream. Leather—use proprietary cleaner. |
| 19 Carpet | Try any cleaner on a test area before using extensively. | | Vacuum-clean or sweep regularly. Shampoo or spot-clean with aerosol liquid or dry shampoos manufactured for the purpose or call in commercial carpet-cleaners. |
| 20 Curtains | When buying ready-made curtains or curtain material enquire as to best method of cleaning/washing. | Windows; doors; alcoves | Vacuum-clean regularly or hang outside in good, dry wind. Wash or dry-clean as suitable for the fabric. |

MICROWAVE COOKER
See page 57.

CONTACT GRILL (INFRA-RED GRILLS)
1  Two electrically heated non-stick plates are hinged together and the food placed between them.
2  Chops and steaks can be cooked in a few minutes.
3  If a baking tin is included with the unit, baking and steaming are possible besides grilling.
4  The toasted sandwich-maker is an adaptation of this cooker.
5  Moderately priced.

ELECTRIC HAND MIXER
1  A small electric motor in a plastic casing, with detachable beaters, designed to be hand-held. A stand may be included in the unit, but it is usually stored on a wall-hanging bracket.
2  Useful for whisking cream, egg whites, cake mixtures.
3  Before buying
a)  check that the handle is comfortable and the weight right for you;
b)  consult friends about their experience with particular types.
4  Reasonably priced.

BLENDER/LIQUIDIZER
1  This is a goblet with high-speed rotary blades in the base, which may fit on to a hand-held mixer or be a separate unit.
2  Useful for blending soups and purées, preparing baby foods and making breadcrumbs.
3  Reasonably priced.
   Together, an electric hand mixer and a blender may be the only aids you need.

TABLE MIXER
1  A much larger and more powerful piece of equipment than an electric hand mixer.
2  Attachments will enable the mixer to mince, chop, shred, make pasta, mix dough, liquidize, etc.
3  To be of real use, the mixer should be kept on a work surface near to a power point, so that it is always at hand.
4  Bulky and expensive.

INDEPENDENT JUICER
1  Citrus fruit and vegetable juice extractor, as a separate unit or an attachment to the table mixer. Of limited use unless your diet demands large quantities of fruit or vegetable juice.
2  Reasonably priced.

FOOD PROCESSOR
1  Will do all the jobs which a table mixer will do (except, sometimes, whisking egg whites) but more quickly and efficiently.

2  Fitted with blades rather than beaters.
3  Available in several sizes: choose the size for which you have space. If it is not always ready to plug in you will not get the best use out of it.
4  Before buying, read the manual carefully and decide whether you will really benefit from its functions.
5  Expensive.

SLOW COOKER
1  An electric casserole which can be left on for 8–10 hours (therefore particularly suitable for the long, slow cooking of cheaper and tougher cuts of meat).
2  Food should be eaten immediately on completion of cooking *or* cooled quickly and stored for a short time in a refrigerator or for longer periods in a freezer—this is to minimize the danger of food poisoning.
3  Usually two heat settings are incorporated—read the instructions carefully.
4  Very economical to run, using the same amount of power as an ordinary light bulb.
5  Bulky to store but should be kept easily accessible.
6  Moderately priced.

MULTI-COOKER/TABLE-TOP COOKER
1  See page 58.
2  Heated by an element underneath the pan.
3  Reasonably priced.

TOASTER
1  Cheaper to run than an electric grill but more expensive than a gas grill.
2  May be a 'good buy' if toast is required every day; bread is not wasted as it pops up when ready and does not become burnt.
3  Reasonably priced.

*A food processor*
*(Toshiba UK Ltd)*

*A slow cooker*
*(TI Tower Housewares Ltd)*

ELECTRIC KETTLE
1 Before buying
a) decide which capacity best suits your needs;
b) survey costs in electrical goods shops, department stores, etc.— prices vary;
c) assess the grip you can make on the handle.
2 If filled through the spout, the danger of your hand being scalded by steam is considerably reduced.
3 Automatically switched-off kettles are more expensive than non-automatic but reduce the danger of the element being damaged by the kettle boiling dry.
● Note that it is worth having a spare non-electric kettle for use on a camping stove in the event of power cuts.

ELECTRIC CARVING KNIFE
1 Hand-held powered knife with twin blades.
2 Very sharp; cuts without effort at any angle.
3 Blades operate as soon as button is pressed; warning light on good models indicates that knife is ready to work.
4 Reasonably priced.

VACUUM CLEANER
*Upright*
Sweeps, beats and cleans at once. Very good if you have a large expanse of carpet which needs this type of cleaning. Tools are available.
*Cylindrical*
As popular as the upright, slightly cheaper. Tools are supplied; automatic flex re-wind available. More versatile than the upright— carpets, corners, curtains, pelmets, furniture and stairs may be cleaned.
Before buying
a) shop around—prices vary considerably;
b) test the weight, particularly if the cleaner will have to be carried upstairs.

CARPET SWEEPER
1 Useful for daily cleaning (it is not necessary to vacuum clean every day).
2 Buying—choose a sturdy, efficient model which is easy to empty. Test on a carpet surface first.

IRON
1 Available as dry or steam models. Also capable of spraying and providing extra steam as required; the more versatile the more expensive.
2 Before buying
a) remember that most fabrics are more successfully ironed if slightly damp;

b) check that controls are easy to identify;
c) make sure that the iron will stand safely when vertical;
d) feel the weight and make sure that it is suitable for you;
e) if you are left-handed choose an iron with the flex coming from the handle instead of from the side.

IRONING BOARD
1 These vary in length and width.
2 Height should be adjustable so that any member of the family can use it.
3 Choose one light enough to move without difficulty but strong enough to be firm in use; try it before buying it.
4 Reasonably priced.

## HOME MAINTENANCE

You will be wise to make complete checks all round your home twice a year; convenient times would be late autumn, before winter aggravates wear and tear; in the spring to check that bad weather has not caused fresh disrepair. Check that
a) gutters are clear of leaves and other debris;
b) gutters are not leaking or, if iron, not rusty;
c) all exposed pipes and tanks are well insulated to protect them from frost;
d) all stop-cocks are working easily so that they can be turned off in an emergency;
   ● It is very important that you know the position of *all* your mains inlets—gas, electricity, water.
e) paint is in sufficiently good repair to withstand weather;
f) latches and locks work efficiently;
g) doors are fitting snugly;
h) the central heating system is working satisfactorily—an annual professional service is a good investment.

Employing professional help for small repairs can cost you a great deal of money and for some repairs expert advice is essential. However, there are a number of jobs which you can carry out yourself with a little effort and, if necessary, the help of one of the many excellent D.I.Y. books available. Some of the most common minor repairs required are described below, but before undertaking any kind of maintenance equip yourself with a basic tool kit:

three screwdrivers: one small with an insulated handle for electrical work;
one larger for general purposes;
one Philips 'pozidriver' for cross-top screws
one hammer
one pair of pliers

one pair of wirecutters
one chisel
one adjustable spanner (the 'Stillson' type is best for plumbing jobs)
one steel tape measure
one drill (hand or, preferably, electric)
one set of drill bits
several masonry bits

## Mending a Blown Main Fuse

This is usually caused by a faulty plug or incorrect size of fuse. Before taking steps to repair a main (or circuit) fuse:
1 Make sure that it is not just one appliance which has failed; if this is so, change the fuse in the plug. Should it 'blow' again as soon as it is switched on seek expert advice.
2 Check that other premises nearby have electricity—it could be a general power cut. If yours is the only dwelling without any power at all call the Electricity Board.
3 Make sure that all the lights are without power and that it is not one socket or switch which has failed. If it is, seek expert advice.

To facilitate the repairing of fuses, it is advisable to have by your meter (where the main circuit fuses are found) a box containing: a torch or a candle (in a safe holder) and matches, a screwdriver, fuse wire or spare cartridge fuses (5 amp for lights and small plug circuits, 15 amp for large plug circuits, 30 amp for cookers and ring mains).

METHOD
1 TURN OFF THE MAIN SWITCH.
2 Open the fuse box, remove each of the row of blocks which you will find inside in turn and identify which one is carrying a broken fuse wire. (It would be helpful if you were able to label which fuses are concerned with lights, heaters, cooker, etc.)
3 If your fuses are
a) of the new cartridge type, all you need to do is to replace it with a new one of the same rating;

*Figure 4.1  A main fuse*

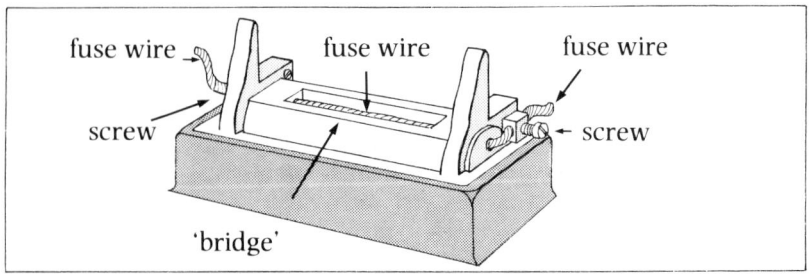

b) rewirable (as in Figure 4.1), select a new piece of fuse wire of the same gauge.

4 Loosen the screws at each end of the carrier and remove the old pieces of wire.

5 Wind one end of the new wire round one of the screws once and cut off a length long enough to traverse the carrier and be secured at the other end. Tighten the screw.

6 Thread the wire through the 'bridge' of the carrier; do not pull too tightly.

7 Secure the wire to the second screw and tighten it.

8 Replace the fuse carrier in the socket.

9 Secure the fuse box.

10 Switch on the main switch. Should the fuse(s) blow again when the lights/power are switched on once more, seek expert advice.

● Some premises have miniature circuit breakers (MCBs) with which you can restore the power simply by pushing a button or flicking a switch into a position different from the rest.

## Rewiring a Plug

1 Loosen the large screw at the outer end of the plug until the cover can be removed.

2 Unscrew each of the three wire-holding screws until the ends of the wires can be gently pulled out.

3 Loosen the small screws holding the flex-clamp (see Figure 4.2) and remove the flex (if the plug is not of the new type which has a shaped channel from which the flex is easily loosened).

4 Make sure that there are sufficient lengths of unexposed wires to reach each of the pins (the brown wire should be the shortest, the green and yellow one the longest). Each should end in about 5 mm. ($\frac{1}{4}''$) of exposed wire. Use a wire-stripper to bare the wires if necessary.

5 Twist the bare wires slightly to make them more convenient to fix.

6 Insert the flex under the flex-clamp and push it into the depression in the plug until a small amount of the covered flex is visible and each of the exposed wires reaches the appropriate screws.

*Figure 4.2 Wiring a plug*

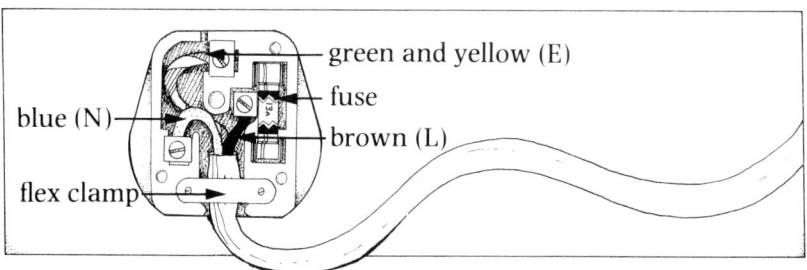

green and yellow (E)

fuse

blue (N)

brown (L)

flex clamp

7 Then
a) connect the green and yellow (earth) wire to the top terminal
marked E or

b) connect the blue (neutral) wire to the terminal marked N or
coloured black
c) connect the brown (live) wire to the terminal marked L or coloured
red.
To do this: push the ends of the wires through the screw holes and
tighten the screws until the wires are secure *or* twist the ends round the
stems of the screws under the washers and tighten the screws until they
are held firmly.
8  Tighten the flex-clamp screws if necessary.
9  Replace the cover of the plug and secure with the large screw.
10  Test the plug by using the appliance. If it does not work it is likely
that the fuse was blown when the wiring was damaged. Remove the
cover of the plug, replace the old fuse with a new one of the same
number of amps, replace the cover and re-test.

## Clearing a Blocked Sink

1  Prevention is better than cure—try to avoid blocking the sink outlet
pipe by not allowing solid matter to be emptied into it with waste water
and by not pouring liquid fat down the outlet which might congeal and
cause a blockage. Even a match can cause a blockage if it jams across
the pipe, then fat congeals around it. Always flush the pipe with clean,
hot water after using the sink.
2  Use the simplest means of unblocking first. After baling out as much
water as possible from the sink:
a)  If you suspect that waste matter has collected, use a rubber plunger
over the sink vent to create suction by working the handle up and
down; this will often be sufficient to cause the trapped water to dislodge
small amounts of solid material.
b)  If you have reason to believe that grease has accumulated, fill the top
of the outlet pipe with soda crystals and pour boiling water over them.
Repeat this until the grease has become emulsified and the pipe is clear.
  After the pipe is cleared by using method a or b flush it with a good
flow of hot detergent water, followed by clear, cold water.
  If a or b is not successful:
c)  Place a bucket underneath the waste trap and remove the screw of
the U-bend *or*, in more up-to-date models, the large nuts of the bottle or
P-trap (see Figure 4.3). Run a length of strong or coiled flexible wire
from the sink to the trap opening and remove the blockage. If necessary,
repeat from the opening onwards (it is unlikely, however, that waste
material will pass the trap). Wash out the bottle or P-trap.

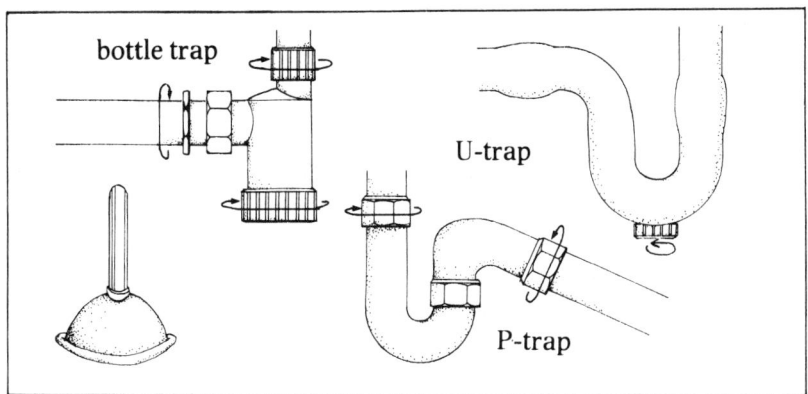

*Figure 4.3  A sink plunger and the different types of sink traps*

Replace screw or nuts and trap tightly and run clear water containing disinfectant from the sink to test that the pipe is clear. Remove the bucket and dispose of the dirty waste water.

### Fixing Screws into the Wall

There are a number of items which you may wish to hang on your walls, from cupboards to paintings and clocks, etc. The safest way, always, is to use screws, but you cannot drive woodscrews straight into masonry. (For light pictures or photographs special masonry nails may be used; these enter the wall at an angle and must be well hammered in.)
1  Use a drill, preferably electric, to make a hole well into the wall, using a masonry bit. Clear the hole of dust.
2  Insert a wallplug—this provides the screw with a surface on to which it can grip. Seek advice on the type to use; some plugs are specially designed for hollow walls and some for solid ones.
3  Secure the screw with a good screwdriver and test it well before hanging anything on to it.

*Figure 4.4  Screws*

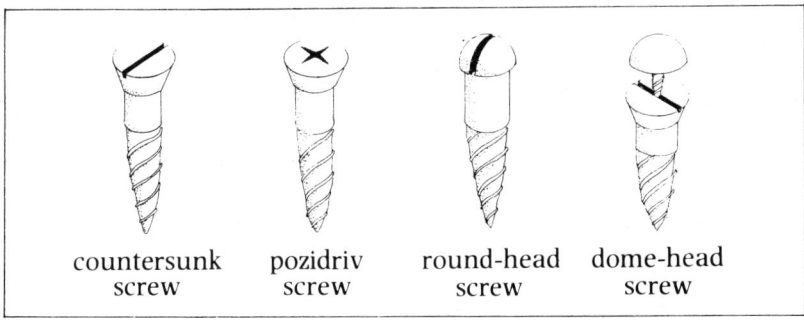

countersunk screw  pozidriv screw  round-head screw  dome-head screw

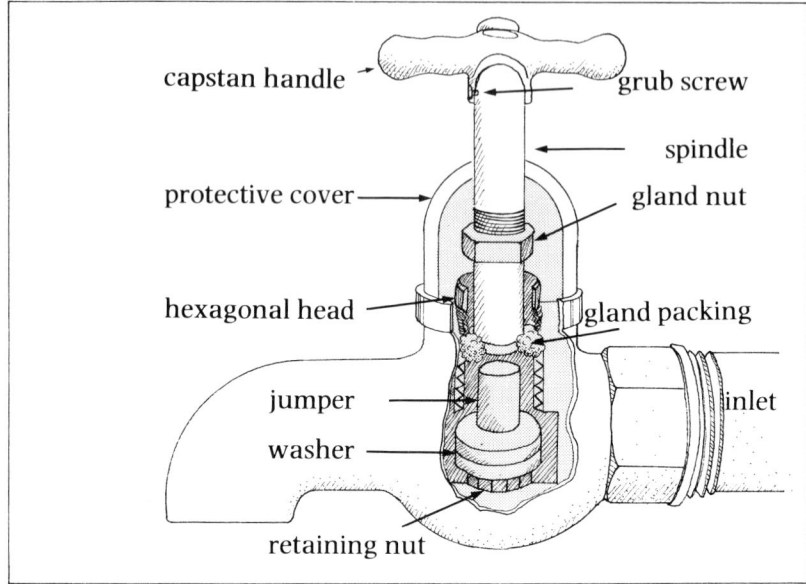

*Figure 4.5  The components of a tap*

**Stopping a Dripping Tap**

A tap drips, wastefully and irritatingly, because the washer inside it is worn and the water continues to flow even when the tap is turned off. Replacing the washer entails taking the tap apart and is not a simple job; perhaps it is advisable to be supervised by someone who has done it before when you do so for the first time.

1  Turn off the water at the stop-cock.

2  Let the water run until the flow ceases—several taps may be turned on at once if more convenient.

3  Wrap masking tape round the tap to protect the surface from being scratched by the spanner.

4  Unscrew the cover of the tap, using the adjustable spanner from your tool kit. Take care not to turn the whole tap—this will damage the sink/basin.

5  Lift the cover and undo the hexagonal nut underneath (see Figure 4.5).

6  Remove the nut which holds the washer in place, using pliers.

7  Replace the worn washer with a new one of the same size.

8  Grease the screwheads lightly with petroleum jelly and reassemble the tap.

9  Turn on the water at the stop-cock.

10  Turn on the tap and let it run for a few minutes to prevent air-locks in the pipes.

—————————————— **FURTHER STUDY** ——————————————

## Things to Do

1 Find out where the following are situated in your own home:
the main water stop-cock;
the hot water system stop-cock;
the main gas tap;
the main electricity switch;
the main fuse box or Consumer Unit;
the gas meter;
the electricity meter.

2 Obtain a spare fused plug and a short length of flex. Practise re-wiring the plug and compare the result with Figure 4.2 on page 83.

3 Obtain an electric main fuse and practise wiring it.

4 Work out two timetables for the daily routine of a family of four, consisting of parents, one schoolgirl and her older brother who is apprenticed to an engineering firm. One timetable is to be for a non-working mother, the other for one who goes out to work every day.

5 Collect as many different examples of metal as you can, together with appropriate cleaners. Discover which metals are
a) the easiest
b) the most difficult
to clean.

6 Collect details of as many different types of furniture polish as possible, including different brands of the same type. Compare prices, quantities in containers and, as far as possible, the quality of performance. Tabulate your findings.

## Questions to Answer

1 Write out and complete each of the following statements with the correct term chosen from the list in the right-hand column.

a) Some woodscrews have crosses on their tops instead of slots and require a _____ screwdriver.

silicones

b) The grinding units inserted into drills for making holes are called _____ .

yellow/green

c) Greasy pans and pipes can be cleaned by adding _____ to the water, so that the grease is emulsified.

Philips

d) Spanners are available in many sizes, the one most useful in plumbing work being the _____ type.

beaters

**e)** A length of weaker wire in an electrical circuit is called a _____ and acts as a 'safety valve' to an overloaded circuit.

soda

**f)** Electric food mixers, whether hand-held or table models, are fitted with _____ which rotate rapidly.

fuse

**g)** Food processors work by the action of their _____ , enabling them to carry out most preparation processes except whisking.

bits

**h)** Labour-saving furniture polishes contain _____ which act as a lubricant in applying wax.

brown

**i)** In an electrical flex the earth wire is coloured _____ .

Stillson

**j)** The wire which must be attached to the L or 'live' terminal in an electric plug is _____ in colour.

rotary blades

**2** If you were to be given a present of any of the labour-saving items mentioned in this chapter, which would you choose? Explain why you have made this choice.

**3** 'Woman's place is in the home.' Discuss this old saying.

**4** Imagine yourself running a home for two people, both of you in full-time employment. What steps would you take to ensure that your accommodation is well kept and that you both have time to enjoy yourself.

**5** How do modern products contribute to good hygiene in the home?

## MEMBERS OF THE FAMILY

In the early days of setting up home together there are just two of you, establishing a way of life that suits you both and working out your joint responsibilities. This is a period of great adjustment for you both and calls for humour, tolerance and a sense of proportion, quite apart from mutual affection.

If you become parents you acquire the added responsibility of the physical and emotional care of your children. It is your job to safeguard their physiological and psychological health and counsel them to the best of your ability, so that they make their way in the outside world with confidence. Eventually your children will feel the need to move away from home, putting into practice the independence which you have tried to develop in them. This will leave just the two of you again and you will have the time and the opportunity to focus your attention and energies upon other matters; to develop your personal interests, take on a job, offer to do some voluntary work or undertake some congenial leisure activity. Life moves on, involving as it goes self-adjustment to cope with it and to enjoy it to the full.

Married daughters used to keep up a close relationship with their mothers but nowadays, for a variety of reasons, it is often necessary for them to move away from the family's locality, and to be without the benefit of familiar support in hours of need. However, society recognizes the necessity for advice and assistance at every stage of life; the special needs of babies, adolescents, spouses, parents and the elderly are met by a large range of public organizations. Your local Citizens' Advice Bureau will be able to help you to locate them and some are listed later in this chapter.

You must begin, yourself, with a basic knowledge about the fundamental needs of people at all stages of their development.

### Babies

The arrival of a new baby is a very emotional event for parents and a unique relationship immediately has to be established with this new member of the family. Human contact is essential to a baby to begin with, and contentment comes with feeling warm, loved and well fed;

being cuddled and talked to are special needs of the baby which *can* be supplied by a number of people, but the best person of all is the mother. Being a parent is a tremendous responsibility and you are going to need a great deal of understanding of the nature of and the means of supplying your baby's requirements. As a simple example, remember that it has been established that a new-born baby fears only two things—noise and being dropped—and then think of the number of things which frightened you when you were very young (and may still do so). You will now have to recognize and quieten your own child's fears.

ADOPTION
To those parents who are denied the privilege of having their own children a system of adoption is available and this can be the answer to marital problems arising from the frustrations of childlessness. Both parents must accept very thorough screening before they are considered to be eligible, and much time may elapse before adoption can actually take place. There are about 70 adoption agencies, societies and organizations dealing with the formalities, but preliminary enquiries can be made through the Children's Department of the local authority, your doctor, district nurse or health visitor.

## Schoolchildren

As the baby grows into a child his need for love and attention remains but now he has to learn, with encouragement, to become independent and confident enough to do things away from the family unit. Remember that a child's emotional development is established during the first few years of life and the ability to communicate with and relate to people outside the family circle is vitally important.

Talking to children is an activity often too little practised by parents— they may be too preoccupied with their own affairs, too wearied with work or just unaware of the necessity; by involving your children in family discussions, being interested in what they do at school and at home, and generally including them in 'family' activities, you will be laying a good foundation for confidence and happiness in a wider circle of human contacts.

## Teenagers

Adolescents experience many and varied problems, and at this time in their lives the security of a good, stable home background and affection which remains steadfast whatever they do is the only thing of which they can feel certain. The physical changes which are going on in their bodies cause (to them) inexplicable moodiness which often leads to them behaving in ways quite foreign to their normal demeanour. This is frequently shown most clearly in their attitudes towards their parents, who must be prepared to accept these without altering their own. Respect, expected and even demanded by parents, should be recognized as earned, not automatically given; many problems can be avoided by showing as well as by exacting respect. Most teenagers prefer to identify with their peer group rather than to become conspicuous individuals; this might well be because they are more sure of understanding and tolerance from their contemporaries than from their elders.

## Parents

Although officially at the head of the family unit, the role of parent is not an easy one. Every member is an integral part of the whole and contributes to the success or otherwise of a happy relationship; giving and taking should be recognized as of equal importance and it is in the privacy of the family that the old saying 'you get out of life what you put into it' is first apparent. The relationships between Mum and Dad and between them and their children stand as examples of love, respect and tolerance which the children should have pleasure in returning.

## The Elderly

The expectation of life nowadays is longer than it has ever been, but this in itself produces problems; one of society's most poignant difficulties is how best to cope with those who can no longer manage for themselves. If the home unit cannot supply their physical needs, social welfare usually will (e.g. Meals on Wheels, Home Helps, financial benefits), but it is their emotional needs which are so desperately unsatisfied in a distressingly large number of cases. Grandparents and maiden aunts used to be the stand-by and anchor in most families, providing a fund of worldly wisdom which only comes with experience. Today's young

*A Senior Citizens' Club (Shelter/Nick Hedges)*

'nomad' families often have to leave them behind and they are deprived of the opportunity to spend their ample time in being involved and giving help; of loving and being loved. If they are mobile, visits to Senior Citizens' Clubs, Day Centres and church organizations should be encouraged. There, whatever else they are doing, they can meet people of their own age and with similar interests. However good these contacts are, though, the personal element of family life is lacking and every effort should be made by young people to keep in touch with the older members regularly if not frequently.

Although much emphasis has been laid upon the art of being together as a family, it is important, as well, to remember that everyone needs some time on their own. People's ability to enjoy this varies tremendously but it is part of becoming a 'whole' person to develop pleasure in being alone without being lonely. It is a time of quiet and reflection during which you are able to think, consider and know yourself, without the pressures of making conversation and projecting your personality. Everyone, at every age, should have somewhere where this can happen when they need it to, without question and without the invasion of privacy.

## GOVERNMENT SERVICES

Government administration is divided into sections, each Department with its own field of responsibility:

DEPARTMENT OF HEALTH AND SOCIAL SECURITY
National Health Service; family and community services; National Insurance; supplementary benefits; child benefits.

DEPARTMENT OF EDUCATION AND SCIENCE
Schools; colleges; universities; scientific research.

DEPARTMENT OF THE ENVIRONMENT
Housing; planning.

HOME OFFICE
Probation and after-care service; community relations.

DEPARTMENT OF EMPLOYMENT
Employment exchanges; disablement resettlement services; redundancy fund.

TREASURY
Control of Government expenditure on welfare services; fiscal (taxation) policy.

● Note that the Scottish Office and the Welsh Office are responsible for housing and planning and for secondary and primary education in their own areas.

Government business is administered by civil servants and local government officials work in close liaison with them.

Local government is the authority which administers national policies to sections of the country defined by county boundaries. Each of these sections is represented in Parliament by elected Members (MPs). It divides its activities between:

Environmental Services; ⎫
Personal Services;         ⎬  see page 231.
Protective Services.      ⎭

## The National Health Service

The aims of the National Health Service are clearly defined as:
1  free universal medical care throughout Britain;
2  integration of hospitals, family doctors and local health services;
3  freedom of individuals to choose the doctor they want;
4  the prevention of ill-health to be as important as the treatment and cure of illness.

GENERAL PRACTITIONERS
You may approach any GP you choose to ask for your name to be added to his list of patients, although you need not necessarily be accepted. GPs usually define their own catchment area and you may not be accepted because you live outside this boundary; or you may be refused for some other reason which violates the policy of the practice. It is obviously advisable to find a GP nearby, for ease of visiting both by him and yourself.

Should you have a complaint to make against a GP you can contact the Community Health Council (Medical Watchdog); the address can be found in your doctor's surgery or at the Post Office.

PRESCRIPTIONS
The cost of medical supplies prescribed by the GP is partly covered by the National Insurance contributions you pay, but most people have to pay a percentage of the cost of the items they receive. Certain people, however, are entitled to free prescriptions. These are:
pensioners (men over 65, women over 60);
children (up to the age of 16);
diabetics (requiring insulin, usually for life);
those on life-saving drugs (i.e. daily medicines without which they cannot live);
expectant and nursing mothers;
war and services disabled.

HEALTH VISITORS
These are qualified State Registered Nurses (SRNs) with midwifery or obstetric certificates in addition, who have completed a year of special

D

training as a health visitor. Health visitors' work is mainly preventive medicine, looking for deficiency diseases, recognizing family problems and providing the after-care of mothers with new babies (in succession to the midwife who attends the mother for ten days). All age groups ('from womb to tomb') come under their care and they liaise closely with social workers and voluntary organizations.

DISTRICT NURSES
Qualified SRNs who have completed six months of training and three months of supervised work with a qualified district nurse. The district nurse visits the housebound to assist in the care of invalids and the acutely ill, to renew dressings, remove stitches, give injections and provide necessary nursing supplies (e.g. pads for the incontinent).

MIDWIVES
If the GP agrees with a woman's desire to have her baby at home, the midwife will call to check her general health prior to the birth and for ten days afterwards, as well as attending the actual birth. She will weigh and bath the baby and check that both mother and baby are progressing as they should. If the mother needs assistance after this she should ask the doctor to contact the health visitor for her.

Health visitors, district nurses and midwives constitute the Primary Health Care team attached to your GP's practice.

HEALTH CENTRES
In many large towns much of the help available under the National Health system is based under one roof, namely a health centre. All the treatment offered in these centres is free and includes:
1 *Dental care*
    This is available for certain categories of the community (e.g. pre-school and school-age children, pregnant women). If you wish to confirm whether or not you are eligible for treatment, ask for advice at the centre.
    All other members of the public are at liberty to go to a National Health Service dentist and pay part of the cost of their treatment and dentures, or to a private dentist and pay the full cost of both.
2 *Chiropody*
    This service is available to certain categories, such as pensioners and the registered handicapped. Doctors may refer patients to the chiropody clinic. Domiciliary visits may be made to the housebound.
    All other people must visit private chiropodists if they require treatment.
3 *Well-women clinics*
    These are more common in some parts of the country than in others. They are run by the District Health Authority and may be attended by any woman; there is no lower age limit; an upper age limit of 65 is suggested.

A series of comprehensive tests is given:
cervical smear,
breast and pelvic examination,
urine test,
blood pressure monitor,
and it is suggested that these tests are repeated every five years.
Appointments can be made in person or by telephone.

4 *Family planning clinics*
Normally, your own GP will advise you about any family planning queries which you may have. If, for any reason, you do not wish to consult your doctor, however, you can go either to a private family planning clinic or by appointment to your local health centre's family planning clinic. If you are over 16 years of age, any advice or treatment you receive will be strictly confidential. Under the age of 16, any action will be at the discretion of the person running the clinic. These clinics are offered both during the day and in the evening and are open to boys as well as girls.

5 *Baby clinics*
These are open to any mother who wishes to have her baby weighed or to avail herself of the powdered milks and the cereals which are sold there at slightly reduced prices. Development checks are made at 6, 9 and 18 months and again at 3 years of age. A health visitor and a doctor are usually in attendance for counselling and reminders with regard to vaccination and immunization.

6 *Ophthalmic, Audio, Psychology, Diabetic, Orthopaedic clinics*
These are usually held at local hospitals for patients referred by GPs.

7 *VD special clinics*
Completely free and confidential clinics for advice and treatment. No GP's letter is required. They are held at most large hospitals, where appointments may be made in person or by telephone.

Other responsibilities of the NHS include:
hospitals—general and specialist;
dentists;
opticians;
ambulances;
food safety and shop hygiene;
social work with the physically and mentally sick;
day centres and clubs for the handicapped;
hostels for the mentally sick;
immunization;
health education;
school medical services;
mass radiography;
homes for unmarried mothers;

health and safety at work;
prevention of infectious diseases;
port health.

## The Education Service

The law in Britain states that every child from the age of 5 to 16 must receive full-time education, geared to his age, ability and aptitude. Each local authority is responsible for providing this, according to the system it favours, assuming that it is approved by the Secretary of State for Education; but it is the responsibility of the parent(s) or guardian to make sure that the child actually receives it. If a parent can supply an education better than that offered by the State (either by his/her own skill or by providing a home tutor) the child need not be sent to school.

PRE-SCHOOL PLAYGROUPS
These must be approved by the local authority in respect of premises (toilet provision, room loading etc.) and ratio of staff to children. If satisfactory, the group is registered. They are run by a rota of mothers and voluntary helpers, and are usually available only in the mornings. Some are attached to Colleges of Further Education or to hospitals but they are mainly held in church halls, community centres or village halls.

NURSERY SCHOOLS
These are administered by the Education Department. The lower age limit for admission is usually 3 years but, according to local provision and resources, may be slightly over or under. Children are taught by qualified nursery school teachers.

SCHOOLS
Each local authority is allowed to submit its own scheme for the statutory education of those between 5 and 16 years of age to the Secretary of State for Education for approval. *The arrangements vary from county to county* and also among the different parts of the United Kingdom but one type of comprehensive system divides school life into three parts: from 5–9 years at a Lower School, from 9–13 years at a Middle School and from 13–16 plus years at an Upper School.

Another common arrangement is the division between the ages 5–11 and 11–16.

Many comprehensive schools, now standard provision, are purpose built to accommodate the hundreds of pupils who attend them; others, for economic reasons, are an amalgamation of previously self-contained schools and buildings. The range of courses and activities offered is considerable and there is a tendency for some schools to become regarded as somewhat superior in some fields than others. The mere size of the establishments overwhelms many people, both pupils and parents,

*Adults learning English at a community college (Frobisher Institute)*

and there is some controversy as to the overall merits of this type of education.

SIXTH-FORM COLLEGES
These exist as such but provision for the over-16s is now generally made in Upper Schools. Curricula usually led to A-level examinations but now new sixth form courses are offered preparing pupils for examination at 17 plus, the Lower Sixth catering for 16–17-year-olds, the Upper Sixth for the 17–18 age group.

TERTIARY COLLEGES
These establishments combine all 16 plus provision, i.e. sixth form and further education courses.

COMMUNITY COLLEGES
Usually attached to a school, these are intended to be used by all age groups in a community, e.g. pre-school playgroups, OAP clubs, and adult education classes. The latter can overlap the provision made in colleges of further and higher education but may be more convenient geographically.

FURTHER AND HIGHER EDUCATION COLLEGES
Most of these colleges are under the control of their local education authority (exceptions are those for specialized study, e.g. law, tele-communications). They offer full-time or part-time education for those school-leavers who wish to continue their education (free until 18 years of age, at present). Courses may lead to qualifications or be taken purely for enjoyment; to fulfil leisure time, to acquire new skills or to pursue an already established hobby. They are open to people of all ages over 16, usually with reduced fees for pensioners. Apprentices to such large organizations as engineering firms, car manufacturers, etc. may be sent to college for a certain number of hours per week as part of their employment—this system is known as 'day release'.

Prospectuses are offered in the spring by most colleges, listing and describing the courses becoming available the following September (the academic year runs from September to June/July), and the fees required for each course.

## COLLEGES OF EDUCATION (MONOTECHNICS)

These are where prospective teachers are trained. Courses are of three years duration and tend to specialize in certain subjects or range of subjects. Application forms are sent to a Central Clearing House where preferences and suitability are sorted. Application must be made early in the year preceding that of commencing training (see above). Grants are available according to the income of your parents.

A one-year course leading to a Certificate in Education may be taken after graduation (PGCE).

Since 1972 many colleges of education have been combined either with other colleges to become colleges of higher education, or with polytechnics.

## POLYTECHNICS

These colleges provide advanced further education and higher education, the minimum age of entry being 18. They often provide opportunities for those who have missed the conventional routes to university. They are financed by local government, supported by grants from the national Government.

## UNIVERSITIES

These are the oldest established seats of learning, usually founded by Royal Charter and offering the highest branches of education in the arts and sciences. It is only in this century that women have been generally allowed entry. The universities are financed through the University Grants Committee.

Advice on your own eligibility and on choosing your course, the universities you should consider and how to obtain application forms should be obtained from your teachers, your careers advisory service, your local authority and/or (last but by no means least) your parents. Many universities and polytechnics hold open days and it is always advisable to see for yourself as well as acquiring as much literature as you can. Your school or college should have the information issued by the Universities' Central Council on Admissions (UCCA), and by the United Kingdom's College, Polytechnic or University (UKCPU).

## THE OPEN UNIVERSITY

The Open University provides degree courses administered by a combination of television, radio, correspondence, tutorials, short residential courses and local audio-visual centres. No entry qualifications are required. The scheme is grant aided by the Department of Education and Science and does not come within the University Grants Committee system.

SPECIAL SCHOOLS
Some children have special needs, which are recognized by local authorities who for many years have segregated them into separate schools for:
a) the slow learners (formerly known as ESN—educationally sub-normal);
b) the physically handicapped;
c) the blind and partially sighted;
d) the deaf and partially deaf;
e) the maladjusted.

The Warnock Report (1978) suggested that councils should try to integrate units for children who fall into these groups into 'normal' schools so that they can, as far as possible, and at their own rate, go through the ordinary schooling system.

Organizations which can provide information and advice about the education of children are:
The Advisory Centre for Education (Cambridge)—publishes a monthly magazine called *Where*;
The British Association for Early Childhood Education (London)—offers a service for children up to 8 years of age;
The National Association for Gifted Children (London).

ADULT EDUCATION
1 See page 97 for council provision.
2 The Workers' Educational Association (WEA) is a national organization which offers evening classes, daytime and day release courses, weekend courses and residential summer schools.

## SOCIAL AND WELFARE SERVICES

### National Insurance

National Insurance is included in the Social Security Act 1975. Some benefits are dependent on payment of contributions to a specified standard, e.g. sickness, maternity, retirement; some are subject to a means test, others are not.

Non-contributory, non-means tested, benefits include:

| | |
|---|---|
| Industrial injury ⎫ | |
| Disablement ⎬ | See leaflets N 1, 5, 6, 12 |
| Industrial death ⎭ | |
| War pensions | See leaflets MPL 151, 153 |
| Invalid care allowance | See leaflet NI 212 |
| Attendance allowance | See leaflet NI 205 |
| Mobility allowance | See leaflet NI 211 |
| Child benefit | See leaflets CH 1, 11 |

*Leaflet FB2 details the kind of benefits that are available (DHSS)*

Non-contributory, means tested benefits include:

| | |
|---|---|
| Supplementary benefit | See booklet NWBH |
| Family income supplement | See leaflet FIS 1 |
| Rent and rate rebates and allowances | See NWBH (appendix) |
| Welfare benefits (free prescriptions, etc.) | See leaflet M 11 |
| Educational benefits (free school meals, etc.) | See leaflet FIS 1 |

Contributory National Insurance benefits include:

*Unemployment benefit* (leaflet NI 12)

As long as you are registered at your local Employment Exchange as unemployed, you are able to draw a weekly benefit.

*Sickness benefit* (leaflet NI 16)

If you are employed and not fit to work, you can draw sickness benefit on production of a doctor's certificate.

*Invalidity benefit* (leaflet NI 16A)

Covers extended periods of chronic illness.

*Maternity benefit* (leaflet NI 17A)

See page 69.

*Widow's benefit* (leaflets NP 35, 36)

A fixed benefit for a limited period; subsequently at 40 according to circumstances.

*Retirement pension* (leaflets NP 32, 32A, 32B)

This is available to women at 60, men at 65 (see also page 142).

*Death grant* (leaflet NI 49)

A lump sum is paid on behalf of the person who has died, to contribute towards the funeral expenses.

*Child benefit (non-contributory)* (leaflets CH 1, 11)

This is paid to every family for every child, without means testing.

## Provision for Children

Social Services have a special duty to look after any child needing special care. As in the case of an elderly person, the aim is to keep such a child in as normal surroundings as possible, preferably within his own family. If the mother is ill, in hospital, or just unable to cope, a Home Help may be sent in to assist; a social worker will visit 'problem families' to give advice and counselling. If the child is still thought to be 'at risk' the local authority assumes the responsibility of the parents and takes him into care.

CHILDMINDERS
By law, any person looking after someone else's children in their own home for more than two hours a day, and being paid for it, must register with the local Health and Social Security Office. Unless you know the minder personally, it is advisable to check that this registration has been made before making use of their service.

A minder is only allowed to care for three children under 5 years of age, and any child of her own under 5 years old counts as one of the three.

DAY NURSERIES
The nurseries are administered by the Social Services. Children are physically cared for from early morning to early evening (i.e. a parent's working day) and can be admitted at the age of 6 months. Charges are made according to the income of the parent(s). Children are cared for by State Registered Nurses, State Registered Children's Nurses or Nursery Nurses.

PRIVATE DAY NURSERIES
Very young children are not usually accepted, the lower age limit normally being 3 years. These must be approved by the local authority and tend to be rather expensive.

## Help for the Aged

The aim of the Social Services is to keep as many elderly people as possible living in their own homes, but they recognize that a certain amount of help is essential. Local councils, therefore, make provision for Home Helps, health visitors (see page 93), and, in some cases, night nurses, to keep the elderly comfortable in their own environment.

MEALS ON WHEELS
This service is provided for the elderly housebound. Volunteers (e.g. the WRVS) deliver the meals but most of the cooking is done on local council premises (e.g. schools, old people's homes).

SHELTERED HOUSING
Local authorities build groups of small flats and bungalows especially for the elderly; they may be warden-supervised. Much thought is given to the planning and special fixtures are installed, e.g. bath and toilet seat handles, wide doorframes and slopes (instead of steps) for wheel-chairs, all designed to help the older person to be independent.

RESIDENTIAL HOMES
If old folk are unable to look after themselves except for their personal physical needs, they are taken into care in residential homes with a warden or matron to keep watch over them, assisted by a number of members of staff. If totally incapable, it may be necessary for them to enter special homes for the mentally or physically infirm, where very specialized care is available.

RATE/RENT REBATES
The council will consider any application from unemployed elderly people who, perhaps because of the death of their partner or other misfortune, cannot afford to pay the rates and/or rents of their homes. Allowances and rebates are based on each person's financial position.

## LEISURE SERVICES

### Youth Clubs

These are usually attached to a community centre or to a church, some being run on a voluntary basis, others by the Education Authority, with the help of paid leaders and assistants. They may be open during part of the day but are almost always available in the evenings for the provision of discos, table-tennis, swimming, badminton, football, drama, hobby clubs, etc.

### Church Clubs and Organizations

The clubs are affiliated to the church but are not necessarily for church members only. They offer a variety of activities, sometimes in the afternoon (e.g. Mother's Union, Bright Hour), sometimes in the evening (e.g. choir practice, bell-ringing, Guides, Brownies, Scouts, Girls' and Boys' Brigades, youth clubs, Men's Fellowships).

### Women's Institutes, Townswomen's Guilds

These are non-political groups which meet in village and school halls all over the country, weekly, fortnightly or monthly. They provide excellent opportunities for women of all ages to meet and exchange ideas and interests. Guest speakers are engaged to introduce a wide variety of subjects. From time to time conferences are held at regional and national levels.

### Business and Professional Women's Clubs

This type of non-political club is composed of representatives of a number of different businesses and professions, together with a mandatory ratio of housewives. Guest speakers are engaged and conferences held at local, national, and international levels.

## Hobby Clubs

These are set up and run by enthusiasts. They meet on a weekly or monthly basis in village halls, community centres or private premises and arrange contests, competitions, exhibitions, rallies, etc. among themselves and neighbouring clubs. Subjects include chess, stamp collecting, wine-making, flower arranging, angling, sailing, sports of all kinds, radio, amateur dramatics/operatics, bell-ringing, snooker, darts, bird watching, rambling, music, art.

OTHER ORGANIZATIONS FOR WOMEN
Soroptimists
Inner Wheel
Embroiderers' Guild
Weavers' Guild

OTHER ORGANIZATIONS FOR MEN
Rotary Club
The Lions
Masonic Lodges
British Legion

## VOLUNTARY ORGANIZATIONS

### Women's Royal Voluntary Service

(Address in local telephone directory.)
This service was inaugurated during the Second World War to run canteens, rest centres, etc. It has continued to cater for the needs of the community, running clothing and furniture dispensing offices, arranging food for public exercises, assisting in emergencies, supplying hospital facilities such as tea-bars, shops, library trolleys, etc.

### National Marriage Guidance Council

(HQ: Little Church Street, Rugby, Warwickshire)
The Council is operated by people who have undergone at least two years of part-time training and who then become voluntary councillors. They offer assistance with marital problems and an educational service in personal relationships, including advice to engaged couples on preparation for marriage. All interviews are confidential.

### Citizens' Advice Bureau

(Address in local telephone directory.)
The Bureau offers a free service of information and advice on almost any

personal problem, sometimes including legal assistance. If the answer cannot be supplied here you will be referred to the establishment which can advise you.

## The Samaritans

(Number in local telephone directory.)
A 24-hour a day telephone service available for advice on any dire problem; *or* appointments may be made for personal interviews. Carefully selected volunteers are trained for this very exacting work. All cases are treated as strictly confidential.

## Alcoholics Anonymous

(HQ: AA General Service Office, PO Box 514, 11 Redcliffe Gardens, London SW10 9BG)
This service provides opportunities for self-help group discussions for people of any age who have lost control of their drinking habits. There are two support groups:

AL ANON
This is a group formed to help wives and partners of alcoholics.

AL ATEEN
This is a group formed to help the children of alcoholics.

## Local Council on Alcoholism

Affiliated to the National Council on Alcoholism, this group is complementary to Alcoholics Anonymous, offering a counselling service to those with drinking problems and to their families. Patients are often referred to the Council by GPs or social workers, the aim being to give advice before the alcoholism problem becomes too great.

## National Council for One-Parent Families

Any single parent (father, mother, unmarried, married, separated, widowed, divorced) may seek help from the Council. Advice is available on housing, education, adoption, legal problems, etc. The Council works as a pressure group to improve legislature for single parents.

## British Red Cross Society

The Society is mainly composed of voluntary workers who provide first aid at large gatherings (e.g. football matches, processions, theatre performances); it also organizes clubs and holidays for the handicapped and the elderly.

## St John's Ambulance Brigade

This is also a voluntary organization offering similar services to those provided by the Red Cross Society. There are some differences, however, in the rules and regulations concerning qualifications.

These are only a few of the better-known organizations and all voluntary bodies are only too anxious to recruit new members. If you have any spare time which you would like to offer to the community you will be welcomed by any of the above.

## PETS IN THE HOME

Children love to have their own pets and it is excellent training for them to take responsibility for an animal and to learn the traumas of reproduction and death while adults are at hand to cushion them from the blows they will receive. However, the addition of a pet to a family brings its own problems and these should be considered before attachments are formed.

1 If the house is going to be empty all day and every day (except during holidays), animals cannot receive the training, care and exercise they require.

2 Their needs continue *every* day and provision has to be made if pets cannot accompany their owners when they go away for visits or holidays.

3 Most animals, particularly dogs and cats, are going to need veterinary treatment, if only for preventive injections. Other conditions requiring skilled attention include illness, accident and neutering; fees for all these occurrences are very high.

4 Feeding cannot always consist of left-overs from your own meals and the cost of proper food appropriate to the breed of pet must be included in the family's catering budget.

5 A pet owner is legally liable for third party damages and for ensuring that pets do not suffer unnecessarily. Adequate insurance to cover these eventualities should be purchased.

## FLOWERS AND PLANTS IN THE HOME

A home is for people, but people feel better when their surroundings are attractive, and few rooms are not improved by the introduction of living plants and flowers. They are like the decoration on a cake—not essential, but adding charm and character.

It is not essential to buy expensive blooms from a florist's shop; flowers may be picked from the garden or even during a country walk. A very few, mixed with appropriate foliage and arranged in an attractive container, can be made to look most effective. There are many illustrated books as well as special classes on floral art available to help with this. Colours should be chosen to complement, not necessarily to match, the scheme of the room; mixed colours and varieties of flowers and leaves are equally as successful as those arrangements using one colour and type. Vases, too, do not have to be expensive—jugs, dishes of all kinds and even ornaments may be used as containers, the stems being supported by blocks of water-retentive synthetic fibre ('Oasis' or similar product) soaked for twenty minutes before use and re-watered daily.

Plants are available in a large range of types, colours and sizes. Care should be taken to choose those which will not wilt in the dry atmosphere of central heating, plus gas or solid fuel fumes. Seek advice from the grower or retailer and read the 'care tag' attached to the plant before you spend money on it. You will then be able to assess whether or not you can supply the cool dark or the warm sun which it requires.

Bulbs can be planted in the autumn and bring a splash of colour in the early spring. Suitable ones for indoors are hyacinths, crocuses, snowdrops, daffodils and tulips, although the last two grow rather tall and usually have to be supported.

## SAFETY IN THE HOME

The homemaker is responsible not only for the health and comfort of the people in the home but also for their safety. In all the chapters of this book so far reference has been made to safety precautions appropriate to the subject, but the details of safety measures for the family will be dealt with in Chapter 10.

———————————————— FURTHER STUDY ————————————————

### Things to Do

1   Find out what the following abbreviations stand for:
    DHSS, NHS, MD, GP, SRN, SCM, SRCN, SEN, HV, NNEB, MRCS, WRVS, AA, PPG, OAP.
2   Discover what provision there is in your own district for children under 5 years of age, provided both privately and by the Council.
3   Obtain a prospectus from your local college of further education and choose
    a)   a full-time course
    b)   a part-time course
    c)   a leisure course

which you would like to follow. Calculate how much each course would cost you, including fees, your travelling expenses, subsistence costs and the amount you would have to spend on materials such as books, notepads etc.

4   Find out what Youth Clubs are available in your locality and how much it would cost you to attend twice weekly.

5   Compare the current provision for statutory education with that which was in force when your parents were at school. Discuss the advantages and disadvantages of each system.

6   Find out how the Open University is administered, the entry qualifications required, the courses available and the method by which they are followed. How much does it cost and how long can you take to gain the qualification you are seeking?

7   Consult your telephone directory to find out where you could get in touch with your local CAB, the Samaritans, the district nurse, the WRVS and your nearest Social Security office.

8   Look around your area and assess the provision which is being made for the elderly and infirm regarding accommodation, reduced fees, clubs, medical and library services.

## Questions to Answer

1   Write out and complete each of the following statements with the correct term chosen from the list in the right-hand column.

a)   Courses for training to become a teacher are held in a _____ and last for three or four years.

chiropody

b)   Parents who wish their children to receive education before the statutory age of 5 may apply for their admission to a _____ .

childminder

c)   If, for any reason, parents are unable to look after their 10-month-old baby while they go to work, they may be able to place him in a

_____ .

health visitor

d)   All public educational services come under the care of the local education authority, but all those which care for the physical needs of the community are administered by the

college of education

_____ .

e)   Free _____ attention is available at health centres for certain categories of the community,

community college

f)   including _____ .

g)   At these centres free dental treatment is available for children and for _____ .

nursery school

**h)** A person who is paid to look after other
people's children in her own home is called a
——————— .

Social
Services

**i)** A ——————— is able to offer to the district
a variety of educational courses, leisure-time
activities and accommodation for hobby
meetings.

pensioners

day nursery

**j)** If you have a young baby, an elderly relation
who requires occasional checks, or a child
with feeding problems you can call in a
——————— .

pregnant
women

**2** What are you most frightened of? How long have you had this fear?
What fears have you grown out of and how did you overcome
them?

**3** The Citizens' Advice Bureau has been referred to frequently, but this
has only been established for a relatively short time. How did people
manage to obtain advice about their problems before it existed?

**4** How do you account for the fact that it has been discovered that
**a)** many young children enter school unable to hold a conversation;
**b)** although they are literate, many adults are unable to compose
a letter?

**5** 'The power of being alone' has been referred to by a poet as resulting
from 'losing solitude'. Describe your own feelings about being on
your own and say whether and why you feel that it is important in
your life.

**6** What is meant by 'a nomad family'? How may their situation have
arisen? What advantages and disadvantages are there in being one?

**7** The Warnock Report recommended that children with special
educational needs should be admitted into ordinary schools and
integrated into 'normal' classes. Give your opinion of this innovation.

**8** In times of national economy, cuts in expenditure for public services
are inevitable. Giving reasons for your opinions, state whether you
think that these are better made in education or in the social
services.

## KITCHEN PLANNING AND EQUIPMENT

In earlier years the kitchen was the hub of family life, large enough for meals to be prepared and eaten in, and still provide accommodation for everyone to enjoy other activities, if only just sitting beside the fire and talking. Today, although there are many more space-consuming pieces of equipment to be fitted in, the kitchen is often one of the smaller rooms of the home. Fundamentally, it is a place in which food is stored, prepared, served and, often, eaten; other activities may go on but these should not be allowed to interfere with its primary purpose.

If you have the opportunity to plan your kitchen from scratch, or even to adapt its present arrangement, bear in mind that:

1  Its main use is to be for culinary purposes, therefore

2  Much time is going to be spent between the sink, the cooker and the work surfaces, so place them as conveniently close to each other as possible.

3  The food storage area should be as close to the door as possible for easy unloading of shopping (see Figure 6.1).

4  The position of electric sockets may not be suitable for such pieces of equipment as the central heating boiler, washing machine, tumble drier, etc. Avoid trailing leads and, if possible, install additional points.

5  If the laundry equipment can be moved into a 'utility room' or the end of an under-used garage, much desirable space can be freed in the kitchen.

With these general principles in mind, continue to plan your arrangement, considering

a)  how much and what type of cooking you intend to do;

b)  how many you will be cooking for;

c)  your height—if you are shorter or taller than average the height of your floor-standing units and wall-hung cupboards must be tested for your convenience;

d)  that utensils are most conveniently stored close to where they are going to be used;

e)  that the position of the sink is important—more than half the work done in a kitchen is at the sink so it should be in an attractive position, usually underneath a window (this also facilitates plumbing to an outside drain);

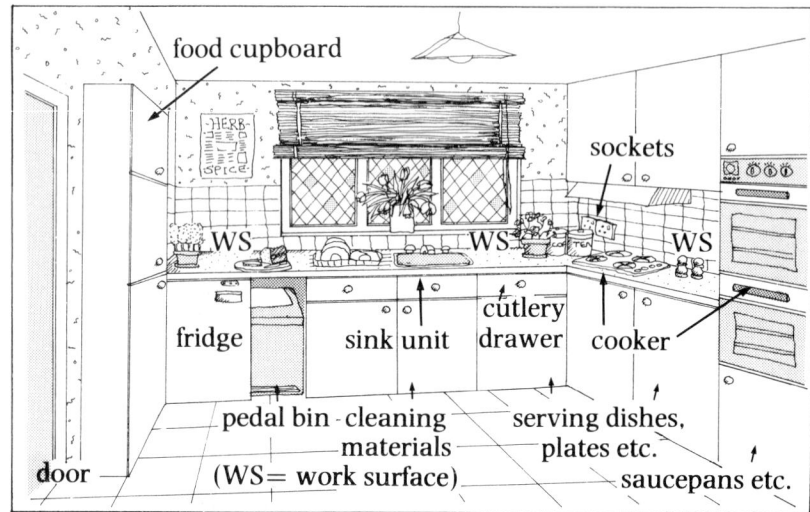

food cupboard

sockets

WS WS WS

fridge

sink|unit

cutlery drawer

cooker

pedal bin - cleaning
————— materials
door
(WS= work surface)

serving dishes,
plates etc.

saucepans etc.

*Figure 6.1 An example of a convenient work-flow arrangement*

f ) that room to move is important, so leave the centre of the kitchen as clear as possible;
g) whether sliding doors will be more convenient than those hung conventionally;
h) whether you need or have room for a double sink.

## Working Surfaces

1 Laminated plastic is probably the best material for these; it is available in a variety of colours and designs and is easy to clean and to keep glossy if required, *but* it will show scratches and react to heat, so does need protection.
2 Ideally, for the average housewife, two different heights are desirable:
a) for chopping and preparing food—900 mm. (3′)
b) for rolling out pastry          —800 mm. (2′ 9″)
but it is more usual to have all the worktops at one height.

## Equipment

The following items are *not* essential but are certainly contributions towards the easy management of the kitchen.

REFRIGERATORS
There are two main types (see Figure 6.2):
1 *Compression*
    This is controlled by an electric pump, which can be heard as it
    switches itself on and off.

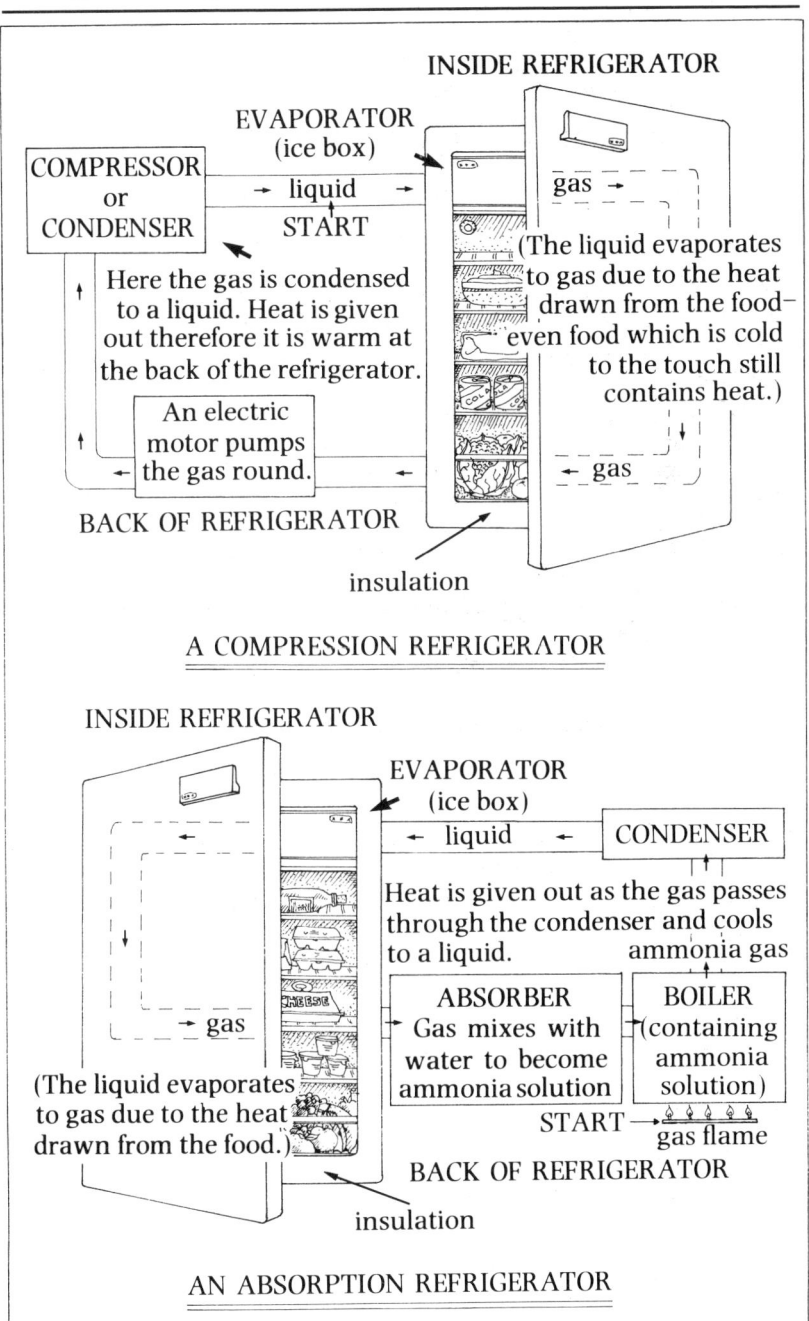

Figure 6.2 How refrigerators work

2 *Absorption*

This depends on a gas jet or an electrical heating element; it runs completely silently.

Today, most refrigerators and all freezers are of the compression type; the absorption type is more expensive to buy initially and to run.

The successful functioning of a refrigerator depends upon the physical facts that

a) as a liquid becomes a gas (i.e. evaporates) it absorbs heat from its surroundings;

b) as it reverts to a liquid it gives off heat.

If the first change of state occurs round an insulated box (i.e. the refrigerator cabinet) the temperature inside it will fall; as the second change occurs the heat produced must be dispelled (through the metal 'fins' behind the cabinet so you must allow room for this). A simple demonstration of this process is the chill experienced when a volatile spirit such as ether or methylated spirit, or a solid-perfume stick is rubbed on the skin: as the liquid evaporates (i.e. becomes a gas) it takes from your skin the heat it requires to change its state.

When choosing a refrigerator, consider:

a) the size you need—allow a capacity of thirty litres per person;

b) how much money you can spend—buy the most highly recommended model within that cost figure;

c) how much space you can allow, in conjunction with the capacity you need;

d) whether a small hanging type or a shelf model would be sufficient and convenient for your needs;

e) whether you need or are able to afford a basic refrigerator, one with a freezer section or a separate freezer.

Having decided on these points, ask the following questions:

1 Does it defrost automatically (a desirable option)?

2 Have you the choice of left/right hand opening doors?

*A refrigerator (Electrolux Ltd)*

3  Are the shelves adjustable?
4  Is there space for standing tall bottles?
5  Is there a crisper for salads?
6  Is it easy to move?
7  Is the interior door flap (if any) easy to open and to keep closed?
8  Are the controls easy to see and to adjust?

*Frozen food compartments*

These are incorporated in most refrigerators. The temperature of the main cabinet is $4°-7°$ C ($39°-45°$ F); in the freezer compartment it is lower and will therefore keep food at freezing point for a certain time. Its capacity for doing this is indicated by the number of stars shown.

  Frozen food can be stored for one week (temperature is about $-6°$ C).

  Frozen food can be stored for up to one month (temperature is about $-12°$ C).

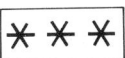  Frozen food can be stored for up to three months (temperature is about $-18°$ C).

Refrigerators with a 4-star frozen-food compartment are more expensive to run and only worth buying if you do not intend to buy but have the need for a freezer.

The freezer cannot be used to freeze fresh foods unless this symbol is also shown:

If you are fortunate enough to have a separate freezer you do not need a frozen food compartment in your refrigerator. Cabinets without these sections are called 'larder fridges' and there is that much more storage space in the refrigerator.

*Care of refrigerators*

1  Make sure that there is room for air to circulate round the cabinet (see opposite).
2  Leave room for the cold air inside the cabinet to circulate round the food (coldest air falls to the bottom of the cabinet, pushing up the warmer air).
3  Wrap solid foods to avoid drying-out.
4  Allow left-over cooked food to cool before storing in the cabinet.
5  Cover liquids so that the atmosphere does not become laden with moisture, causing frost.
6  Defrost regularly if the model does not control frosting automatically.
7  Wash out regularly with water containing bicarbonate of soda (15 ml. : 1 l. of water).

## FRIDGE-FREEZERS

There are three types of fridge-freezer:

1 Two independently controlled units are placed together, usually the fridge being placed on top of the freezer (for convenience in using, the refrigerator being at the higher level because it is used more frequently). There is ample space in both and this arrangement is very suitable if you intend to freeze a fair amount of food.

2 One unit with a small freezer section at the top of the normal refrigerator. There is less storage space for frozen goods but it could be preferable to the above if you are short of space.

3 Three section refrigerator: this is an extension of the fridge freezer, consisting of three compartments at different levels of temperature:

a) freezer;

b) refrigerator;

c) compartment slightly warmer than b for storing foods not requiring as low a temperature, e.g. eggs, canned drinks, butter, etc.

## FREEZERS

The more popular models of freezer are the chest and upright cupboard types. There is also a table-top model but this is more expensive both to buy and to run.

*Chest freezer*

    1 This is cheaper to buy and up to 20% cheaper to run than the upright model.

    2 It accommodates bulky and awkwardly shaped items more easily than the upright model *but*

    3 It takes up more floor space than the upright model.

    4 It is much heavier than the upright cabinet and therefore more difficult to move.

    5 Containers at the bottom are often difficult to locate, especially if you are shorter than average.

    6 Hanging baskets may be slid across the top, to hold small items.

*Upright cupboard*

    1 This is slightly more expensive to run than the chest model *but*

    2 It has the same base dimensions as a refrigerator, so is easier to accommodate than a chest and makes a good twin fitment with a refrigerator of the same make.

    3 It facilitates packing and locating of foods, particularly if the cupboard is fitted with drawer baskets.

    Before buying a freezer:

1 Consider carefully the size you need. It is expensive to keep the freezer filled but it is uneconomical to run if only partially filled. (If, for any reason, you cannot keep it more than half full, fill the spaces with cardboard boxes stuffed with newspaper.)

2 Consider where the freezer is to be sited. If it is to be placed in a garage or under the staircase you will need an interior light.

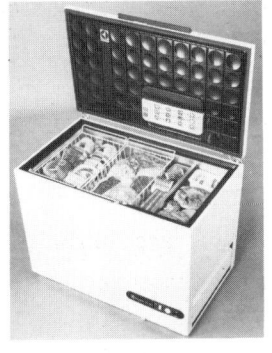

*An upright freezer, a chest freezer and a fridge-freezer (Electrolux Ltd)*

3 Check that the lid of the chest-type freezer is counterbalanced and has a magnetic catch.

4 Check that there are indicator lights
a) to show that the mains electricity is switched on in the freezer;
b) to warn that the power has inadvertently been switched off;
c) to show when fresh food is being frozen—'fast-freeze light'.

*Use and care of freezers*

1 Site away from sunny spots and hot water boilers.

2 Make sure that it is standing level (if in doubt, use a spirit level to check).

3 Place as much food as possible against the refrigerated surfaces.

4 Open for as short a time as possible (the cupboard type loses more cold air than the chest type when opened).

5 Rotate the stored food (label each item with the contents of the container and the date of storing) and make sure of the optimum safe storage time.

6 If a fast-freeze switch is incorporated in the model, remember to switch this on *before* beginning to freeze fresh foods (study the handbook for necessary time to be allowed).

7 If you wish to bulk-buy meat or fish, ask your butcher or fishmonger to pre-freeze the items for you. (They will, if asked, use their skills—regrettably normally underused—to joint, wrap and freeze multiples of individual portions.)

8 Wrap food carefully to prevent drying out and freezer burn. Heavy duty polythene bags or aluminium foil are best for awkward shapes; plastic or foil containers are useful for general purposes.

9 Consult your manual, supplied with the freezer, for advice on all problems, including de-frosting.

10 Thaw food slowly, in either a refrigerator or in a cool place. Never re-freeze uncooked thawed food.

*Insurance*

This is not a worthwhile expense for a small freezer but it is certainly advisable for a large one. Unless you are covered by your householder's policy, take out a separate insurance for the freezer (to cover loss of contents) and shop around for the most advantageous terms.

DISHWASHERS

1 A dishwasher is not really a worthwhile investment unless
a) you are an extremely busy person;
b) your family has increased considerably in size;
c) you are well supplied with china and glass.

2 Most washers are free-standing and of a size which will fit under existing work surfaces, but it is possible to obtain smaller versions which will stand on the top of them.

3 Most models are fully automatic—all you have to do is to load and unload them.

4 Different sized models will take from 4 to 14 place settings.

5 Dishwashers may be plumbed in (to be recommended) or fed from a tap by hose. If plumbed in:

*A dishwasher (Hotpoint Ltd)*

a) they may be connected to the hot or cold water system, but must incorporate a built-in heater if plumbed to the cold water supply;
b) the cycle will be lengthened if attached to the cold water system;
c) check that the Water Board approves a permanent connection.
6 Look for:
a) on/off indicator lights;
b) built-in water softener if you live in a hard water area;
c) an adjustable basket to accommodate the awkwardly shaped dishes you may have to wash.
7 The functions contained within programmes vary so select the one most suitable for your needs.
8 Remember that:
a) you must use a low-suds dishwasher detergent;
b) you should use a rinsing aid to help the rinsing water to run off without smearing glass or cutlery;
c) most water softener units need salt added from time to time to regenerate them (consult the manual for necessary frequency and quantity of salt required);
d) the following items should not be machine washed, because the water becomes very hot and the detergent is very strong:
    hand painted china; gilt or silver-edged china; cutlery with plastic or wooden handles; very delicate china; fine and good cut glass; polythene containers; aluminium and copper items
e) to use your washer economically you may need to buy additional crockery and cutlery—it is extravagant to put the machine into use for a small amount of washing-up;
f) when running, the washer may be noisy; it may be a good idea to switch it on when you are out or in bed (but switch it off as soon as possible after use);
g) prices vary—shop around, compare prices and consult *Which?* reports before making your decision.

MICROWAVE COOKERS
(See also Chapter 3, page 57.)
Your own particular lifestyle should guide you in deciding whether or not one of these cookers is a good investment for you. If you are a career person with little time to spare for cooking you may find that a freezer filled with ready-cooked dishes which can be quickly defrosted and reheated in a microwave cooker will be a very advantageous way of catering. If you have a family in which a number of different members require cooked meals at different times, one of these cookers will enable you to serve fresh-looking re-heated portions at a few minutes' notice.

SMALL EQUIPMENT (ESSENTIAL AND DESIRABLE)
There are on the market today so many different kitchen utensils that it is difficult to differentiate between those which you really cannot do without and those which you would like to own but are not really

necessary. It is a good idea to make out a list of items in order of priority, drawing a line between the essential and the desirable. Whatever you are buying, however, look for

a) good construction and design;
b) quality and safety of materials;
c) BSI and Design Centre award tags;
d) guarantees.

## Saucepans

You need not buy the traditional 'set' of pans—if there are only two of you a milk pan, a frying pan and two medium-sized saucepans will be sufficient as the basis for your collection. You can add to them as and when you need. Whatever pan you are buying:

1 Make sure that it is fairly heavy, with a good flat base (particularly for use on electric cookers) so that heat is evenly distributed.

2 Check that handles are securely fixed and are made of heat-resistant material.

3 Lids should fit tightly. Some pans nowadays are fitted with lids incorporating vents so that excess steam can escape and the pan will not boil over.

4 Make sure that you have full instructions for care and cleaning.

5 Purchase the best you can afford; it is false economy to use cheap, light pans. The even conduction of heat prevents 'hot spots' which cause food to stick and burn and the better pans are usually the most efficient in this respect.

Here is a list of materials in descending order of heat conduction efficiency:

copper, aluminium, cast iron, carbon steel, stainless steel, earthenware, porcelain, glass

NON-STICK FINISHES
Saucepans (and baking tins) with non-stick linings are more expensive than the unlined variety, so consider whether the extra cost is worthwhile to you.

British Standards cover the quality of non-stick coatings:
BS 4861 for those with which only plastic spatulas may safely be used;
BS 5206 for hard-based coatings which will withstand the use of metal tools.

Unfortunately few manufacturers quote the BS number of their products, so those which have passed British Standards or equivalent continental tests have to be identified by their trade names: Fluon, Teflon, Tefal, Armourcote, Xylon.

*Care*
1 Wash in warm, soapy water before using.
2 Cook food over a medium heat: fierce heat can shorten the life of the lining.

| Saucepan Materials | Special Points | Advantages | Disadvantages |
|---|---|---|---|
| 1 Aluminium | Available in varying thicknesses, the heavier the better. | A good long-term investment. | Initially expensive. May be pitted by alkalis and a few acids. After a long period of neglect, rust appears on outside as a white deposit, very difficult to remove. |
| 2 Stainless steel | | Not easily dented. Corrosion resistant. Not affected by ordinary scouring, acids or alkalis. Very durable. The best buy, if copper bottomed. | Not a good conductor of heat, so base is usually covered with aluminium or copper. Expensive. |
| 3 Vitreous enamel | Glass-like substance sprayed on to steel or aluminium and baked. Price indicates the quality of the coating and the thickness of the metal. Initial high cost ensures good quality and durability. | Beautiful colours and designs. May be oven-to-table ware. Metallic coating on the base will ensure even heating. | Enamel (inside and out) may become scratched (abrasives must be avoided). Poor quality pans heat food too quickly and will cause it to stick and burn. |
| 4 Vitramel | Cast iron coated with glass-like substance. | Good for long, slow cooking. Can be used in the oven and on the hob. Oven-to-table ware. Decorative appearance. | Very heavy. Enamel may chip or become scratched (abrasives should be avoided). Will break if dropped. Expensive. |
| 5 Copper | Usually lined with tin, nickel or aluminium. | Excellent heat conductor. Attractive, durable. | Reacts to certain foods if not lined. Lining may become scratched (avoid abrasives and metal tools). Very expensive. |
| 6 Glass ceramic | Can withstand direct hob heat as well as oven heat. | May be used on gas or electric cookers. Inert, non-porous, easy to clean. Reasonably priced. Cooking process can be watched. | Some pans have hot spots, so should be used on moderate heat only. |

3  Avoid sharp-edged tools which may scratch the lining.
4  Let the pan cool after use before filling with cold water.
5  Soak burnt or dried-on food remains in hot salt water before washing.
6  Avoid abrasive powders and pads.

## Casseroles

1  These may be made of vitreous enamel, vitramel, porcelain, ceramic or glass.
2  All may be used as oven-to-table ware.
3  Instructions for use must be carefully followed, especially for porcelain, ceramic and glass.
4  Most are reasonably priced.
5  'Ovenproof' means that the casserole may be safely heated in the oven. 'Flameproof' means that the casserole can withstand the direct heat of the hob.

## Cutlery

When choosing:
1  Handle the items critically, especially the knives which should be 'handle heavy' (i.e. the weight of the handle should keep the blade off the cloth).
2  Look for makes stamped with a well-known name.
3  Check that your choice is of a standard pattern so that you can match it when you wish to extend your stock over a number of years.
4  Remember that handles which are not integral can present a hygiene hazard at the joint; also they may become detached.
5  Make sure that kitchen knives are made of a steel which you can sharpen yourself; jobs are much more easily carried out with the correct knife than with an all-purpose one.

| Kitchen Knife Materials | Special Points | Advantages | Disadvantages |
|---|---|---|---|
| 1  High carbon steel | Good buy if looks are not important. | Sharpens to an excellent fine edge (use a butcher's steel or a carborundum block). | Tends to discolour; will rust if left wet. |
| 2  Stainless steel | | Easy to clean; will not stain, will not rust. | Difficult to sharpen yourself. |
| 3  Vanadium steel | High carbon steel alloy. Resembles 2. | Easy to sharpen. Tough; durable. | |

| Cutlery Materials | Special Points | Advantages | Disadvantages |
|---|---|---|---|
| 1 Stainless steel | Most commonly used metal. Look for the British Standards mark. | Easy to look after. Good resistance to corrosion. Can be washed in a dishwasher. | May become scratched. |
| 2 Silver | Buy from reputable dealers. Study hallmarks (booklet available from jewellers). Not suitable for everyday use. | Good investment. Beautiful to use. | Needs regular cleaning. Should be stored in a lined box or tray to avoid scratching. Should not be washed in dishwasher. |
| 3 Silver plate | Steel coated with silver. | Looks attractive. Less expensive than 2. May be washed in a dishwasher. | Coating may wear off eventually. |
| 4 Bronze | An alloy of copper and tin. Currently very fashionable. | Looks attractive when table is set. Reasonably priced. | Not very functional —metal is soft; blades may bend easily and cutting edge becomes blunt. Requires regular cleaning with metal polish. Shows fingermarks readily. Contact with vinegar causes corrosion which cannot be removed. Do not wash in dishwasher. |

*Figure 6.3  Kitchen knives*

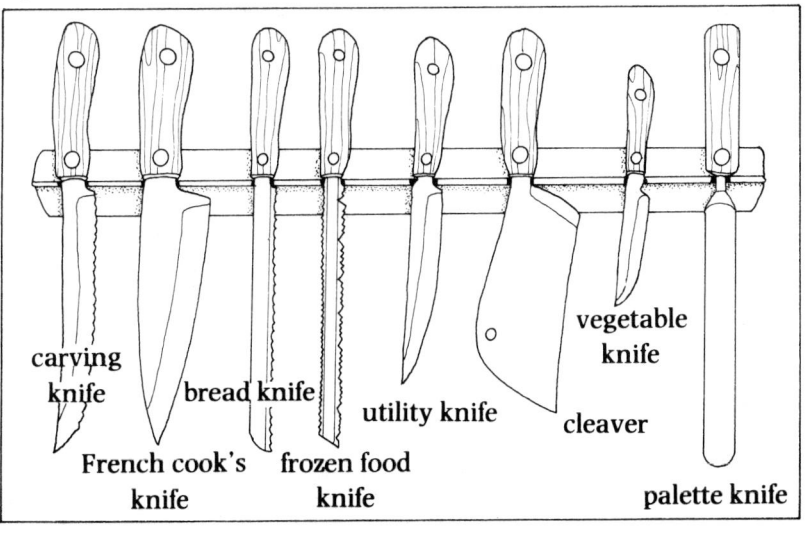

carving knife    French cook's knife    bread knife    frozen food knife    utility knife    cleaver    vegetable knife    palette knife

## Tableware

Possible materials for tableware include bone china, porcelain, pottery, pewter, melamine, wood (for bowls), glass (heat-resistant). Before making a choice from the very extensive and attractive range available, consider:
a) whether you are going to have two sets—one for everyday use and one for special occasions—or one set which will cover both usages;
b) that if you are hoping to add to it as and when you can, you must check that it is a line which will be available in the future;
c) the way you live and the type of meals you enjoy;
d) the design—do the cups fit the saucers well?, are the handles comfortable to use?, do the lids fit well?;
e) the initial cost and how much you can afford—remember that earthenware smashes as easily as bone china does;
f) that simple shapes without crevices are the easiest to keep clean;
g) that your taste in tableware is a very personal matter. If you are not sure of what you want, buy at first a set of attractive, inexpensive and durable ware which will be suitable for all occasions, and give yourself time to think, look, judge, and save while you are using it.

## Glassware

There is a very extensive range of glassware available—chunky, fine, cut, engraved, plain and coloured. Again, your choice is a very personal one, but it is only commonsense to use cheaper, thicker and plain glass for every day and to keep fine, cut or engraved glass for special occasions.
   Glass is made in four types:
1 Soda-lime—all purpose glass, the better quality being made by hand, the cheaper range being machine moulded.
2 Plain crystal—better quality than soda-lime type, containing a small percentage of lead oxide which is responsible for the clarity, weight, brightness and strength of glass.
3 Lead crystal—heavier and denser than 2, containing 25% lead oxide.
4 Full lead crystal—heavy and lustrous, containing a minimum of 30% lead oxide.

DRINKING GLASSES
Although there are traditionally 'proper' shapes for specific uses, it is quite possible to manage very satisfactorily with merely a set of tumblers and one of general-purpose large wine glasses. If you wish to start a complete collection, begin with sherry glasses and add the others according to your needs.
   Flute—tall, slender glass for sparkling wines
   Port glass—short-stemmed shaped glass

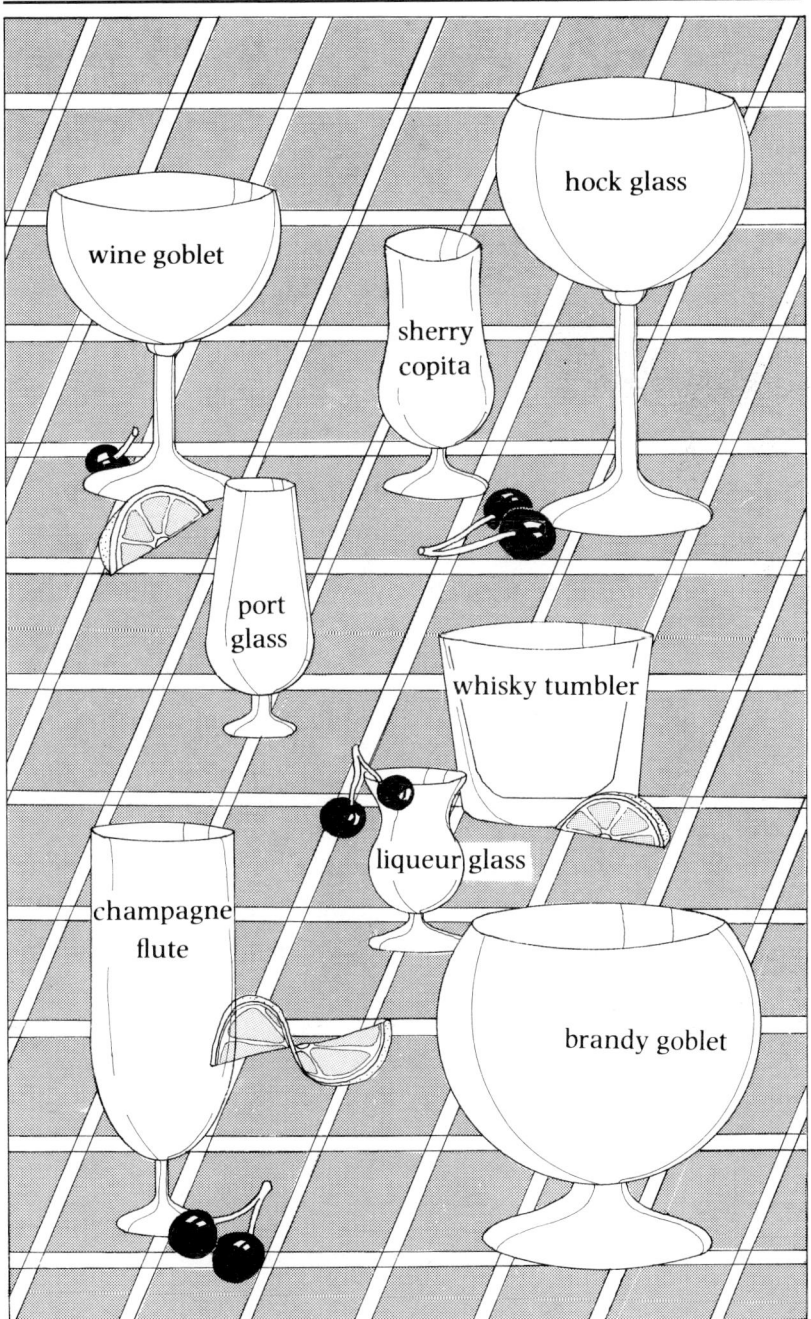

*Figure 6.4  Glasses*

Wine goblet—large bowl-shaped glass
Tumbler—squat, thick-based glass for whisky
Hock glass—long-stemmed, shallow bowl (often with coloured stem)
Brandy goblet—bulbous-shaped glass
Copita—for sherry
Liqueur glass—miniature wine glass
*When choosing*
1 Select a standard repeatable pattern if you intend to enlarge your collection.
2 Remember that metal or earthenware goblets look attractive and are more durable for everyday use.
*When washing*
1 Do not use a dishwasher to clean good glassware. Wash in hot detergent water and rinse in hot clear water (glass does not contract and expand evenly and quick changes of temperature can cause it to crack).
2 Use a lint-free cloth for wiping and polishing. Do not polish by twisting the bowl in the hand by the stem—the most vulnerable part of the glass is the join between them. Hold each part separately to remove smears.

## Table Linen

The cloth you use on your table acts as a background for your china, glass and cutlery and can make the simplest meal attractive and the most exotic one distasteful.

TABLECLOTHS
These may be:
a) damask—elegant but difficult to launder;
b) cotton—any colour, plain or patterned as preferred;
c) seersucker—requires no ironing so good for everyday use;
d) lace—luxurious and very effective used over a dark coloured plain cloth.

Tablecloths should be hung evenly on the table with creases, if any, running the length of the table. They may be protected by a plastic traycloth or matching napkin at a place used by a child. They should have a felt pad underneath if the tabletop is polished *or* heat-resistant tablemats may be placed on top of the cloth at each setting.

TABLEMATS
These are very useful on a table with a good finish; they are much easier to launder than cloths and obtainable in very decorative styles. Unless heat-resistant in themselves, thick protective mats should be placed between them and the table.

NAPKINS
Each member of the family can have his own table-napkin, which should be rolled and stored in a distinctive ring between uses. (Guests should leave theirs unfolded on the table when leaving it.)

Small decorative paper serviettes may be used at tea-time and larger, thicker ones for other meals if necessary. These are thrown away after one use, which reduces the amount of washing necessary, but they are becoming rather expensive items.

Some tablemats and tablecloths have matching napkins in the same material which give a very attractive appearance to the table setting.

TRAY/TROLLEYCLOTHS
Trays tend to become rather stained with use while still being perfectly functional. The use of traycloths not only disguises the wear but adds some distinction to the tray setting. (There are very pretty lace-like plastic ones available, which only need wiping over after use.)

## Small Kitchen Equipment

| Necessary Items | Desirable Items |
|---|---|
| Tins: baking, roasting | Fluted flan ring |
| Mixing bowl | Plain flan ring |
| 2 medium-sized basins | Icing bag and nozzle |
| Pie dish | Tongs |
| Graduated jug | Potato masher |
| Set tartlet/biscuit cutters | Garlic press |
| Cooling tray | Egg poacher |
| Set of scales | Set of basins |
| Collander or sieve | Mincer |
| Chopping board | Soufflé dish |
| Wooden spoon | Mouli grater |
| Potato peeler | Glassware (heat-resistant) |
| Pastry brush | |
| Fish slice | |
| Pair kitchen scissors | |
| Spatula | |
| Balloon whisk | |
| Grater | |
| Rolling pin | |
| Washing-up bowl | |
| Swing-top refuse bin/pedal bin | |

## NUTRITION

Your health and well-being, and that of your family, depends to a considerable extent on what you eat; it is therefore very advisable for

E

you to have a basic knowledge of the functions of food. Food does three things for us:
1  It builds up and repairs cell tissue.
2  It provides energy and warmth.
3  It controls and regulates all bodily functions.

## Body-Building and Repairing (excluding bone tissue)

These functions are carried out by substances called *proteins* and these are composed of combinations of *amino acids*. There are 22 different amino acids, some of which can be synthesized by the body from those it does not need, but 10 of them must be provided as such. These are called *essential amino acids* and foods which contain all 10 are known as *complete proteins*—these are all animal products, i.e. meat, fish, cheese, eggs and milk. *Incomplete proteins* lack one or more of the essential amino acids and are found in pulses (peas, beans, lentils), cereals (wheat, barley) and nuts.

Any left-over protein—that which is not required for building and repairing cell tissue at any one time—is used to supply energy, but this is an expensive way of obtaining it. (See below for energy-giving foods.)

*Bone tissue* is laid down by calcium and phosphorus, with the help of vitamin D.

## Warming and Energizing

There are two types of foods which supply warmth and energy:

1  Carbohydrates
These are starches and sugars obtained from flour (bread, cakes, biscuits, etc.), other cereals, potatoes, cane sugar, jam, honey and fruit. These foods are the bulky, filling elements of our diet and tend also to be the cheapest items. Overweight is most commonly due to eating too many carbohydrate foods and using too little energy to counteract them. Unfortunately, such foods are those which many people find the most attractive.

2  Fats
These are found in butter, margarine, lard, dripping, oils, oily fish, meat. They supply twice as much energy as carbohydrates provide but cannot be so easily digested and are not eaten in such large quantities. The body's intake of fats is thought to be related to blood cholesterol, which is laid down in arteries and other blood vessels rather as fur collects in pipes carrying hard water. This can be decreased by eating only polyunsaturated fats, i.e. those of vegetable rather than of animal origin.

## Controlling and Regulating

The food substances which carry out these functions are required in very small quantities, but are absolutely necessary for the health and efficiency of the warm and moving body. If the body is regarded as a well-organized machine, assembled and repaired by proteins and kept moving with carbohydrates and fats, these elements act as the oil in the works, keeping all parts running smoothly and ticking over efficiently.

If you are eating a well-balanced diet (i.e. one containing some food from each section every day) you only need to supplement your meals with commercially produced additives (e.g. vitamin pills) under exceptional circumstances such as during pregnancy or convalescence.

The nutrients (i.e. the elements in food which actually do the job) which keep the body in good working order are
a) vitamins;
b) mineral elements.
See the table on page 128.

Water (to lubricate all the processes) and roughage, or fibre as it is now more often called, to keep the digestive system well toned, are also necessary.

## Planning Meals

ORDINARY MEALS
Having established that some of each of the three classes of foods should be included in the diet every day, preferably at every meal (this is what is referred to as a 'well-balanced' diet), good eating habits should now be developed. Everyone beginning to arrange their own meals tends to continue the pattern of eating which was established in their first few years of life, but this form may have to be modified at least once when pressures of work plus housekeeping and, later, parenthood make it less convenient.

As a rule-of-thumb guide, the total meals eaten every day should include protein items (for growth and repair), some carbohydrates and fats (for warmth and energy) and vitamins and mineral elements (for the regulation of bodily processes)—in other words, a meat, fish, cheese or egg dish; potatoes, bread (or some other flour-based dish), butter or margarine; fruit and vegetables as preferred and at least a pint of liquid (non-alcoholic). So, when planning meals, bear in mind that:
1 Some of each of the above items should be included every day, preferably spread over each meal.
2 Following this arrangement, nibbling between meals should be avoided (if sweets or chocolate are craved for, these should be eaten at the end of a meal, not between meals).
3 The most important and the most expensive item is the protein (meat, fish, cheese, eggs) dish; start planning from this, add your carbohydrates

| Name of Vitamin | Functions | Sources |
|---|---|---|
| A<br>(fat soluble) | Keeps all mucous membranes (moist linings) of the respiratory system and the eyes healthy. Essential for the perception of light in dimness. Assists in the growth of children. | Butter, cheese, eggs, oily fish, fish liver oils, fresh and powdered milk, liver, kidney. As carotene (converted by the body into vitamin A): carrots, turnips, green vegetables, tomatoes, dried apricots, prunes. |
| D<br>(fat soluble) | Assists the combination of calcium and phosphorus to form sound bones and teeth. (When the skin is exposed to sunlight, ergosterol is converted into vitamin D.) | Dairy fats, fish liver oils, eggs, vitaminized margarine. |
| E<br>(fat soluble) | Little is known about the exact function in the human body, although it appears to be necessary for reproduction in some animals. | Wheatgerm oil. A little in most foods present in a well-balanced diet. |
| K<br>(fat soluble) | Enables blood to clot. | Foods supplying vitamins A and C. |
| B Group (1–12)<br>(water soluble) | Assists normal growth of children. Releases energy from carbohydrate foods. Keeps skin healthy. Stabilizes the nervous system. | Yeast products, offal, cheese, milk, eggs, pulses, potatoes and other vegetables. |
| C<br>(water soluble) | Keeps skin healthy. Assists the quick healing of wounds. Keeps teeth and gums healthy. Assists normal growth of children. | Fruit and vegetables, particularly citrus fruits, rose hips, blackcurrants, cabbage, spinach, cauliflower. (Easily destroyed by heat and exposure to air). |

| Name of Mineral Element | Functions | Sources |
|---|---|---|
| Iron | Necessary for the formation of haemoglobin which gives blood its colour and carries oxygen round the body. | Liver, kidney, corned beef, curry, cocoa. |
| Calcium | Essential for the formation of bones and teeth in conjunction with phosphorus and vitamin D. Helps the clotting of blood. | Cheese, milk, eggs, fish (those of which the bones are eaten, e.g. sardines, tinned salmon), hard water. |

and fats (potatoes, bread, butter), then your vitamins and mineral elements (vegetables and fruit).

4 Carbohydrates, particularly bread and potatoes, are satisfying 'fillers' and are easy items to include. These are the foods which are usually first to be avoided in slimming 'diets' but, in fact, potatoes are a good source of vitamin C and, if boiled and not fried, do not contribute as many

calories/joules as fats do. Bread, particularly wholemeal or bran type, can also be low in calorific value, especially if butter or margarine is spread only thinly. A better way of regulating calorific intake is not to cut out specific foods but to decrease the amount eaten of all of them.

5 Special people require special feeding and the attention they need is described on the following pages.

6 All foods look more appetizing if presented attractively. See page 133.

## SPECIAL MEALS
### *Babies*
1 Mother's milk is traditionally and irrefutably the best food for the early days of a baby's life, but there may be very good reasons why it is not available or sufficient for the baby. In this event, consult your health visitor or your doctor as to which commercially produced substitute milk will be best for you to use.

2 Babies are normally endowed with sufficient iron and vitamin C in their system to last them for the first 6 months of their lives. After this, puréed liver and eggs (to supply iron) and orange or rose-hip juice (for vitamin C) may be introduced.

3 It is inadvisable to over-salt babies' food and very unwise to over-sweeten it. A baby may develop a sweet tooth at a very early age and this may cause overweight which continues well into adolescence. Remember how early eating habits are established.

4 New flavours, as many as possible, should be introduced gradually but regularly, so that the baby accepts a wide range of 'taste sensations' as a matter of course.

### *Pre-school children*
1 These are crucial years for eating habits, setting a general pattern for life. Make sure that it is a good one!

2 The child is growing rapidly; developing bones and teeth demand good supplies of calcium, phosphorus and vitamin D.

3 The energy expended by children of this age does not need to be emphasized, but this requires replacement and care should be taken to ensure that they receive plentiful supplies of energy-giving and process-regulating foods while avoiding overeating of sugary items.

### *Schoolchildren*
1 Energy expended and attendant appetites are mutually dependent and it is often difficult to satisfy the needs of energetic, fast-growing youngsters. Again, commonsense must be used in supplying plenty of filling foods (not forgetting fruit) which are not also sugary or greasy.

2 A satisfying breakfast is important, particularly when journeys to school are lengthy and require an early, sometimes cold, start. Missing breakfast can mean a gap of well over fourteen hours between meals and the child arrives at school jaded and chilly,

unable to make the most of either his mental or physical potential.

3 School meals are very carefully planned and nutritionally balanced; meals supplied at home either supplement or substitute for these and should include a high proportion of protein (to ensure good growth) and plenty of energy-giving foods to make good the demands made by the super-activity characteristic of this age group.

4 At this stage, encouraging both boys and girls to cook will help them to appreciate the value of food.

*Adolescents*

1 This period (between 12 and 19 years of age) is a time of great 'growth spurt' and energy drive. A diet of high protein (body-building) and energy-giving content is essential.

2 There is a strong temptation at this time to fill up on 'empty calories' and 'junk foods' (i.e. items high in calories but low in real food value) such as sweet fizzy drinks, sweets, crisps, etc. Ensure that a good supply of milk, fresh fruit and fruit juice, and 'filler' foods such as cheese and wholemeal bread are available.

*Adults*

By now eating habits are established and well-balanced meals are a matter of course. Providing that your health is good there should be few dietary problems.

*Pregnant women/new mothers*

1 The unborn baby relies on the mother's diet to supply the nutrients it needs to develop into a well-formed, healthy being. Therefore, the type and amount of food the mother-to-be eats is very important.

2 Although literally 'eating for two' the expectant woman should not be eating twice as much as usual. What she must do is to be certain that her intake of protein, calcium (which will ensure that there are adequate supplies of phosphorus as well), iron and vitamins is sufficient to keep them both healthy. The doctor or health visitor will advise if required.

3 If the new baby is breast-fed the mother's diet must contain plenty of milk, cheese, fish, eggs, fresh fruit and vegetables. Alcohol should be avoided.

*The elderly*

1 This is a very vulnerable section of the family—less active, often with a small appetite, but still needing a very nutritious diet. The problems are often ascerbated by living alone, frequently with a much reduced income, poor mobility and lack of incentive to bother.

2 Bones become brittle and digestion less efficient as the years advance, so the diet should include good supplies of calcium and of foods eaten in easy-to-chew forms, e.g. fish, poultry, eggs, grated cheese, milk, fresh vegetables and soft fruits.

*Invalids*

Those who are ill or convalescent will have poor appetites which require tempting so, unless a specific diet is prescribed by the doctor, follow these general rules:

1 Include plenty of body-building and repairing foods, as well as ample fresh fruit and vegetables to supply vitamins and mineral elements.

2 Serve foods known to be favourites of the patient.

3 Present dishes cleanly, attractively and in small portions.

4 Avoid very strongly flavoured foods and those with distinctive smells.

5 Serve meals punctually.

6 Never serve 'warmed-up' dishes.

7 Keep the content as light as possible; serve small meals more frequently rather than large ones at longer intervals.

8 Include copious fluids—milk, soda water, fruit juices or cordials.

*Vegetarians*

There are two types of vegetarian: *lactovegetarians*, who will not eat animal flesh, and *vegans*, who will not eat any animal product at all.

1 Lactovegetarians—The acceptable diet includes animal proteins in the form of milk, eggs and cheese (which contain all the essential amino acids), so it is not an inferior diet and should present few problems.

2 Vegans—

a) Vegetable proteins all lack one or more of the essential amino acids, so it is very difficult to ensure an adequate protein intake. A variety of vegetables will supplement each other's amino acid content, but a large quantity of mixed vegetables is tedious to prepare and bulky to consume. Nowadays, textured vegetable protein, commercially prepared from soya beans to resemble meat, can add variety to the diet in a compact form. (Soya beans, alone of known edible vegetables, do contain all the essential amino acids.)

b) Because of the omission of blood-containing flesh from the diet, there may be a danger of anaemia. Iron-containing supplements may be necessary.

c) Margarine is a good source of vitamins A and D but normally contains whale oil. There is, however, a special blend produced for strict vegetarians which contains the vitamins but no animal fat.

d) Nuts will add bulk to meals, besides contributing additional vegetable protein, oil and vitamins.

e) The distinctive flavours of meat and fish, as well as of cheese, may be compensated for by the use of good seasoning and free employment of herbs and spices. Insipid meals are not appetizing and the vegan must be protected against the lack of incentive to eat.

f) Vitamin B may be deficient because of the lack of animal proteins and, again, may require supplements.

## ENTERTAINING

The secret of entertaining is enjoyment, not only by your guests but by you, as well. A warm welcome, relaxation and pleasure in each other's company are of greater importance than food served—these are the essence of the purpose of all social occasions.

The nature of your hospitality will depend entirely on your accommodation and resources. There is no need to aim at ambitious catering, for instance, if you are living in a bed-sit where preparation, presentation, space for outdoor clothing and seating arrangements all have to be fitted into a very limited area, and food served provided from a slender budget. Very successful parties for your friends can consist of nothing more than sitting on the floor, eating potato crisps out of bags, dunking pieces of French bread into a cheese dip and drinking coke from bottles through straws.

It is not even essential for you to supply all the items yourself. A 'get-together' at which you provide space, plates, cups or glasses, and your visitors bring their own 'take-away' type contributions can be as successful as and far less exhausting than the more formal type of dinner party.

If, however, you are sufficiently fortunate to have the space, the time and the money to indulge in more stylish entertaining occasionally and you do wish to provide food, it does not have to be elaborate—cheese and wine, sandwiches and drinks or even tea or coffee and biscuits are all that are necessary to welcome your visitors. In either case, a little planning in advance will prevent you from becoming flustered as your guests arrive.

1 Check that the room in which you are going to meet is warm, aired, softly lit and tidy.

2 Make sure that there are plenty of ashtrays available if you expect smokers.

3 If drinks are to be served, place drink mats on polished surfaces that could become marked.

4 As guests arrive, introduce them to anyone they do not know.

5 Circulate among your guests and make sure that no one is ignored or singled out. To some people it is highly embarrassing to be announced as in any way different and it is part of good hospitality to put everyone at ease.

If a meal is to be included:

1 Prepare as many dishes as possible in advance, preferably the previous day. A 'hostess trolley' which enables you to serve and keep hot all the dishes you make (so that you are free to mix with your guests until it is time to eat, and also to wash up all the saucepans as soon as

they are emptied) is a boon but it is an expensive luxury and is certainly *not* essential.

2 Serve a cold 'starter' or soup which only needs heating up at the last minute—again to give you freedom to be with your visitors.

3 Remember that casseroles can go on cooking safely without attention during the preliminaries of the occasion and make good meals when accompanied by a selection of fresh vegetables.

4 Tolerate visitors who may have put themselves on slimming diets and have cheese and biscuits available for them if they do not wish to eat a sweet dish. Cold sweets may be prepared in advance and stored in the refrigerator until required, but desserts are not absolutely essential. Your own knowledge of your guests will enable you to judge.

5 Prepare your cutlery and other tableware as early as possible and lay the table so that you have nothing else to bother you when the food is prepared.

## Laying a Table

Although the following suggestions are made to ensure pleasant hospitality, the basic principles should be followed at meal times when only the family is present. Table manners and etiquette are often disregarded in these days of pressures of time and activity but they should not be ignored if young people are to be able to attend functions, eat in restaurants and stay in hotels with confidence.

1 Make sure that the tablecloth or tablemats are clean. The cloth should be placed evenly on the table, with a level overhang all round and with the fold creases running along its length.

2 Use heat-resistant mats if hot plates and dishes are to be placed on polished surfaces.

3 Ensure that cutlery is absolutely clean and free from smears, and that there are sufficient pieces for all the food to be served. Settings, or 'covers', are arranged with the utensils to be used first on the outer sides and the sweet spoons/forks at the top (see page 134). The ends of the handles should be at least an inch ($2\frac{1}{2}$ cm.) from the edge of the table.

4 Place a small plate on the left-hand side of each place—napkins may be folded and placed on these plates or made into fancy shapes and placed on the plates, in the glasses or on the centre mat of the cover. Bread rolls may be placed inside the napkins or served in a basket.

5 Polish all the glasses which are to be used and place them at the top right-hand side of the cover. If the table is laid well in advance they may be turned upside-down until just before use, but they must be standing upright when the meal is served.

6 Check that there are plenty of salt and pepper containers so that people who will be needing them do not have to wait too long.

7 Place sauceboats on small plates with their own spoons, to prevent drips on the cloth or table.

*An informal table setting for lunch/supper*

*A formal table setting for lunch*

*A formal table setting for a dinner party*

*A breakfast tray setting*

*A coffee tray setting*

*A tea tray setting*

8 Fill the water jug last of all, adding ice if possible.

9 Use a central decoration of flowers or candles if possible, to add interest and beauty to the table, but do not let it be so tall that there is the danger of knocking it over when plates are being passed, or so dense that people cannot see those who are sitting opposite them.

10 If patterned china is being used, arrange it so that the same motif is at the bottom of each item; place cups in saucers with their handles to the right and the teaspoons with their handles in the same position.

## Serving the Meal

1 As host or hostess, come to the table yourself as smart in appearance and as calm in manner as you possibly can. It is too late to change the food and any unforeseen calamities can be offset with humour and aplomb on your part.

2 Make sure that plates are warm if food is to be served hot, and cold if it is to be chilled.

3 Serve soup from a tureen or present each person with individual bowls, covered if possible.

4 Serve the main dish on to plates piled before you, pass them round and allow everyone to help themselves to accompaniments.

5 Keep vegetable dishes covered after the first serving and encourage second helpings as required.

6 Keep the atmosphere of the meal light and pleasant—avoid controversial subjects which are going to spoil the diners' appetite, impair their digestion and cause your efforts to be ignored.

7 Remove all traces of one course before serving the next.

8 Allow guests to leave the table and sit more comfortably if coffee is to be served. The tray or trolley should be already prepared.

## BUYING FOOD

You should agree and stick to a definite sum which you can spend on food each week, and budget accordingly. If you have a job outside the home you will probably not have time to shop around for the most advantageous terms and will have to rely on supermarkets for quick service and reasonable prices. Both these and the more personal smaller establishments have their advantages and disadvantages, and you have to decide which is the better for you.

## Supermarkets

1 The company's objective is to make you spend your money, so they provide a comfortable, relaxed atmosphere with:
a) spaciousness and room to stand and consider (and chat!);
b) warmth in winter and air-conditioning in summer;

c) sometimes 'piped' background music;
d) a trolley to carry your goods to the check-out (and to your car if necessary).
2 There is a large range of colourful goods on display and it is very easy to be influenced by pretty packaging into buying a trolleyful of expensive goods, *but*
3 If you shop at 'off-peak' times you can complete your shopping quickly.
4 You can spend as much time as you like comparing the prices of similar commodities under different brand names; there is a far wider range of products available than at any smaller shop and, because they are purchased in bulk, the prices are more reasonable.
5 You can pick and choose your own items, even pieces of fruit and vegetables, so any sub-standard purchases are your own responsibility.
6 'Cut price' offers may be made from time to time, made possible because goods are purchased in very large quantities and are not required to stay long in stock.
7 Because of the rapid turnover of stock, you are unlikely to have cause for complaint about out-of-date foods.

## Smaller Shops

1 Personal service is available and this is particularly appreciated by elderly people who sometimes speak to no one but the shopkeeper all day.
2 The shopkeepers will wish to keep your custom so will do their best to provide what you want, in amounts convenient to you, and to keep items in stock especially for you.
3 The establishments are likely to be nearer to your home than the supermarkets, so you can save bus fares or petrol costs, *but*
4 Goods are likely to be a few pence dearer than those in the super-market, because the retailer cannot afford to buy in such large quantities.
5 The choice of products is small.
6 Shopping may take you longer because of the personal service and the limited numbers of assistants.

Whichever way you shop, make a list of the items you require as the need arises, take it with you and do not be tempted away from it. Keep a watch for 'special offers' and take advantage of them if you consider them to be genuine. You will need to be aware of the normal prices of these goods to judge them fairly.

If you buy your meat from your local butcher and find that you can rely on it being of good quality and fresh, make the most of the assistance he can give you. Butchery is a specialized craft and your retailer can advise you on cuts of meat, methods of cooking, boning and the use of nutritious cheap cuts.

## Convenience Foods

1 A 'convenience food' is any item packed in a tin, jar, bottle or packet in the process of which some preparation has been carried out by the manufacturer. In some cases all that remains to be done is to heat it. Examples of convenience foods are:
canned meats, fish, fruit, vegetables, sauces, pie fillings, soups; packets of soup, suet, cake mixes, sauce mixes, desserts; frozen pastry, jellies, flan glazes, savoury glazes, stock cubes, instant potato, dehydrated fruits and vegetables, baby foods, freeze-dried foods, jams, marmalade, sauces, pickles, chutneys

2 These foods *are* convenient and at times it is *necessary* to make use of them but they should not be regarded, as a whole, as substitutes for freshly prepared ones.

3 In order to preserve many foods, it is necessary to add chemicals to improve the texture, enhance the flavour, sweeten and colour them. Manufacturers are controlled by the Food Standards Committee which states the amount of additives allowed. The names of these chemicals must be shown on the labels of the items and you should read these carefully and decide how much you are prepared to eat.

ADVANTAGES OF CONVENIENCE FOODS
1 The food value is not necessarily less than that of 'fresh' foods.
2 Foods are available out of season.
3 Much preparation is avoided, saving time and labour.
4 They are useful in emergencies (illness, bad weather, visitors).
5 They add variety to the diet.
6 They are valuable on self-catering holidays.
7 Using them, children will quite happily prepare themselves a meal.

——————————— FURTHER STUDY ———————————

## Things to Do

1 Visit some old houses (i.e. stately homes, various private dwellings) and examine the kitchens. Compare the size, furnishings and equipment with those of a modern kitchen and discuss how they reflect contemporary society.

2 Draw a plan of your own kitchen and plot the journeys you have to make to enter it and to prepare and serve a tray of tea and biscuits (assuming that everyone takes milk and sugar).

3 Discover exactly how a refrigerator, of either the compression or the absorption type, works. Illustrate the processes which take place.

4 Find out the meaning of the words 'calorie' and 'joule'.
    a) How many calories/joules do you need each day?
    b) How many did you gain from your last meal? (*The Manual of*

*Nutrition*, published by HMSO, will provide you with tables to help you to work out your answers.)

5 Make a list of the items you would like to have in your own kitchen and calculate the amount of the bill.

6 Read the labels on some of the goods in your kitchen cupboard and make a list of the preservatives used in their preparation. Find out what function each serves.

7 Find out what a hallmark is and make a list of as many as you can with a note of what each one indicates.

## Questions to Answer

1 Write out and complete each of the following statements with the correct term chosen from the list in the right-hand column.

a) A frozen food compartment in a refrigerator is marked with _____ if it will keep food fresh for a week.

anaemia

b) Frozen food compartments which will safely keep food for three months are marked with _____ .

good

c) A material which will not react chemically with other materials is described as _____ .

fibre

d) Nearly every metal is a _____ conductor of heat and this makes it a very suitable material for cooking pans.

one star

e) A dishwasher should not be used to clean glasses as the water becomes very hot and glass is a _____ conductor of heat.

vitamin A

f) Calcium and phosphorus are necessary for the formation of sound bones and good teeth, but they need _____ to act as a catalyst.

vegan

g) A deficiency of iron in the diet may cause _____ which is shortage of red blood corpuscles, not the shortage of blood.

poor

h) A person who will eat no meat, fish, dairy produce or eggs is called a _____ .

i) _____ is not a nutrient but is required by the body to keep the evacuation of waste products from the digestive system regular and complete.

three stars

j) Carotene, found in fruit and vegetables, can be converted into some of the _____ which the body requires for the health of mucous membranes.

vitamin D

inert

**2** Why is it important to buy good quality saucepans? Say which type you would like to have for yourself and give your reasons.

**3** Assuming that you begin with no equipment at all, list the items which you consider essential in fitting your kitchen. Tabulate your answer, with reasons for your choice, under the headings: Furniture, Cooking Equipment and Utensils, Cleaning Agents and Kitchen Cloths.

**4** What do you understand by a 'well-balanced' diet? Plan a day's menus for your family, indicating:
   **a)** what nutrients you are supplying;
   **b)** any provision you are making for a 'special' member.

**5** List the convenience foods used in your own home. Plan a main meal using as many different types of such foods as you can.

**6** Plan an evening's entertainment for yourself and friends to celebrate your birthday. Include a meal and show:
   **a)** what preparation you would make beforehand;
   **b)** your day's timetable;
   **c)** what steps you would take to make your friends feel welcome.

Budgeting and Spending

7

## MONEY MANAGEMENT

Management of money is something which has to be carefully considered—no good management 'just happens'. Unfortunately, it is also a part of life which can cause untold problems but, with some understanding, planning and commonsense these should be reduced to a minimum. Certain terms are frequently used when talking about money and these are emphasized in the following pages—knowledge of exactly what they mean may save a good deal of confusion.

First, consider your *income*, i.e. the amount of money you receive weekly or monthly, almost always your earnings, paid to you by your employer. If you are paid weekly this sum is usually referred to as a *wage*, if monthly as a *salary* (in either case this is based on a yearly rate for the job, paid to you, as a convenience, in instalments of 1/52 or 1/12). Your *gross earnings* are the amount of money credited to you *before* deductions are made, your *net earnings* are the remainder, *after* deductions.

### Deductions

Deductions made 'at source', i.e. before you receive your money, are
a) compulsory—PAYE (income tax); National Insurance (NI); pension contributions
b) voluntary—union fees: these are voluntary unless a 'closed shop' operates, meaning that every employee must belong to the union; savings schemes; BUPA or similar scheme (private health scheme); social club contributions

PAYE (INCOME TAX—'PAY AS YOU EARN')
With the exception of the self-employed, this is the way in which most people pay their income tax to the government. Your employer deducts the amount which your *code number* indicates and pays it to the Inland Revenue Department. Your code number is calculated from your income tax return form and it is important that when you receive your form annually (the tax year runs from 6 April one year to 5 April the following year) you fill it in correctly, claim all the *allowances* to which you are entitled and return it promptly. *All* your income must be

declared on the form and you should notify the Inland Revenue Office immediately if your circumstances change, e.g. if you marry or take out a mortgage.

There is a certain amount of your earnings which is not taxed; this is called your *personal allowance* and depends upon your own particular circumstances. It can change from year to year with the Government's financial policy.

NATIONAL INSURANCE (NI)
Everyone who is employed must pay National Insurance contributions, except people who have reached pensionable age, are under 16 years of age, or those whose earnings are below the *lower earnings limit*. This is the statutory amount which you have to earn before you need to pay NI contributions. If you are eligible for supplementary benefits you do not pay either.

The amount of the contribution paid is fixed by the Government and once you have reached the *upper earnings limit* it does not change. Between the lower and upper earnings limit the amount you pay depends on the amount you earn until you reach a fixed limit called the *weekly earnings limit*, when you begin to pay the full fixed amount. The *benefits* which you can receive from the National Insurance Scheme depend on the amount you have been paying and the number of contributions which you have made. Some of these are:

National Health services
unemployment benefit
Social Security benefits
maternity benefit
industrial injuries benefit
pensions
death grant

Self-employed people (e.g. contract workers, nannies, etc.) should seek professional advice regarding their contributions; it is very important that payments should be kept up.

PENSIONS
When you are young, talking about retirement pensions seems to be pointless but you should make sure of exactly what your pension will be eventually, because it will determine your lifestyle when you finish your working life. Provision for this when your earnings are good will be much appreciated when your income is considerably reduced.

The State Retirement Pension is available for most people when they retire—for women (at present) when they reach 60 years of age and for men at 65 years. Should either men or women continue to work beyond this age, their pension is not available until they finally stop. The amount of pension to which you become entitled depends primarily on your National Insurance contributions; on the number you have paid and the length of time you have been paying them. Many firms run their own pension schemes and you should seek information about these when you enter their employment.

For details of other pensions see pages 99–100.

## Budgeting

When all the necessary deductions have been made you should aim at making the best possible use of the remainder of your income. At a national level, the Chancellor of the Exchequer presents his budget and your own domestic one is no less important.

If you are living alone, providing that you can meet all your bills and remain *solvent* (i.e. not in debt), you are at liberty to spend your remaining money as you wish without consulting anyone else. However, when finances are joint matters, more thought must be given and the family budget must be a mutually satisfactory arrangement to you both. Remember, as a basic fact, that there is no fun in worrying about unpaid bills; plan your expenditure to balance your expenses with, preferably, a little left over for emergencies, luxuries and savings. (Remember Mr Micawber's advice to David Copperfield: 'Annual income twenty pounds, annual expenditure nineteen, nineteen six, result happiness. Annual income twenty pounds, annual expenditure twenty pounds ought and six, result misery.' Currency and incomes have changed, but the advice is still sound.)

You will find your own best way of using your income but initially the following general guide will be useful.

1 As some of your expenses will be weekly, some monthly, some quarterly and some annually, it will be advisable to work on a yearly basis and spread your expenditure over 12 monthly periods. List these.

2 Write down what you expect your income for the year to be (excluding bonuses and overtime payments as these may not materialize) and beside it the payments you will have to make; this will give you a guide to your financial position and you will be able to economize or indulge accordingly. Dividing your expenditure on a percentage basis as shown in Figure 7.1 may be a helpful plan. The items included in each of the sections are as follows:

*Figure 7.1 Suggested allocation of spending*

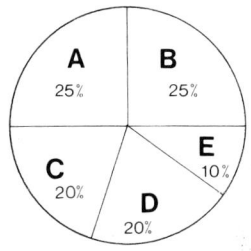

A   25%
Rent or mortgage
Rates
Water rates
Insurances—house and contents
Hire purchase payments (if any: preferably only one item at a time, e.g. washing machine, TV set)
Car tax, insurance, petrol or fares for public transport

B   25%
Fuel and lighting bills: keep account of your bills so that you can consider economies or adjustments
Insurances—personal
Maintenance—paint, wallpaper, repairs, etc.
Car repairs
Servicing contracts for central heating, TV, washing machine, etc.

C   20%
Food: actual amounts spent will depend on
a)  the number of people being catered for;
b)  the number of meals eaten at home (many firms offer a good catering service);
c)  how much produce can be home-grown;
d)  the appetites of the individuals being fed.
Toiletries
Cleaning materials

D   20%
Clothes (including shoe repairs)
Telephone: keep a check on calls made (a timer or even a lock may be useful!); make as many as possible during the cheap rate period
TV licence
Laundry/dry cleaning
Entertainment
Newspapers, magazines
Pets: licences, food, veterinary care
Personal expenditure

E   10%
Savings
Holidays
Hobbies
Presents—birthdays, Christmas
Impulse buying: a budget which does not allow for this (occasionally) may need revising

These percentages can only be a rough guide and you may need to keep your own weekly or monthly accounts to see exactly where your money is going and where economies can be made if necessary. Although this may appear to be a tiresome chore it may be made easier by using indexed file boxes for keeping household bills and important documents in good order.

You may decide to pay bills as soon as they arrive or to take advantage of the various credit facilities available. If you do the latter take care not to become too deeply involved (see Chapter 8 for further information). Remember that delay in settling accounts can result in further charges, e.g. an ignored final demand for electricity charges can mean the cutting off of the service and, at present, a charge of £23 to re-connect it.

## EFFECTS OF ADVERTISING

Every day we are bombarded with advertisements in newspapers, magazines, leaflets and circulars; and on hoardings, the radio and television. Every advertiser tries to convince us that his advertised product is the best and skilfully tempts us to buy it. Remember that advertising is big business; a great deal of money is spent on the advertisements and often the 'voice over' of a famous personality is used to make an even greater impact. Every possible ploy is used to persuade the consumer (each one of us) to buy the product displayed.

Advertising is, in essence, an agreeable and entertaining form of brainwashing and only the individual customer can control its success. There are two safeguards, however, which aim to protect the public from actual deception. These are The Trade Descriptions Act and The British Code of Advertising Practice: between them they ensure that advertisements contain nothing that breaches the law, that they are truthful, include only claims that can be substantiated and do not exploit fear, violence or superstition.

Advertisements on television and the radio are the responsibility of the Independent Broadcasting Authority which has its own code, similar to that used for printed advertisements, but its code is statutory rather than being voluntary.

As it is virtually impossible to ignore the tempting and colourful advertisements which abound, you need to use and practise your own commonsense to distinguish between:

a) the informative advertisement, i.e. that which gives factual details of size, colour, price, etc.;

b) the persuasive advertisement, i.e. that which appeals to emotive factors such as sex and status to sell products; and sometimes makes appear acceptable certain undesirable social behaviour, e.g. smoking and excessive drinking.

Be advised to look and enjoy but do not be misled. Use your own discretion when purchasing any item whether it be a packet of cereal or a washing machine.

## CONSUMER RIGHTS

It is not easy these days to be a 'good shopper'.
1  Pre-packed foods cannot be fully seen.
2  Synthetic fibres may need special care in washing.
3  Electrical gadgets may be unreliable or dangerous when used.
4  Within each range of goods there is a bewilderingly wide variety of choice.
As with advertisements, however, the consumer is protected; make sure that you know what help is available to you and do not hesitate to use it.
1  Leaflets give information and should be read carefully before expensive purchases are made.
2  Local organizations such as the Trading Standards Consumer Protection Department or the Citizens' Advice Bureau are ready and pleased to assist.
3  Laws have been passed by the Government to protect the public:
a)  The Trade Descriptions Act 1968 forbids any trader to make a false description (verbal or written) of any goods or services offered.
b)  The Sale of Goods Act 1893, as amended by the Supply of Goods (Implied Terms) Act 1973, states that goods sold must be of merchantable quality and fit for the purpose for which they are sold.
4  Should you have bought goods from a catalogue or newspaper advertisement *or* at a 'sales' party in a private house (where you are dealing with a trader, not a private seller), you have the same protection under the Supply of Goods Act, providing that you can supply the name and address of the trader.
  The Unsolicited Goods and Services Act 1971 protects the consumer from demands for payment for goods not ordered, e.g. records, books, Christmas cards, etc. which are delivered to your home by post. You can:
a)  return the goods immediately, marked 'Unsolicited', without paying postage;
b)  write to the senders giving your name and address and asking them to collect the goods; if they do not do so within 30 days the goods become your property;
c)  do nothing: the goods become your property after 6 months.
5  The Trading Standards (including Weights and Measures) Department:
a)  lays down standards of safety, e.g. regarding oil/gas/electric fires;
b)  makes checks on stated weights of foods displayed in shops.
6  Food Labelling Regulations 1980 (new regulations made under the old Food and Drugs Act 1955) state that:
a)  a full list of ingredients, in descending order of quantity, must be displayed on all pre-packed foods;
b)  the name and address of the seller and the importer must be displayed clearly on all products.

Since 1 January 1983 all foods with a life of between 6 weeks and 12 months (this will be extended to 18 months in January 1985) must show a 'Best Before' mark with the relevant month and year. Foods of a perishable nature, i.e. those intended for consumption within 6 weeks of packaging, must show a 'Sell By' mark above the day and month. This indicates the minimum life of the item. The following must also be observed:
a) water content over 5% must be declared;
b) colourings, additives and preservatives must be quoted;
c) if a food is advertised as being 'special', e.g. 'low-fat', 'contains Gin-seng', etc., the percentage of the 'special' content must be stated;
d) special conditions of use or storage must be indicated.
Catering foods are covered by the same regulations.

Certain items such as deep frozen foods, fresh fruit and vegetables and bread do not need date marks.

The above are the most important of the ways in which the consumer is protected, but some of the responsibility still rests with you. Making complaints about faulty goods or poor service is never easy. People generally dislike making a fuss, but if you have been supplied with a faulty product which does not perform its task, inform the vendor. It is his responsibility to take your complaint seriously and to compensate you for faulty goods or inadequate services. He is the person with whom you have made a contract.

## Complaints

1 Be methodical about keeping receipts; you will need them for any purchase you wish to return.
2 Should you have a complaint about any goods bought from a shop, ask to see the Manager and explain to him why you are returning them. Most retailers will exchange goods or return customers' money for the sake of goodwill. (Note that they are not *obliged* to change anything because you do not like it or because it is the wrong size.) Reasonable behaviour on your part is likely to result in co-operation.
3 If the retailer offers you a credit note instead of refunding your money, you do not have to accept it; you have the right to ask for your money back.
4 If you do not receive satisfaction, return the goods to the manufacturer with a letter (keep a copy) giving details of your complaint.
5 If you discuss complaints by telephone make sure that you ask the name of the person to whom you are talking, so that you have someone to refer to if need be.

## METHODS OF SHOPPING

Shopping in shops and supermarkets—see Chapter 6.

## Bulk Buying

Time and money can often be saved by buying in bulk, but before doing so, make sure that
a) you can afford to make the purchase;
b) you have adequate storage space.
If possible, share your purchasing with a friend or neighbour, so reducing the initial cost and diminishing storage problems.

Be especially careful when tempted to buy a complete animal carcass; this will include head, tail and trotters, which you will probably not want to use. The saving in money is considerably reduced if the whole animal is not used and you could be better off by paying more per pound but choosing your joints according to your taste.

## Mail Order

Magazines, newspaper supplements and the beautifully illustrated mail order catalogues all offer goods for sale which can be delivered to your door by post. The catalogues are a pleasure to browse through and a boon to the housebound or elderly, but they have their drawbacks.
1 Clothes cannot be tried on before ordering them.
2 The quality of the goods cannot be appreciated until they arrive.
3 The cost of postage and packing can cancel any apparent saving.
4 If you decide that you do not wish to keep the article you may have to pay the return postage.

Any mail order advertisement must conform to the British Code of Advertising Practice; when money is paid in advance the advertiser must deliver the goods within 28 days unless a longer delivery date is stated. If goods are returned undamaged within 7 days of receipt, your money must be refunded, but proof of posting must be retained.

## Discount Trading

Discount warehouses offer a large selection of merchandise—furniture, electrical goods, decorating materials, D.I.Y. equipment, food, etc., and, because of their size, they can display more varieties of the same type of goods than most stores. They are, therefore, excellent places to see a whole range of products and to compare prices. Having done this, shop around your usual stores since, because firms have to be competitive, you may find a better buy 'on offer'. Check whether there is a delivery charge or not, as this can sometimes cancel out the saving in price.

## Buying on Credit

This form of credit is similar to that enjoyed by the hire-purchaser (see Chapter 8) but there are differences.

1  Unlike the arrangements for hire-purchasing you, the buyer, own the goods from the time of the initial payment and if you fail to keep up the payments your purchases cannot be reclaimed. You can, however, be sued in court for the money you owe.

2  Payments for credit sales usually extend over a shorter period of time, from 6 to 18 months.

Read the agreement form carefully—it should show you

a)  the cash price;
b)  the amount and due date of each instalment;
c)  the number of instalments required;
d)  the total purchase price.

Remember that the interest required on money borrowed is likely to be high.

●  Note that if you buy on credit away from trade premises, e.g. from a doorstep salesman, you have a 'cooling-off' period of a few days in case you wish to change your mind.

It is now a legal requirement that the interest rate on any money that you borrow must be shown on any quotation you receive. It is shown as APR—the annual percentage rate of the total charge for credit. Be on the lookout for this figure and, if you do not understand it, seek advice before signing any agreement. You are not obliged to sign anything on the spot and your Trading Standards Department will be prepared to help you.

### Trading Checks and Vouchers

The use of this method of purchasing goods is more common in some areas than in others. You can have a 'check' for any amount between £1 and £30 and, providing you use shops which accept trading checks, you can buy goods without passing over any money. The amount you have spent will be entered on your check by the shop assistant and it is then sent to the trading company. The company pays the shop and deducts your debt from your original check. An agent calls weekly to collect your money, the original cost together with the interest usually being paid back over 20 weeks. Larger sums of money can be used as trading 'vouchers' and these are paid back over a longer period.

This is quite an expensive way of borrowing money and if you do not spend the check immediately you may be paying interest on money you have not spent.

### Savings Stamps

Stamps are available to be stuck on to special cards to make it easier to pay fuel and television licence bills. They may be purchased as often as you wish and are credited to you when offered as payment when the bills are presented.

Gas token stamps and electricity token stamps are available from the respective showrooms, while TV licence stamps are available from the Post Office (local or head).

## Direct Debit

Any recurring quarterly or annual bill can be paid in monthly instalments by arrangement between the supplier and your bank. The amount you pay can be varied and may be debited on any date you wish to specify. A small fee is debited from your account for this service unless you are exempt from bank charges. This is a convenient way of paying for your gas, electricity, rates and other standing commitments you may incur.

## Commodity Labels

For date stamping, see 'Food Labelling Regulations', page 146.

## Unit Pricing

Unit pricing is the price per pound or the price per kilogram of a commodity and manufacturers and retailers do not make price comparison easy for the uninformed shopper. The problem arises because traders are still using a mixture of imperial and metric weights and measures. One large supermarket at present marks a few of its products with the unit price as well as the selling price so that it is possible to compare, for example, two washing powders:

| POWDER A | | POWDER B | |
|---|---|---|---|
| Cost of item: | 79p | Cost of item: | 73p |
| No. of ounces: | 32.8 | No. of grams: | 0.930 |
| Price per pound: | 38.54p | Price per pound: | 35.61p |

## Stock Control Code

On many commodities you may see a mark showing a number of lines and a series of figures which is a computer number, as shown opposite. As each item is sold, a light pen passed across this band of marking reads it as a stock item number. This information is fed automatically into the computer which registers the sale and deducts it from the appropriate stock, so that a stock check is always available at source.

## Guarantees

Most of the larger household items you purchase carry a guarantee. These are for your protection and you should read them, sign them and send them back to the manufacturers as soon as possible after you have

*An example of the stock control code (Article Number Association)*

purchased them. The period of guaranteed satisfaction can vary from 6 months to 10 years, occasionally for a shorter time.

Make a habit of keeping your receipt safely, together with any literature relating to the item, so that you can find it whenever the need arises. Reference to your guarantor, providing that the stated period has not elapsed, is often the quickest and most satisfactory way of having faulty goods repaired.

—————————————— **FURTHER STUDY** ——————————————

## Things to Do

1   Find out from your local DHSS office how many National Health contributions you must have made to qualify for any of the benefits listed on pages 99–100. What benefits could *you* obtain, if necessary, through the National Health Service?

2   Look at the 'Situations Vacant' pages in a newspaper and select a job which states the salary offered. Read the details carefully so that you can estimate the amounts you (assuming that you held this position) would have to put aside for travelling, clothing and eating away from home. Bearing in mind compulsory deductions, discover what your net income would be.

3   Make a list of your present items of weekly expenditure and apportion them according to the pie chart shown on page 143. Set these against your income and compare your percentage expenditure in each 'slice' with that suggested.

4   Collect examples of informative and persuasive advertising from as many magazines and newspapers as possible. Discuss the merits of each and decide what it is about them which 'sells' the product.

5   Watch a series of television advertisements and list which are informative and which persuasive.

6  Find out which stores in your area have adopted the 'unit pricing' system. For a similar commodity from each store, give an example of unit pricing and state which is the best buy.

## Questions to Answer

1  Write out and complete each of the following statements with the correct term chosen from the list in the right-hand column.

| | | |
|---|---|---|
| a) | Advertisements for jobs quote a wage or salary figure which is the amount of _____ earnings received. | credit buying |
| b) | Deduction from salary which is paid to the Government's Department of Inland Revenue is shown as _____ . | direct debit |
| c) | The amount of money deducted from your income which allows you to collect payment when you are sick is shown as your _____ contribution. | net |
| d) | Your _____ is calculated from the information you give to | current |
| e) | the Department of _____ when you fill in your income tax return. | income tax |
| f) | The amount of money you actually receive in your pay packet or which is paid into your bank is your _____ earnings. | National Insurance |
| g) | It is now illegal for any food product to be sold which does not show a list of the _____ in descending order of proportion. | code number |
| h) | Hire purchase and _____ are both ways of buying goods in which you pay for them by instalments. | Inland Revenue |
| i) | Money may be deducted from your _____ account at specified intervals to pay recurrent bills such as those for gas and electricity supplies. | ingredients |
| j) | This method of payment (i) through your bank is called _____ . | gross |

2  What advantages are there in paying your bills as soon as you receive them? If you could not manage to do so, which of the alternative methods would you choose? Give your reasons.
3  If you had to make some drastic economies in your expenditure, in which area(s) would you attempt to do so? Which items would you consider to be worth exemption from economy?

4  Consider the advertisements you have seen on TV and describe the ones which you have found most persuasive. Why is this so?

5  What would you do about the following problems:
   a)  a shirt (labelled 'polyester') which shrinks on its first washing;
   b)  a tin of 'beans and pork sausages' containing only one sausage;
   c)  a large cardboard packet of herbs containing a very small cellophane package of the product;
   d)  an electric food mixer which fuses after being used twice;
   e)  a pre-packed tray of plums of which the lower layer contains three unusable ones.

6  Why has it become obligatory to describe the ingredients of food products on the packaging? What can you gain by reading this information?

## BANKING

Many young people nowadays open an account with one of the 'Big Four' main banks: National Westminster, Barclays, Lloyds or the Midland.

### Accounts

CURRENT ACCOUNT
This is the most obvious way of opening an account. It means safe keeping for any money which you wish to be kept readily available to you
a) by handing it over the counter together with a paying-in slip;
b) by having your wages or salary paid straight into your account by your employer. In this case you will be given a payment slip by your employer, stating how much you have earned, what deductions have been made and the amount which has been paid into your account (this is your net income—see Chapter 7).

When you first apply to open the account you will be asked to nominate someone who will give you a reference. A bank employee will write directly to this person, merely asking him/her to sign a form stating that in his opinion you are a fit person to have an account, and possibly how long you have been known to him.

After you have made your first payment into the bank you will be given a cheque book and with this you can draw money out of your account as you need it, safeguarding you from the necessity of carrying large numbers of notes about which can be lost or stolen. You can pay your bills by using cheques and these are made payable to the firm or person who has sold you goods or service. If you wish to draw out cash for yourself you write 'Cash' in the space which says 'Pay_____' and tell the cashier the denomination of the notes or coins you want (e.g. 2 £5 notes, 10 £1 notes and 10 50-pence pieces).

Whenever you write a cheque you must enter:
a) the date;
b) the name of the person to whom the cheque is to be paid (or 'Cash' if that person is yourself);

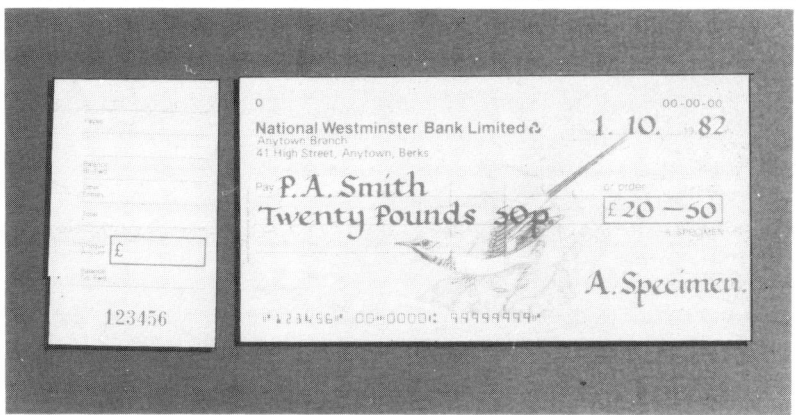

*A cheque and counterfoil (National Westminster Bank plc)*

c) the amount of the payment in words; ⎫
d) the amount of the payment in figures; ⎬ These must agree.
e) your own signature. ⎭

You will find it helpful to fill in the counterfoil or record slip with the date, the value of the cheque, to whom it was paid and what it was payment for.

When you wish to pay money into your account you should use your own paying-in book as this will bear your account number. If you use an open slip (obtained from the counter) you will need to enter the number yourself, so it is useful to keep a note of this number in your diary. (If you are in doubt, your cheque book will show the number of the account as well as that of the branch holding it and the serial number of the cheque.)

When filling in the slip, enter on the front:
a) the date;
b) the amount paid in and whether it is by cheque, notes, coins, etc.;
c) the account number if not shown;
d) the signature of the person paying-in; so long as the other details are correct, it need not be yourself;
and on the back:
the name(s) of the people drawing the cheques made out to you and the amount of each cheque.

When you pay in a cheque or any form of cash, your account will be credited with the amount; when you draw a cheque your account will be debited with the amount.

A *statement* from the bank is issued at intervals (usually at periods requested by you: at the Midland Bank statements are presented when the sheet is full *or* quarterly, whichever is first) which sets out exactly how your account is standing. If you find that you are drawing out more than you are putting in—in other words, if you become *overdrawn*—

you may find it necessary to apply to the Manager for an *overdraft*. This will allow you to draw money up to a specified limit but interest will have to be paid on what is virtually a loan.

These services take up the time of bank employees and therefore a small charge is made for every transaction; these are referred to as 'bank charges' and are shown on your statement. However, if

a) you are a student and remain in credit *or*
b) you are under 21 and remain in credit *or*
c) your account is always in credit of £100

no charges are made.

When you receive your statement, tick off the cheques shown against the details recorded on your cheque book counterfoils/record slips. You will then be assured that your account or name has not been confused with that of someone else, and it may put your mind at rest that cheques you have sent by post have been received. Check figures shown under 'Remittances' against your payslips and your paying-in book counterfoils.

As a holder of a current account, you are usually offered a card with which you may obtain cash at any time of the day or night. You must remember the code number allotted to you because this is used in conjunction with your card in the automatic dispensing machines installed outside most of the larger branches.

CHEQUE CARDS

When you have proved yourself to be credit worthy, you can apply for a 'cheque card', which is a guarantee from your bank that the cheque you are presenting for payment (e.g. in a shop or garage) will be honoured. In addition, this card will enable you to cash cheques to the value of £50 at any bank in the United Kingdom and in many abroad. (Some banks are now, however, introducing a system where you will have to apply for a special renewable card if you wish to cash cheques abroad.)

You *must* sign your card as soon as you receive it and, if possible, keep it somewhere separate from your cheque book. If you mislay one or other of these items they are of little use to anyone else, but if you lose them both together it is relatively simple for an unscrupulous finder to draw money from your account. If you should lose either or both, notify your bank *immediately* and all payments will be stopped at once.

When you receive the period replacement card sign it *immediately* and destroy your old one. It cannot be torn up, so either burn it or cut it in half.

BUDGET ACCOUNTS

This service is intended to ease the difficulty of paying regular bills which are presented periodically, your income remaining at the same level throughout the year. A small charge is made but, if the account is used sensibly, this amount is worth considering favourably.

Only those over 18 years of age may apply for this service and it is available only at the discretion of the Bank Manager. If you wish to open a budget account you must first list the amounts you expect to pay out for various items throughout the year (e.g. fuel, electricity, holidays, clothes, repairs, etc.). Add these up and divide the result by 12. This figure will be the value of a debit automatically made from your account each month, but you may write out cheques for payments in full. To apply for such an account ask an assistant (at the 'Enquiries' counter) in your own bank for the necessary form(s).

DEPOSIT ACCOUNT
A current account does not normally accumulate interest on the money paid into it, being a convenient method of day-to-day transacting. Any surplus credit built up in the current account, 'windfalls' or savings can be used to open a deposit account. This account accrues interest half-yearly at a rate fixed by the bank. Under special schemes, interest may be paid at a higher rate if you guarantee to make regular payments and limit your withdrawals. This interest must be declared on your income tax return.

You cannot draw cheques on a deposit account but if your current account is becoming very much diminished you may request a certain sum to be transferred from your deposit to your current account. This must be made in the form of a written, signed application but it is possible to arrange for the transfer to be made automatically when your current account becomes low.

## Other Banks

There are other smaller banks that are worth considering before you finally decide where to place your account.

CO-OPERATIVE SOCIETY BANK
There are 'Handy Banks' in most large co-operative stores and these will offer the same counter services as the large banks, together with certain advantages.
1  They are open on Saturdays until 5 o'clock (17.00 hours).
2  Providing you are 1 penny in credit no bank charges are made.
3  No charges are made on standing orders or direct debit arrangements providing you are in credit. (Should you become overdrawn, bank charges are imposed for a quarter year.)
   Statements are sent out monthly or when the sheet is full, whichever comes first.

GIROBANK
There is almost certainly a branch of Girobank in your local Head Post Office, and this can be used in the same ways as the large banks except that it does not arrange mortgages. A cheque book is issued to you and,

F

subject to favourable references, a cheque card as well. This bank, too, has certain advantages.

1 Free banking is offered as long as you are in credit.

2 Without a cheque card you can cash a cheque valued up to £50 every other business day at either of two Post Offices you choose.

3 With a cheque card you can cash a cheque for up to £100 at the Post Office designated as your first choice on your application form; or a cheque for up to £50 at any other Post Office with a Girobank.

4 It is open on Saturday mornings and until 5 o'clock (17.00 hours) on weekdays.

5 Statements are issued every time you make a payment in and after every 10 withdrawals.

TRUSTEE SAVINGS BANK
These banks offer the same facilities as the large banks with the exception of budget accounts (see page 156). Bank charges are made if your account falls below £50 in credit. Opening times are the same as those of the 'Big Four'—normally 9.30–3.30 Monday to Friday. Saturday morning opening is being introduced in some banks. Statements are presented either when the sheet is full or quarterly, whichever comes first.

**Credit Cards**

The major banks, together with other commercial concerns, are also involved in running credit card schemes. In the United Kingdom the principal cards used are 'Access' and 'Visa' (Barclaycard). When the scheme was initiated cards were sent out to bank account holders by post, without application being made. Now, however, if you wish to hold such a card you must apply for it.

*A credit card (Barclays Bank plc)*

Many stores, petrol stations, discount warehouses, restaurants, hotels, etc., display credit card signs (large facsimiles of the individual cards) indicating that they are prepared to be paid according to this scheme. You will be asked to sign an invoice when you produce your card. Each month the credit card company will send you a detailed statement of your purchases and the total amount of debt outstanding; it will also show the minimum payment (about 10%) which you have to make— you may exceed this or pay off the debt completely but you are not permitted to pay a lower amount.

You are allowed to have interest-free credit if you pay off your debt within 25 days from the date of your statement (this does not include cash transactions at the bank).

Although this is an extremely convenient way of paying bills, it is very easy to allow debts to mount up alarmingly, so use it with care within the set limit.

STORE 'CREDIT CARDS'
Many large stores, including some supermarkets, operate their own credit card schemes. They are operated in various ways, but the two most common types are:
1  *Budget/subscription account*
    You decide how much you can afford to pay each month and the store will allow you to spend up to 24 times that amount, e.g. if you decide to allow yourself £10 a month you may spend up to £240. As you pay off your debt you can 'top up' your credit again; *but* your monthly statement will include interest charged.
2  *Option account*
    This operates in the same way as a bank's credit card system. You can settle your debt in full or make a regular repayment each month; interest will be charged on the balance outstanding each month.
    Remember that, when using this system, you are limited in choice to the goods which the store sells.


## SAVINGS

Many schemes are available, including bank deposit accounts, mentioned on page 157. Here are some alternative schemes.

### Post Office Savings Bank

This is organized by the Government and administered by the Post Office. It is a very convenient way of saving small sums of money as you can open an account with £1 and withdraw up to £100 on demand (providing that you have £101 in your account—complete withdrawal will close the account).

All interest is taxable and must be included in your tax return. The Post Office also offers an investment savings scheme wherein the first few pounds are tax free (e.g. £70) and the interest rate is much higher than that on the normal savings scheme. You must, however, give one month's written notice before you can make any withdrawal.

## Index-Linked National Savings Certificates

During periods of high inflation, the disadvantage of saving money is that by the time you withdraw it, even with the accrued interest, its value is less than it was when you put it aside—i.e. you cannot buy as much with it as you would have been able to when you first had it. Index-Linked National Savings Certificates are designed to protect lump-sum savings from these effects.

The certificates are purchased in pound units and there is a limit to the number of certificates you may hold (a maximum holding). When you cash them the money you receive should buy the same amount of goods and service as your original investment would have done. You must, however, wait for one year after buying them before your certificates will attract interest—if you cash them within 12 months you will receive only the purchase price. After one year their cash value will be increased each month in line with the rise in the cost of living since the time of buying. This rise is monitored by the Retail Prices Index. Interest gained on these certificates is not taxable and you do not have to declare it on your tax return.

There have been many issues of National Savings Certificates (each one has a number shown on the part you retain) and each one matures after a specified number of years. This is the time at which it ceases to attract interest at the advertised rate. Interest will continue to accrue in subsequent years but at a lower rate. There is no compulsion about

*A National Savings Certificate (Director of Savings, Crown copyright)*

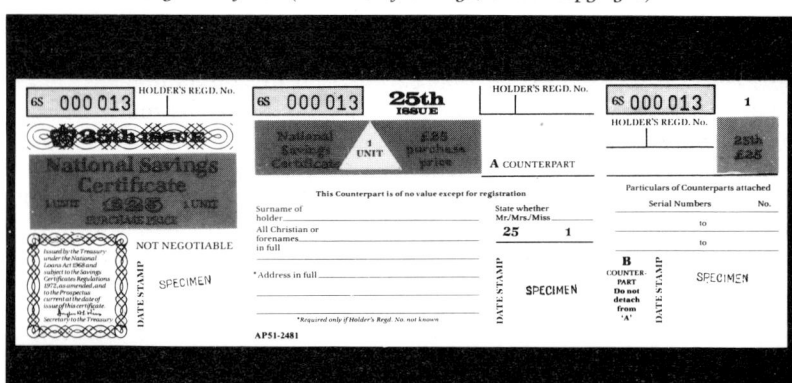

encashing your certificates at any time but it is to your advantage to withdraw them (the purchase price plus the interest) when they reach maturity and re-invest the proceeds.

## Building Societies

You can open a normal savings account with any of the many Building Societies which now operate. Interest rates vary so it is worth comparing these before choosing the one you wish to save with—choose a reputable company and one which has Trustee Status.

There is currently a good deal of competition between the banks and the building societies. It is now possible to obtain a mortgage from a bank and, shortly, building societies will be issuing cheque books and cheque cards to savings account holders. Interest on your savings is usually paid out at half-yearly intervals, but it is now possible to receive it monthly. You can elect to draw this every month or half year, leaving your capital (i.e. your investment) at a constant value (this is 'simple interest'), or, your interest can be added to your capital and the next interest will then be gained on the capital *and* the interest (this is called 'compound interest'). You will be notified of the amount of interest paid to you in either case and this must be shown on your income tax return.

## CREDIT

### Hire Purchase

This is probably the best known method of buying 'on credit'. You are actually 'hiring' the goods until all the instalments are paid, and this means that
a) the goods can be reclaimed if you fall behind with your payments, and the money you have already paid is not refunded;
b) you cannot sell the goods while you are still paying for them.

Usually, you are required to pay a deposit and then a series of equal instalments at weekly or monthly intervals over a period of months or years. The retailer or dealer himself may put up the money for the full payment of the merchandise *or* the agreement may be made with an outside finance company, arranged by the trader.

On the surface, this appears to be a very convenient and attractive arrangement but look carefully at the interest rates involved. Hire purchase is big business and can be very expensive: it is worth considering whether or not a bank personal loan may be cheaper.

### Insurance Policy Loan

If you hold an insurance policy with a 'cash-in' value, endowment or life, you can ask for a loan of up to 90% of the current cash-in value.

This is an easy way of raising money as long as you are prepared to continue to pay premiums and interest after most of the nest-egg has gone.

You do not *have* to pay back the loan until the repayment of your policy becomes due, although this is the more expensive way as you have to pay interest throughout on the full amount of the loan. Any debt outstanding on your death will be deducted from the assured sum.

—————————————— **FURTHER STUDY** ——————————————

## Things to Do

1 Visit a local bank and collect one of each of the forms for use by the public. Fill in one of each with reasonable figures and check with an unoccupied cashier that you have done so correctly.
2 Collect leaflets explaining the services offered by each of the 'Big Four' banks and compare them.
3 Find out the interest rates offered by each of 6 different Building Societies and compare them with those available from deposit accounts in each of the 'Big Four' banks.
4 Find out which issue of National Savings Certificates the present index-linked ones are, how many of them you are able to purchase, when you can do so and what interest is paid on them. Compare this with previous issues.
5 Find out and make a note of the exact meaning of the following terms:
a maximum holding; a holder's card; a counterfoil; a dividend; a warrant; encashment; a premium; instalments; capital; 'in the red'

## Questions to Answer

1 Write out and complete each of the following statements with the correct term chosen from the list in the right-hand column.

a) Details of payments made to and withdrawals from your bank account are sent to you periodically as a bank _____ . — budget account

b) You may pay bills by cheque instead of by cash as long as you hold a _____ account. — maximum holding

c) If you wish to save money in a bank you may gain interest on it by putting it into a _____ account. — Girobank

**d)** At branches of _____ it is possible to draw out £1 to £50 every other business day without a cheque card.

National Savings Certificates

**e)** In order to spread out payments of bills over the year instead of having to pay several at once you may open a _____ with one of several major and minor banks.

statement

**f)** To preserve the cash value of your savings, certificates may be purchased which are _____ .

mortgages

**g)** You are only allowed to buy a certain number of savings certificates; this number is referred to as the _____ .

index-linked

**h)** The only way in which your savings may attract interest which is not taxable is by buying _____ .

bank charges

**i)** The bank which is run by the Post Office offers most of the facilities available at major banks except _____ .

current

**j)** The administration of your financial affairs by a bank is free under certain circumstances but otherwise _____ are made to contribute towards the cost of the service.

deposit

**2** Thrift used to be regarded as a virtue. Discuss the value of saving money today.

**3** If you unexpectedly received a legacy of £500 on condition that it was invested, which method would you use? Explain the reasons for your choice.

## METHODS

The family wash day used to be a steam-filled occasion of soaking, scrubbing, boiling, rinsing, blue-ing, starching and drying, followed by a marathon ironing session, a festoon of airing and a ritual folding and putting-away. Today, easy-care fabrics and modern appliances have taken most of the hard work out of the task and some procedures have become quite obsolete.

To carry out the family wash may be a matter of doing it by hand, using one of a variety of machines, sending the goods to a commercial laundry or taking it to the nearest laundrette (these are now established in most built-up areas), according to your circumstances and your means. You may even find it useful to use more than one facility.

Table 5 on pages 166–7 sets out the relative advantages and disadvantages of each method.

The table below sets out the functions of washing and drying machines.

| Machine | Functions | Average Load (dry) | Special Points |
|---------|-----------|--------------------|----------------|
| 1 Wash boiler | Heats water to boiling point. | 1.8–2.7 kg. (4–6 lb.) | Portable. |
| 2 Twin-tub machine | Soaks; washes; boils; rinses; spin-dries. | 2.7 kg. (6 lb.) | Load must be lifted from tub to tub. Each operation must be hand set. Fed from taps by hose. Drying-off required. |
| 3 Single-tub machine | Soaks; washes; boils; rinses. | 1.8–2.7 kg. (4–6 lb.) | Used with wringer. Does not sprin-dry—complete drying is required. Each operation must be hand set. Fed by hose from taps. |
| 4 Automatic washing machine | Pre-wash treatment; up to 12 different programmes; rinses; spin-dries on appropriate programmes. | 2.7–5.5 kg. (6–12 lb.) | Most efficient if plumbed in. Once programme is set by hand every operation is automatic. Drying-off is required. |

| Machine | Functions | Average Load (dry) | Special Points |
|---------|-----------|--------------------|----------------|
| 5 Automatic washing and tumble drier machine | As above; complete drying. | 2.5–4 kg. ($5\frac{1}{2}$–9 lb.) | Should be plumbed in. Venting hose to remove steam may be necessary. Automatic operations once washing and drying programmes are set. |
| 6 Tumble drier machine | Dries completely or partially as required by tossing clothes through warmed air. | 2.7–4.5 kg. (6–10 lb.) | No further drying is required. May need a venting hose. |
| 7 Spin drier | Sometimes includes automatic rinse; spin-dries. | 2.7 kg. (6 lb.) | Fed from taps by hose if rinsing is included. Further drying required. |

*Figure 9.1  Washing machine actions*

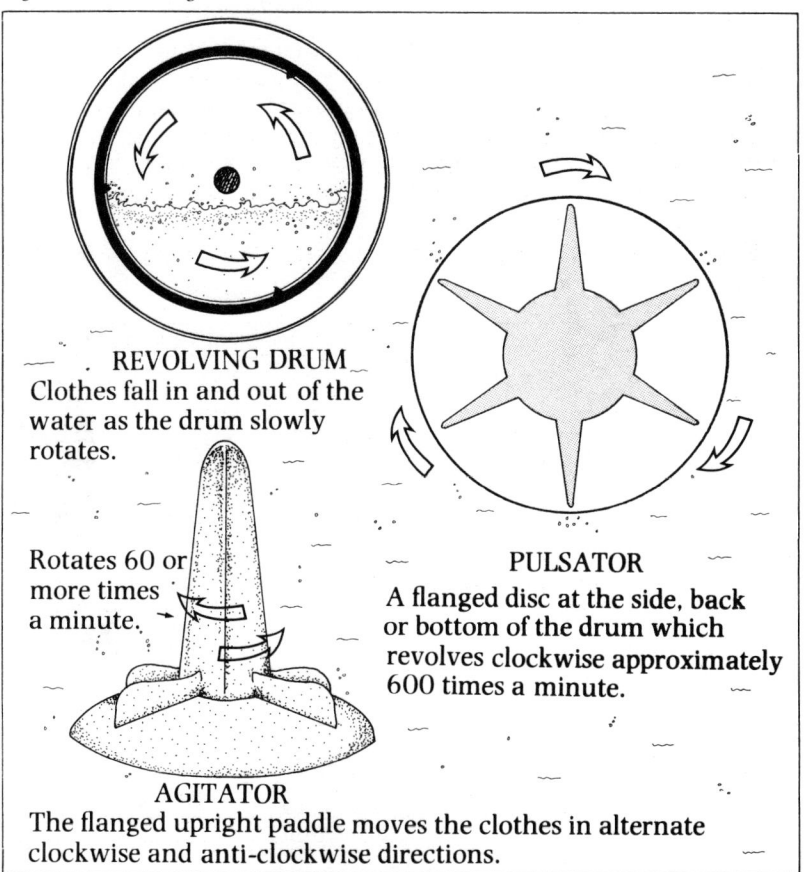

. REVOLVING DRUM
Clothes fall in and out of the
water as the drum slowly
rotates.

Rotates 60 or
more times
a minute.

PULSATOR
A flanged disc at the side, back
or bottom of the drum which
revolves clockwise approximately
600 times a minute.

AGITATOR
The flanged upright paddle moves the clothes in alternate
clockwise and anti-clockwise directions.

TABLE 5: METHODS OF DOING THE FAMILY WASH

| Method | Advantages | Disadvantages |
|---|---|---|
| 1 Hand washing | No initial outlay is involved. No space is taken up in the kitchen by mechanical equipment.<br>Special care can be taken of delicate articles, e.g. special finishes, loose colours, special trimmings or easily-shrunk fabrics. | Time-consuming if there are more than a few items to be laundered. Hard on the hands. Difficult to keep whites a good colour unless they can be boiled. Hot water limitations may present difficulties. |
| 2 Laundry (commercial) | No initial outlay in purchasing machines. Space is saved in the kitchen.<br>Clothes are returned washed, dried and ironed. No domestic electricity or gas is used. Bad weather does not affect ability to have washing done. | Clothes have to be parcelled up, entered into the laundry list and checked on return. Items may be mislaid—marking with a laundry pencil or woven name tapes is important. Clothes do not have a 'fresh air' feel about them as those have which are home laundered. Cost is quite high. |
| 3 Laundrette | No initial outlay for machines. Kitchen space is not used for equipment.<br>Clothes can be tumble-dried, ready for ironing. No domestic gas or electricity is used.<br>Weather does not affect the ability to wash except that the load has to be transported. Machines are very large so will take big items such as blankets.<br>Visits to the establishment may become social occasions. | Time is spent away from home which cannot be used for any other household purpose (unless you are fortunate enough to find one with staff paid to oversee the machines).<br>Programmes are limited and may not be suitable for all your fabrics, necessitating *some* hand washing. The tumble driers may be too hot for some man-made fibres. Clothes have to be ironed as normal. |
| 4 Wash boiler | Cheaper to buy than a washing machine. Because water actually boils it sterilizes as well (important for babies' nappies). Can be easily moved so could be kept in a garage or outhouse to save space in the kitchen. | Will only take small loads. Cannot be used for delicate items. A separate spin drier is necessary if drying ground/space is not available. |
| 5 Twin-tub machine (one for washing, one for rinsing and spin-drying)<br>Should be serviced regularly—preferably every year. The instructions in the accompanying manual should be carefully followed. | Cheaper than an automatic washing machine—both to buy and to run.<br>May be filled with cold or hot water—need not be plumbed in, but fed by a hose from a tap and pumped out by a hose into the sink (therefore must be light enough to be pushed close to the sink).<br>Convenient enough to make it worthwhile doing a small amount of washing frequently rather than one | Will not take very large loads or items. Rinsing is not so efficient as in automatic machines. Heating time may be lengthy—up to two hours from cold for a hot wash. 30–40 minutes from hot.<br>Constant supervision is required. Some physical activity is involved in lifting the load from the washing to the spinning tub. |

| | Advantages | Disadvantages |
|---|---|---|
| **6  Single tub machine** As 5. | usually more effective than those in automatic machines. Machine will fit under a work surface. Similar method of working to that of a twin-tub. A wringer may be attached to the machine or some models are available with a 'bridge' linking them to a matching spin drier. | There is no spin drier facility. |
| **7  Automatic front loading machine** (plumbed to cold to cold water system or to both hot/ cold water supply depending on your water pressures) As 5. | Several sizes of tub to choose from. Very sophisticated programmes allow a full range of fibres to be correctly washed and rinsed. No physical effort is required once the clothes are loaded into the drum. No supervision is required while the machine is working. Machines will usually fit under a work surface. | Expensive to buy; fairly expensive to run but becomes more economical as the load exceeds 1.8 kg. (see page 164). Plumbing-in adds to the initial expense. Floor may require strengthening as machines are very heavy. Washing cycles may be lengthy. Spinner is not so efficient as that in a twin-tub model. Loading the machine necessitates bending. The load cannot be added to once the programme has started. Requires low-foam washing powder because: a) lather is not essential; b) it can damage the mechanism. |
| **8  Automatic top loading machine** As 5. | It is possible to add items once the programme has started. As versatile as front-loading model. Any washing powder may be used. No bending is required for loading. Smaller models may be found than in front-loaders. | Expensive to buy. Any work surface over the machine must be hinged to allow access. Spinner is not so efficient as that in a twin-tub model. |
| **9  Tumble driers** (sometimes an integral part of an automatic machine; usually a separate item) As 5. | May be placed on top of other washing machines, often specially designed to do this. Clothes are dried by tumbling through warm air and may be removed when still damp enough for ironing or when completely dry. Choice of 2 or 3 heat settings for different fabrics—man-made fibres may be cooled after warm drying to prevent creases from forming. | Should be placed near a window or door so that moist air escaping through the vent can be dispersed. |
| **10  Spin drier** As 5. | Useful if you are without a washing machine as it saves wringing; a) spout type—small and light; drains into a bowl; b) pump type—larger, heavier, more expensive; pumps water into the sink. | Small items may be lost between the drum and outer casing—can be avoided by using the spinner mat if available, a folded tea-towel if not, placed over the top of the load. |

If you decide to buy a washing machine:

1  Look around at those on show in stores, compare prices and functions and decide which is going to serve your needs most satisfactorily.

2  Measure the space you have available and take a tape measure with you when you go to buy the machine.

3  Make sure that you have a convenient space close to an outside wall if you wish your machine to be plumbed in.

When using your machine:

1  Read the instructions carefully before you use it and follow the recommendations for water temperatures, loading and use of washing powder.

2  Read the care labels on your garments and treat them accordingly.

The Home Laundering Consultative Council (HLCC) established a labelling system in 1966 and has now combined with the continental care labelling system (introduced in 1974) to form the new International Textile Care Label Code (see opposite). These symbols appear on detergent packets and indicate

a)  the type of fabric to be treated;

b)  the temperature of washing water recommended for both machine and hand washing;

c)  the degree of machine agitation required (minimum, medium or maximum);

d)  the rinsing temperature recommended;

e)  the length of spin necessary;

f)  the iron setting required.

The care label actually affixed to the garment (see below) will usually show

a)  the fibre content of the garment;

b)  where it was made;

c)  specific laundering instructions, using symbols from either HLCC or international codes.

*A garment care label (Marks & Spencer plc)*

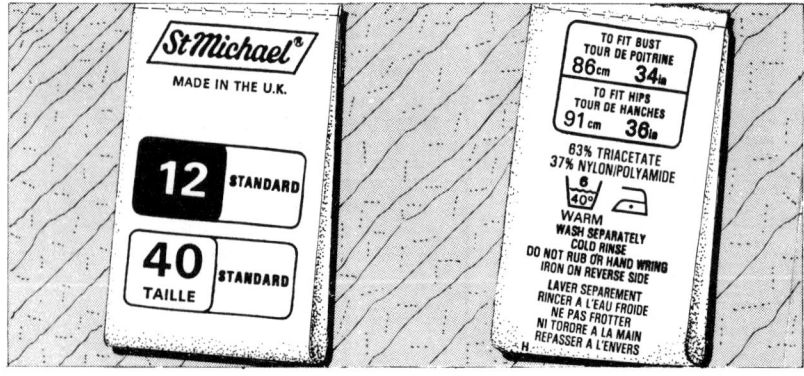

**TUB**
Machine Washing
Instructions

**TRIANGLE**
Bleaching Instructions.

**IRON**
Ironing instructions.

**CIRCLE**
Dry Cleaning Instructions

**SQUARE**
Drying Instructions

CI May be treated with chlorine bleach.

Do not use chlorine bleach.

Use hot iron (max:210°C)

Use warm iron (max:160°C)

Use cool iron (max:120°C)

Do not iron

| Symbol | Washing Temperature | | Rinse | Spinning/ Wringing | Fabric |
|---|---|---|---|---|---|
| | Machine | Hand | | | |
| 1/95 | very hot 95°C to boil | hand hot 50°C or boil | normal | normal | White cotton and linen articles without special finishes |
| 2/60 | hot 60°C | hand hot 50°C | normal | normal | Cotton, linen or rayon articles without special finishes where colours are fast at 60°C |
| 3/60 | hot 60°C | hand hot 50°C | cold | short spin or drip dry | White nylon; white polyester/cotton mixtures |
| 4/50 | hand hot 50°C | hand hot 50°C | cold | short spin or drip dry | Coloured nylon; polyester; cotton and rayon articles with special finishes; acrylic/cotton mixtures; coloured polyester/cotton mixtures |
| 5/40 | warm 40°C | warm 40°C | normal | normal | Cotton, linen or rayon articles where colours are fast at 40°C, but not at 60°C |
| 6/40 | warm 40°C | warm 40°C | cold | short spin | Acrylics; acetate and triacetate, including mixtures with wool; polyester/wool blends |
| 7/40 | warm 40°C | warm 40°C | normal | normal spin do not hand wring | Wool, including blankets and wool mixtures with cotton or rayon; silk |
| 8/30 | cool 30°C | cool 30°C | cold | short spin do not hand wring | Silk and printed acetate fabrics with colours not fast at 40°C |
| 9/95 | very hot 95°C to boil | hand hot 50°C or boil | cold | drip dry | Cotton articles with special finishes capable of being boiled but requiring drip drying |
| | DO NOT MACHINE WASH | | | | |
| | DO NOT WASH | | | | |

*The International Textile Care Label Code*

## Loads

You need to be able to judge the weight of the load you are putting in your machine since you may well damage it by overloading. The table below will act as an approximate guide.

| Item | Approx. Weight | Item | Approx. Weight |
|---|---|---|---|
| HOUSEHOLD ITEMS | | CLOTHING | |
| Tablecloth: linen | 575 g. ($1\frac{1}{4}$ lb.) | Apron | 150 g. (5 oz.) |
| Towels: bath | 650 g. ($1\frac{1}{2}$ lb.) | Baby's napkin | 175 g. (6 oz.) |
| hand | 225 g. (8 oz.) | Blouse: woman's | 150 g. (5 oz.) |
| tea | 75 g. (3 oz.) | Dress: child's | 75 g. (3 oz.) |
| | | woman's | 225 g. (8 oz.) |
| BED LINEN | | Jeans: boy's | 375 g. (13 oz.) |
| Bedspread: candlewick | | man's | 525 g. |
| (single) | 1300 g. (3 lb.) | | (1 lb. 3 oz.) |
| Bedspread: candlewick | | Pants: man's | 50 g. (2 oz.) |
| (double) | 2.5 kg. ($5\frac{1}{4}$ lb.) | woman's/boy's | 25 g. (1 oz.) |
| Blanket: cot | 425 g. (15 oz.) | Pyjamas: cotton | 450 g. (1 lb.) |
| single | 1300 g. (3 lb.) | Shirt: man's (cotton) | 250 g. (9 oz.) |
| double | 2.5 kg. ($5\frac{1}{4}$ lb.) | Sweater: boy's (Orlon) | 300 g. (11 oz.) |
| Pillowcase: cotton | 150 g. (5 oz.) | woman's | |
| Terylene/ | | (Orlon) | 425 g. (15 oz.) |
| cotton | 120 g. (4 oz.) | T-shirt: boy's | 120 g. (4 oz.) |
| nylon | 100 g. ($3\frac{1}{2}$ oz.) | Vest: boy's | 50 g. (2 oz.) |
| Sheet: cot | 300 g. (11 oz.) | man's | 75 g. (3 oz.) |
| cotton (single) | 650 g. ($1\frac{1}{2}$ lb.) | | |
| cotton (double) | 1150 g. | | |
| | ($2\frac{1}{2}$ lb.) | | |
| Terylene/cotton | | | |
| (single) | 600 g. | | |
| | (1 lb. 5 oz.) | | |
| Terylene/cotton | | | |
| (double) | 1000 g. | | |
| | ($2\frac{1}{4}$ lb.) | | |
| nylon (single) | 225 g. (8 oz.) | | |
| nylon (double) | 525 g. | | |
| | (1 lb. 3 oz.) | | |

## DETERGENTS

A look at the shelves of the laundry/soap powder section of your supermarket will give you an idea of the number of products available— how do you choose? It will help if you know a little about what they contain and what they do.

The dictionary definition of 'detergent' is 'that which cleans'. Any substance, therefore, which will help to remove soiling from either clothes or skin can be called a detergent (including water).

## WATER

You will probably have noticed, when visiting other parts of the country, that when you wash, the lather varies (either more plentiful or less easy to obtain) from what you get in your own home. Water which requires a considerable amount of soap to form a lather is called 'hard water', whilst that which only needs a small amount is known as 'soft water'. Hard water causes a scum to form when soap is used before it begins to lather and this, besides requiring extravagant use of soap, causes clothes to feel somewhat stiff, even after rinsing, and can cause scale to collect on the heating elements of your washing machine as it does in your kettle. Hard water can be softened by adding soda but you need to know the exact degree of hardness to be able to add the correct amount of soda: excess soda causes the water to become very alkaline and quite unsuitable for washing woollens and some coloured fabrics. A commercial water softener inserted into the system is preferable but this is an expensive procedure initially (see Chapter 11, page 224).

Synthetic detergents or blends of soap powder and synthetic detergent do not react in the same way as pure soap to hard water so, if you use these, a water softener is not so necessary as far as washing is concerned. However, with very hard water more detergent is required than with soft water.

## Soap

Soap is manufactured from the natural oils of animals and vegetables with added alkalis—if you add soda to the water with which you are soaking a greasy frying pan you will see a similar result (if you agitate it you will find a very small amount of lather forming). It is marketed in the form of bars (e.g. 'Fairy' for kitchen use), cakes (e.g. 'Lux' for toilet use, with added colouring and perfume), flakes (e.g. 'Lux' for hand washing woollies and delicate fabrics) or powders. As described above, it does form a scum with hard water which is very difficult to rinse out. As a powder (e.g. 'Persil', 'Fairy Snow') it can be used in washing machines and will remove some stains (see page 183 and Table 6).

## Synthetic Detergents (non-soap detergents)

These are made from the by-products of the petroleum industry, with the addition of complex chemicals and bleaches. They are produced as
a) powder which foams freely—'heavy duty' for hard-water areas (e.g. 'Omo', 'Surf', 'Tide') and 'light duty' for use with soft water (e.g. 'Dreft');
b) flakes for 'light duty' in hard-water areas (e.g. 'Dreft' flakes);
c) liquids for the same use as b; (e.g. 'Stergene', 'Lux', 'Fairy'.
These detergents can be blended with soaps for use in automatic washing machines which do not require copious lather (e.g. 'Persil Automatic' and most products including 'Automatic' in the name).

## Biological Powders

These are specially designed to remove the most common types of soiling (e.g. gravy, egg yolk, blood and other body stains) and they are effective because of the inclusion of enzymes which break down or 'digest' proteins and which work most efficiently at about 55° C. The most successful use of them, therefore, is in automatic machines which have a 'biological soak' or 'pre-wash' treatment which allows clothing to remain at the best temperatures for a specific time. They can then go on washing in the usual way without the enzymes' effect, which will be inactivated at about 60° C.

Most are suitable for heavy duty, high foaming (e.g. 'Ariel', 'Radiant', 'Biological Omo', plus most brands including 'Biological' in their names) or low foaming (e.g. 'Bold Automatic'). 'Biotex' is a useful overnight soaking agent for delicate fabrics (the cooler the water the longer the soaking time) in hand basins only. Manufacturers' instructions should be followed carefully. Some of these powders also contain *fluorescers* which help to brighten colours (e.g. 'Ariel', 'Bold').

The following items should not be soaked in biological products:
woollens—it may cause stretching;
coloured articles which are not known to be colour-fast (test a small section first);
any specially finished garment or article;
any item with metal buttons, fastenings or trimmings.

There is now on the market a liquid detergent for use in some washing machines that operates efficiently in cold water. This means that you do not have to heat the water and so you save electricity; it is also kinder to your clothes.

● Housewives expect their washing powders to lather so, although synthetic detergents (NSD) do not rely on the action of suds for their cleansing properties, manufacturers add lathering agents to satisfy the consumers' expectations.

## How a Detergent Works

Have you ever wondered how it is possible for some insects to 'walk' on water, or how it is that a drop of water can remain suspended beneath a tap without falling off? It is because the water is exerting a tension causing it to appear as if it is enveloped in an elastic 'skin'—this is called 'surface tension' (see Figure 9.2). Detergents break this tension and make the water 'wetter'. You can prove this to yourself by cutting two identical lengths of wool yarn and placing one on the top of a small dish of cold water and the other on the top of a similar amount of water containing detergent (see Figure 9.3). While the first piece will float, the second will become saturated with water and sink. When soiled articles are immersed in water containing detergent, the detergent can cause the separation of the material and the dirt, which becomes loosened and can float away. This is why it is so often useful to soak clothes before actually washing them.

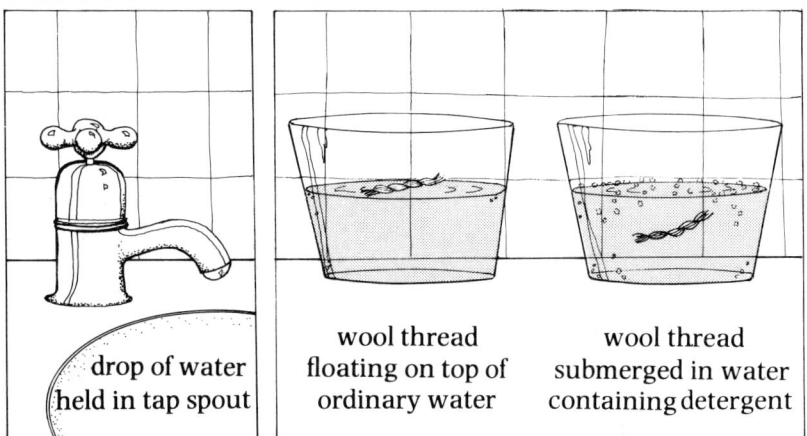

*Figure 9.2  Surface tension*    *Figure 9.3  Surface tension experiment*

| drop of water held in tap spout | wool thread floating on top of ordinary water | wool thread submerged in water containing detergent |

## Other Aids to Laundering

FABRIC WHITENERS
Although most detergents contain sufficient bleaching agent to keep clothes white, hard water, wear and careless sorting of washing can cause white articles to acquire a yellowish or greyish discoloration. Certain products can be used to restore whiteness during washing or rinsing. Each has its own specific use:
Dylon Super-White—for nylon and wool;
Dylon Nylon White—for nylon;
Dylon Curtain White—for net curtains;
Dylon CC Curtain White—for use with cold water.

FABRIC SOFTENERS/CONDITIONERS
These can be added to the final rinsing water and used for soaking for about 5 minutes. Their functions are:
a) to prevent fibres from becoming matted together and so preserve the softness of towels and woollens, for example;
b) to reduce static electricity which causes many man-made fabrics to cling to the wearer and to attract grime.

STARCH
Usually used only on cottons and linens, this has a stiffening effect, replacing the original crispness. Nowadays it is mainly used for table linen, man-made fibres having reduced the difficulties of laundering most clothing.
*Traditional hot-water starch*
    This is made by mixing starch powder with sufficient cold water to form a smooth, thin white paste and then pouring on boiling water, stirring continuously, until the mixture thickens and clears.

This liquid is then diluted according to the degree of stiffness required—the thicker the starch the stiffer the result. Items are then evenly soaked in the mixture and ironed with a hot iron while still damp—the starch grains, gelatinized by the hot water, actually cook in the fabric (in the same way as they cook on the outside of a cake mixture).

*Cold-water starch*
This will dissolve and then thicken in cold water, having been 'pre-cooked'. It is then used in the same way as hot-water starch.

*Spray-on starch*
Packed in an aerosol container, it can be localized in application. It is an expensive method of starching and will last for one wash only, but it is a very convenient way of stiffening small areas, for freshening collars, etc. between washes, or for using when only a few articles are to be treated.

BLEACHES
Hypochlorite bleaches (e.g. 'Parazone', 'Domestos') will whiten complete articles which have become discoloured or remove stains from specific areas. Certain precautions must be observed, however.
1  Do *not* use on wool, silk, rayon or strongly coloured cottons.
2  Consult the care label to see whether the fabric will withstand bleaching (see symbols on page 180).
3  If there is no such information available, test-bleach an inconspicuous portion in a weak solution first.
4  Never use neat bleach—dilute it according to directions on the container.
5  Rinse fabric thoroughly after use.
6  Several weak applications are as effective as, and safer than, one stronger one.
7  Warm water will accelerate the action of the bleach.
   Hydrogen peroxide (20 vols.) may be used on wool and other very delicate fabrics unsuitable for treatment with chlorine bleach. Again, follow the directions on the bottle; be prepared for the bleaching action to be a slow one. Rinse the article thoroughly afterwards.

## LAUNDERING PROCEDURE

A family of several people will accumulate a very mixed collection of dirty clothing during a week and this will be increased by the addition of bed linen, table linen and towels. All these items will require different types of laundering processes and care should be taken to ensure that each class of goods is dealt with separately. Before detailing these precautions, however, remember that the more soiled the articles are allowed to become the more difficult it will be to get them clean and the more wear will be imposed upon the fabric.

## Sorting

1 Separate the items according to their fibres:
woollens;
cottons—white;
cottons—coloured;
man-made fabrics—white;
man-made fabrics—coloured;
delicate items of unknown origin or uncertain dye.
2 Group together according to the treatment they require; use as a guide the more gentle (i.e. the higher programme number) of the appropriate programmes (see table on page 169) e.g.:
    white man-made fabrics and cotton/polyester mixtures—wash as 3;
    coloured man-made fibres and coloured cotton/polyester mixtures —wash as 4;
    wool/wool mixtures—wash as 7;
    white and coloured cottons—may be washed as 2.
3 Soak very soiled garments in cold water.
4 If in doubt about the fastness of colours dip an inconspicuous part of the garment into a bowl of warm suds, squeeze it and press it with a warm iron between two pieces of white blotting paper or old cloth.
5 Make sure that all pockets are empty.
6 Mend rips, tears or splits that may be aggravated during washing.
7 Tie belt ends and apron strings together to prevent the garment from bunching during washing.
8 Close zip fasteners and do up hooks-and-eyes so that they do not catch in other garments or the perforations in the drum.
9 Treat any stains so that they are not spread from garment to garment or become irrevocably set (see Table 6).

### Washing/Rinsing

1 Set the programme according to the processes required if a machine is to be used. Make up loads to the maximum, referring to the list on page 170.
2 Wash by hand if necessary, remembering to:
a) sort according to the care labels' indications, bearing in mind that water at 30° C is cool to the touch,
  ,,   ,, 40° C feels warm to the hand,
  ,,   ,, 50° C is as hot as the hand can bear;
b) wash woollens by kneading and squeezing the fabric in warm suds. Do not rub. Rinse in warm water. Pat into shape;
c) wash other garments by rubbing gently, more firmly on very soiled portions. Cotton collars and cuffs may be scrubbed, using hard soap and a nail brush if necessary;
d) rinse thoroughly in warm water until water remains clear.

## Drying

1 Drip-dry garments should be placed on coated or plastic hangers and hung up, outside if possible, with a peg over the hook to prevent it from blowing down.

2 Spin-dry remaining garments, then hang them outside on a clothes line or umbrella (rotary line) to blow in the air and make them feel and smell fresh. If you must dry them indoors, you should:

a) hang them on a plastic-coated or wooden clothes horse and place it in a warm, dry room;

b) use a heated drying cabinet; there are several types available, some free-standing, some wall-mounted. The clothes are hung over rails and heated by gas or electricity at a low temperature until dry. Some problems may arise with condensation;

c) hang them over retractable lines fixed from wall to wall above the bath.

3 If a tumble drier is available, there is no problem with complete drying but the clothes do not feel or smell as fresh as those dried in the fresh air (see pages 165, 167).

## Ironing

Many garments made from man-made fibres *need* no ironing but there are few which are not improved by finishing in this way. Exceptions are those which have fluffy, napped or embossed surfaces which would be ruined by flattening.

THE IRONING BOARD
This should be firm, adjustable to your height, covered with a lint-free cloth and have a heat-resistant mat for the iron to be rested on. See also page 81.

A SLEEVE BOARD
An optional extra, not essential but very useful for ironing sleeves, babies' garments and for pressing pleats.

THE IRON
It should be of a comfortable weight and shape, either dry or steam type. See page 80.

1 If a steam iron is used, fill it with distilled water before connecting it to the power socket.

2 Switch the iron on and let the thermostat settle to the temperature required while you erect the ironing board and sort the washing into groups requiring a hot, medium and cool iron. Work with the iron first set at the highest temperature required and allow it to cool further as you complete each group; *or* begin with the coolest setting required and turn up the heat as you go.

3 Pull flat articles into shape before ironing them.

4 Damp down dry cottons and linens by squirting them with water from a pressure spray or sprinkling from the finger-ends (not necessary if a steam iron is used).

METHODS
*Sheets*
Fold in half lengthwise, right sides together;
Iron from both outer sides;
Fold each side back;
Pull edges flush with each other;
Iron on both outer sides;
Fold in half widthways and then in half again, with the upper edge of the sheet on the outside.
*Tablecloths*
Iron as for sheets, lengthwise;
Do not iron in widthways creases; fold lightly.
*Serviettes*
Iron as a square;
Fold in 3 one way and iron in the creases; repeat the other way.
*Garments*
Turn inside out and iron seams, hems and double parts (do not complete the finish of the collar);
Iron frills, bows or other trimmings;
Iron sleeves (on right or wrong side, according to whether a matt surface or a sheen is required). Use the point of the iron to go into gathers. Place the sleeve on a sleeve board if available—otherwise place the head of the sleeve over the pointed end of the ironing board to remove creases without difficulty;
Holding the garment by the neck edge, iron the bodice, then the skirt;
Finish the collar;
Do up fastenings and place the garment on a coathanger to air *or*
Turn the garment on to its front, laid flat, and fold each side towards the middle of the back from the middle of each shoulder. Turn the sleeves downwards. Fold the bottom of the skirt to the waist and then again to the shoulders. Turn to the front and store flat.
(This method of folding can easily be adapted for shirts, jumpers, sweaters, blouses, pyjama jackets.)
*Handkerchiefs*
Pull into shape;
Iron on one side;
Fold in half from bottom to top;
Iron;
Repeat folding;
Iron;

Fold in half from side to side;
Iron;
Repeat;
Iron.

*Pleats*
Unless the garment is permanently pleated (i.e. heat set), pleats should be tacked in before washing;
Press lightly to define the edges;
Remove tackings;
Re-press to sharpen the edges. Remove press-marks by ironing underneath the pleat folds on the wrong side.

*Embroidery*
Iron on the wrong side, pressing firmly;
Use a thick pad to press into if the embroidery is 'crusty'.

## Airing

Articles which are ironed when dry do not really need airing, but to be on the safe side, hang them over the rails of a clothes horse, without disturbing any but the last few folds, and leave it in the sun or in a warm room; *or* store them in the airing cupboard.

## Storing

HOUSEHOLD ARTICLES
Blankets, sheets, pillowcases, towels and tea-towels, for example, can be stored in the airing cupboard. To avoid dust marks collecting on the folds, line the shelves with pieces of old sheeting, leaving sufficient surplus to wrap over the front of the shelves and contents and to cover the top.

UNDERWEAR
This should be stored in drawers personal to the wearer. Storage drawers should be lined (with paper *or* adhesive plastic *or* wallpaper remnants *or* commercial perfumed liners). Spare tablets of scented toilet soap or bath cubes placed among the contents keep them smelling pleasant. The use of nylon or plastic bags to store different items of the same kind keeps drawers well organized, separating 'everyday' from 'special' items.

JUMPERS/PULLOVERS
These should be folded as described earlier and slid into plastic bags before storing in drawers or on shelves.

BLOUSES/SHIRTS
These should be stored like jumpers *or* on hangers.

DRESSES
These should be hung on padded or coated hangers in a wardrobe or cupboard with the buckles of the belts (if any) hung over the hook.

TROUSERS
Hung on rails or laid flat in drawers, these should be folded along the leg creases.

SKIRTS
These should be hung by the waist loops on hangers *or* placed between the slats of special skirt hangers *or* folded lengthwise and stored flat in a drawer.

## Pressing

Tailored garments and others which cannot be washed may be freshened by
a) shaking in the air;
b) brushing well;
c) pressing with a hot iron on the wrong side, using a damp cloth between the garment and the iron if a steam iron is not used. Pressing differs from ironing in that the iron is lifted between each movement and not slid from side to side. Press until the cloth is dry;
d) setting pressed-in pleats by beating them with the back of a clothes brush;
e) hanging the garment to air.

## Care of the Iron

1  Always plug it into a heating, not a lighting, socket.
2  Use a 3-pinned (earthed) plug with a 13 amp fuse.
3  Make sure that your hands are dry before handling plugs.
4  Store the cool iron standing on its heel. Let it become quite cold before storing, unless a wall-mounted iron bracket is used.
5  Do not wind the flex round the iron while it is hot.
6  Clean starch marks off the sole plate with a little oil while it is still warm. Other stains should be removed with warm water and detergent or by rubbing very gently with fine wire wool (but not on non-stick sole plates).
7  Add water to a steam iron *before* plugging it in. Use distilled water (*or* boiled water *or* melted frost from the fridge) to prevent the element from collecting 'fur'.
8  Empty surplus water from a steam iron immediately after use.

## DRY CLEANING

Because of their nature some articles cannot be washed, e.g. some heavy curtains, men's suits, duvets, etc., but they will, nevertheless,

*The Association of British Launderers & Cleaners Ltd*

require cleaning from time to time. They should be taken to a Dry Cleaner's and the assistant informed, if possible, of the fibre content of the articles and the nature of any apparent stains. Look out for 'Special Offers' of reductions in the cost of cleaning specific items and take advantage of them—cleaning can be a costly item.

The Association of British Launderers and Cleaners (ABLC), together with the Office of Fair Trading, has produced a Code of Practice which lays down the standards of service its members should give you. Over 75% of the cleaners and launderers in England, Wales and Scotland belong to the ABLC and if you see their sign displayed you will be protected by their Code, should anything go amiss with your property. Leaflets are available from the Citizens' Advice Bureau, the Consumer Advice Centre and Trading Standards or Consumer Protection Departments, setting out their liability. Cleaners also work to the International Textile Care Label Code (see page 169).

Sometimes garments look as if they are washable but they, in fact, carry a 'Dry-Clean Only' label (see Figure 9.4). This may be because:
1 Some fabrics, e.g. jersey, tend to stretch when wet.
2 Silks and cottons used for elaborate embroidery are not always colour-fast.

*Figure 9.4 Dry cleaning symbols*

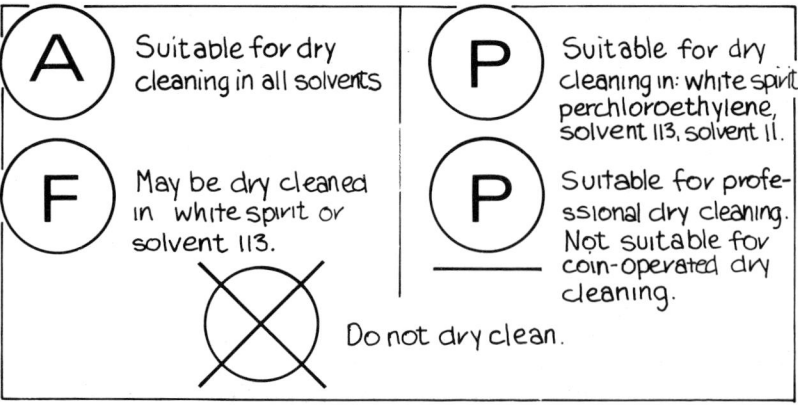

3 Interlining fabrics are not always washable.
It is, therefore, wise to follow manufacturers' instructions and have the garment cleaned, but if, after inspecting it very carefully, you can see no reason for not washing it, do so very gently, by hand in warm water. Handle it very carefully while wet—but remember that the risk is yours!
● When buying a garment such as that described, consider whether the amount of use you are going to make of it justifies the additional expense of frequent cleaning.

### Dry Cleaning in a Laundrette (coin-operated machine)

1 Find out which day the cleaning fluid is changed and try to use the machine as soon afterwards as possible, as it will become very dirty by the end of its use.
2 Weigh your garments/articles before you take them to the laundrette, having first discovered how much you can clean at one time.
3 Remember that curtains and blankets can be effectively and cheaply cleaned by this method; heavily soiled articles will not be satisfactorily cleaned.
4 Do not use this method of cleaning for children's soft toys—toxic fumes as well as the smell may linger.

PREPARING GARMENTS FOR DRY CLEANING
1 Empty pockets and remove fluff from inside.
2 Remove any trimmings likely to be damaged, including decorative buckles and buttons.
3 See that all remaining fasteners are securely attached.
4 Attach belts firmly if they need cleaning.
5 Let down the hems of skirts and sleeves which are going to need lengthening anyway—the pressed-in crease will be difficult to erase after cleaning.
6 Attach a label stating the fibre content of the article and the cause of any obvious stains.

AFTER DRY CLEANING
Before wearing:
1 Remove all cleaner's labels.
2 Air thoroughly out-of-doors to disperse the cleaning fluid smell.
3 Replace buttons, etc.
4 Re-press if necessary.
5 Store as previously described.

### STAIN REMOVAL

Washing will remove the natural soiling that comes from daily wear but when fabrics are stained with a substance that has bonded to the fibres, the treatment has to be different. Although different stains may ultimately require different treatments, always start with the easiest method of removal.

Providing that the article is washable, soak it as soon as possible after the staining happens, in cold or lukewarm water (any body stains are most easily dispersed in water at body temperature—37°C, 98.4°F). This will prevent the stain from 'setting' and may disperse it altogether. If it does not do so, more drastic treatment may be necessary—see Table 6 on page 184. Before carrying out any further methods, though, read the care labels carefully, to avoid accidental damage to the fabric.

If the fabric is not washable or the label indicates risk, take the garment to the professional Dry Cleaner's and make sure that you state the nature of the stain.

Solvents used to remove oil or grease stains by dissolving them (e.g. carbon tetrachloride, methylated spirits, acetone), whether used at home or in the dry cleaning establishment, are highly inflammable, so take care to keep them away from naked flames. *Never* use a liquid solvent and then iron over the fabric concerned; the fumes released by the heat evaporating the fluid may be toxic.

If you cannot or do not want to wash the cleaned article before using it, make sure that you give it a good 'blow' in fresh air.

## General Guide to Stain Removers

How to use
*Absorbents*
> Spread the powder over the affected part and work in with the handle of a spoon. Leave for an hour. Shake or vacuum surplus off. (See nos. 18 and 26 in Table 6 beginning on page 184.)

*Dry cleaning fluids*
> Test on an inconspicuous portion first. Leave for 15 minutes. If safe, place an absorbent pad underneath the stain and apply cleaner with another small, clean pad, working from the outside inwards with a circular motion. Change the pad frequently. Wash or dry clean the article as normal. (See nos. 1b, 3, 6, 7, 8, 10, 11, 16, 17, 18, 19, 20, 25, 26, 27b,c, 33 in Table 6.)

*Wet removers*
> a) Washables—Rinse the item immediately in cold or warm water, then soak in suggested cleaner (unless wool, silk or loose colours), *or* stretch the fabric over a basin, sprinkle borax or detergent over the stain and pour boiling water through it and rinse, *or* (for persistent stains) rub cleaner into the stain, rinse and wash as normal.
>
> b) Non-washables—Sponge the stain with cold water or pour cold water through the fabric stretched over a basin, *or* work in cleaning fluid or detergent lather with a clean pad, sponge with cold water and blot dry.

● *Note that these should be very carefully labelled before storage.*

| Stain Remover | Use | Dangers |
|---|---|---|
| Absorbents (for grease deposits): talcum powder, starch powder, French chalk | | |
| Acetone/amyl acetate (for cellulose deposits) (Do not use on acetate/viscose fabrics.) | | Inflammable. |
| Ammonia (for scorch marks, etc.) (May affect colours.) | Use 15 ml.: 600 ml. warm water. | Poisonous fumes. |
| Borax (for fruit and milk stains) (May affect colours.) | As above. | |
| Detergents (heavy duty—for gentle bleaching; enzyme for protein stains) (May affect colours.) | Use only the lather on non-washables. | |
| Dry cleaning fluids (for grease stains) (Commercial) | Use as directed. Do not smoke while using. | Inflammable; toxic fumes. |
| Eucalyptus (for heavy oil and tar stains) | Use neat. | Unpleasant smell lingers. |
| Glycerine (for softening stains) | Apply neat and rinse in warm water. | |
| Lemon juice (for alkali stains) | Acts as a mild bleach. | |
| Lighter fuel (for dissolving grease) | Use neat. Rinse well. | Inflammable. |
| Methylated spirits (for grass/ink stains) | Use neat. Rinse well if possible. | Inflammable. |
| Paint remover (for soaking paint brushes and removing spots) | Use neat. Rinse well if possible. | Inflammable. |
| Peroxide (for use as a mild bleach on white and delicate coloured fabrics) | Use 1 part 20 vol. peroxide: 4 parts cold water+few drops of ammonia. | |
| Turpentine/white spirit (for paint spots) | Use neat. Rinse if possible. | Inflammable. |
| Vinegar (counteracts discoloration from alkalis) | Use 15 ml.: 600 ml. warm water. | |

c) Carpets/upholstery—Check that fibres may be treated with shampoo. If so, dissolve liquid carpet or upholstery shampoo in lukewarm water to form a foam. Sponge the stain with the foam, blotting frequently then rinse in a similar way, using cold water. (See nos. 4, 5, 8, 9, 10, 12, 15, 17, 25, 28, 30, 32 in Table 6.)

Follow directions on packets or bottles of proprietary cleaners very carefully. Several gentle applications at intervals may be more effective and less damaging to the fabric than one drastic cleaning.

TABLE 6: METHODS OF REMOVING STAINS

| Stain | Method of Removal | Special Points |
|---|---|---|
| 1 Adhesives<br>a) contact/clear | Use acetone/amyl acetate or nail varnish remover. | Will dissolve some cellulose fibres (e.g. Tricel); inflammable. |
| b) latex | Remove solid with a spatula; use dry cleaning fluid. | Inflammable. |
| c) resin | Use acetone/amyl acetate or lighter fuel while still soft. | Cannot be removed once it has dried. |
| 2 Animal droppings | Remove deposit with spatula and then an absorbent. Treat stain with enzyme detergent/borax solution/carpet cleaner. | |
| 3 Ballpoint pen (biro) | Use methylated spirits on a clean pad. Rinse in warm water or wash as usual. | Inflammable. Most writing inks can be removed by soaking in cold water immediately. |
| 4 Beer | Use detergent or carpet shampoo. For dried-in stains add white vinegar (1 egg cup: 600 ml. water). | |
| 5 Blood | Soak in cool salt water (15 ml.: 600 ml. water) while fresh or soak in lukewarm water with enzyme washing powder if dried in. | |
| 6 Candle wax | Scrape off solid wax with the back of a knife. Place a slightly damp tissue or blotting paper over and under the stain and press with a warm iron. Finish with dry cleaning fluid if necessary. | Liquid wax spilt on to upholstery may be solidified with an ice cube and scraped off immediately. |
| 7 Chewing gum | Scrape off as much as possible. Solidify the remainder with an ice cube; scrape; finish with dry cleaning fluid. | Take the article to a professional cleaner for advice if it may be damaged by this method. |
| 8 Chocolate/cocoa | Use an enzyme detergent or borax solution. Use dry cleaner on persistent stains. | |
| 9 Coffee | Loosen dried-in stains with glycerine. Use borax or peroxide on fresh stains not removed with cold water. | |
| 10 Cream | On washables, use an enzyme detergent or borax. | Dry cleaning fluid is inflammable. |

| Stain | Method of removal | Special Points |
|---|---|---|
| 11 Creosote/tar | Scrape off as much as possible *or* loosen old stains with glycerine, rinse with lukewarm water then use: a) eucalyptus oil; b) white spirit; c) dry cleaning fluid. | White spirit and dry cleaning fluid are inflammable. |
| 12 Deodorant | Use a white vinegar solution. If persistent, use methylated spirits. | Methylated spirits is inflammable. |
| 13 Egg | See blood. | |
| 14 Faeces | See animal droppings. | |
| 15 Fruit juice | Pour salt on to the fresh stain to prevent spread. Rinse with boiling water. Use peroxide or borax if the stain persists. Use carpet shampoo if necessary. | |
| 16 Grass | Use methylated spirits, eucalyptus oil or glycerine. | Methylated spirits is inflammable. |
| 17 Gravy | If it is a colouring stain only, use enzyme detergent. If greasy, use dry cleaning fluid. | Dry cleaning fluid is inflammable. |
| 18 Grease | Remove as much as possible with an absorbent, then use dry cleaning fluid. On wallpaper, dust with talcum powder or try holding blotting paper over the stain and pressing quickly with a warm iron. | Dry cleaning fluid is inflammable. |
| 19 Hair lacquer ⎫ 20 Nail varnish ⎬ | Try warm water first. Otherwise, use methylated spirits, acetone, amyl acetate or commercial nail varnish remover. | These are inflammable and may dissolve some cellulose fibres (e.g. Tricel). |
| 21 Heat/water marks | On polished wood: sprinkle brass polish on to a clean cloth and rub wood in the direction of the grain. Re-polish as usual. | |
| 22 Ice-cream | See cream. | |
| 23 Iron mould | Use lemon juice; pour boiling water through. | |
| 24 Mildew | Expose the article to the sun and air to destroy the | Almost impossible to remove if not treated quickly. |

| Stain | Method of Removal | Special Points |
|---|---|---|
| | fungus. On books: use an absorbent. On white washables: use peroxide (chlorine bleach may be used on white cottons). On other washables: rub with hard yellow soap, leave to dry off before washing. On non-washables: use fungicide ('Mystox'). | mildew is caused by a fungus which flourishes in a damp, warm atmosphere and will grow on many different surfaces (e.g. on damp washing left in a warm room). Because man-made fibres do not retain moisture they are less likely to be affected than natural fibres. |
| 25 Milk | Fresh stains: rinse in lukewarm water. Dried-on stains: use borax solution or carpet shampoo. | |
| 26 Oil | Soak up as much as possible with an absorbent: use dry cleaning fluid. Bicycle/motor oil: use eucalyptus oil then dry cleaning fluid. | Dry cleaning fluid is inflammable. |
| 27 Paint a) cellulose | Use acetone/amyl acetate. | Inflammable. |
| b) emulsion | Scrape off while wet and rinse with cold water. If dried on, use methylated spirits. | Methylated spirits is inflammable. Dried on paint is difficult to remove. |
| c) gloss | Sponge with paint remover, turpentine or white spirit. | Inflammable. |
| 28 Perspiration | Everyday stains should wash away. If dried, use enzyme detergent or ammonia or white vinegar solution. | Ammonia is poisonous. If colour runs seek professional advice. |
| 29 Rust | See iron mould. | |
| 30 Scorch marks | Use borax, peroxide or ammonia solution. | Proprietary cleaner 'Moval' may be used for either. |
| 31 Tea | See coffee. | |
| 32 Tomato juice | See fruit juice. | |
| 33 Transfer outlines | Use methylated spirits. | Inflammable. |
| 34 Urine | Use enzyme detergent or carpet shampoo plus white vinegar (1 egg cup : 600 ml. water). | |
| 35 Vomit | See animal droppings. | |

——————————————— **FURTHER  STUDY** ———————————————

## Things to Do

1   Collect pieces of as many different fabrics as you can, both coloured
    and white (e.g. wools—woven and knitted; cottons and cotton
    mixtures; rayons; nylons; polyesters; silks; linens, etc.). Place each set
    in an envelope, labelled with the name of the fabric—cut ten
    squares for each, approximately 6 cm. × 6 cm. Prepare squared charts
    on which to mount your specimens (one chart for each fabric),
    making each square approximately 2 cm. larger each way than the
    squares of fabric. Mount one square of each fabric on the left of each
    chart under the heading 'Original Fabric'. Treat one piece of each
    type as follows and mount the resulting square in the chart, labelled
    according to the treatment:
    a)   wash with detergent by hand, do not rinse;
    b)   wash with detergent in a washing machine;
    c)   wash with soap flakes by hand, do not rinse;
    d)   repeat a and give a hot rinse;
    e)   repeat a and give a cold rinse;
    f)   repeat c and give a hot rinse;
    g)   repeat c and give a cold rinse;
    h)   soak in chlorine bleach solution;
    i)   press with a hot iron.
    Draw up a set of conclusions as to the correct treatment for each
    fabric.
2   Draw out single fibres from the trimmings of fabrics used above and
    make microscope slides of each. Draw their appearance.
3   Visit a commercial laundry and observe the methods used.
4   Visit a supermarket and find as many types of washing powders as
    you can. Make notes while you are there and construct a table on
    your return to show:
    a)   the proprietary names;
    b)   the price of small size, regular size and giant size packets;
    c)   the volume contained in each of these sizes;
    d)   the use recommended for each product;
    e)   the limitations of each.
5   Repeat exercise 4 with as many types of fabric conditioner as
    you can.
6   Visit your local laundrette/dry cleaning centre and discover:
    a)   the cost of using a washing machine for a load;
    b)   the cost of using a tumble drier for a load;
    c)   the cost of using a dry cleaning machine for a load;
    d)   the weight allowed of articles to be washed per load;
    e)   the weight allowed of articles to be cleaned per load;

    **f)**    the time each process takes to wash one load of mixed articles *or* clean one load of goods.

**7**  Discover as many examples as you can of items of laundry equipment which are no longer in use. Describe the articles and say what each one was used for. Illustrate your answer with sketches or pictures.

**8**  Collect leaflets relating to as many different washing machines as you can find. Discuss their merits and decide which is the 'Best Buy'.

## Questions to Answer

**1**  Write out and complete each of the following statements with the correct term chosen from the list in the right-hand column.

| | |
|---|---|
| **a)**  Flat-dwellers and tenants of bed-sitting rooms find a _____ very valuable in enabling them to do their own washing. | biological |
| **b)**  Apart from a machine in which clothes can be washed, a _____ is available in which they can be completely dried by warm air. | carbon tetrachloride |
| **c)**  If you have a garden or similar drying space a _____ will remove sufficient water from your washing to allow it to be dried in the fresh air. | solvent |
| **d)**  Any substance which removes dirt from fabrics and other surfaces is known as a _____. | laundrette |
| **e)**  'Dry Cleaning' cleanses fabrics without making them wet, generally by removing grease with a _____ and thus releasing the dust it holds. | spin drier |
| **f)**  Washing powders contain substances known as _____ which brighten the colours of patterns, giving the fabric a 'new look'. | enzymes |
| **g)**  Substances which remove colour from fibres of any kind are known as _____ ; two gases are responsible for this in laundering processes, namely chlorine and oxygen. | tumble drier |
| **h)**  The most commonly used dry cleaning fluids which are used in the home contain a solvent called _____. | detergent |
| **i)**  Food stains are easily removed by certain washing powders which contain _____ to digest the particles and make them soluble. | fluorescers |
| **j)**  The detergents which are able to break down and disperse food and body stains (i.e. those containing proteins) are described as _____. | bleaches |

2 Compare the procedures carried out in 1900 with those used today when a family wash is in progress. How do you account for these changes?

3 What special precautions would you take when laundering the following items:
   a) a cotton/polyester pillowcase stained from a nose-bleed;
   b) a rayon blouse with an embroidered frill;
   c) a linen/polyester dress with a pleated skirt;
   d) a woollen skirt with a coffee stain on the front?

4 If you were to be given one large piece of laundry equipment, which would you choose? Give your reasons for making this decision.

5 What do you understand by the term 'dry cleaning'? Why is it necessary? Describe exactly how you would prepare the following items for cleaning and what you would do with them after they have been cleaned:
   a) a child's large teddy bear with one loose eye;
   b) a georgette evening blouse with gilt buttons and belt;
   c) a pair of cotton-lined curtains with a grease splash on one of them;
   d) a man's suit comprising trousers, jacket and waistcoat;
   e) a linen jacket of your own with a 'Dry Clean Only' label.

G

A home should not only be a place of comfort but a place of safety as well. Unfortunately, this is very often not so, and a large proportion of the accidents which occur every day take place within the so-called 'safety' of the home. However, safety must not be regarded simply in the negative sense of injury-free, but in the wider positive view of overall security. The range of danger areas is unlimited and can be extremely worrying, but if a commonsense attitude of mind is developed, all precautions become matter-of-course. While being well aware of risks and dangers, habits become safeguards which are unconsciously copied by all the members of the family.

Children can be taught how to use potentially dangerous items such as knives, scissors, kitchen and workshop equipment just as they are taught how to use chemicals in school, *providing that* they also learn respect for them and what can happen if they are abused. The first path to this comprehensive realization of and deference to security is learning to be tidy, to clear up spillages and to put away tools and toys immediately they are finished with.

## GOVERNMENT LEGISLATION

Outside our own homes we, the general public, are protected by many laws, more than a dozen of which are directed at the shopper alone. We have already described the Association of British Launderers and Cleaners (page 180) and there are other similar organizations applicable to different areas of our buying which are co-operating with the Office of Fair Trading in producing 'Codes of Practice' which give us protection over and above our legal rights.

### MAIL ORDER PUBLISHERS' ASSOCIATION (MOPA)

Members of this association display the sign shown opposite and their code covers the way in which goods are advertised and conditions regarding their dispatch. They publish books, magazines and records which are sold by mail order.

### SHOES

The Code of Practice for Footwear aims to improve the quality of footwear offered to the public. In addition, shops displaying the sign opposite train their staff to advise and assist customers when they are buying shoes.

*Reproduced by permission of the Footwear Distributors Federation, MOPA and the BSI*

BSI SAFETY MARK

This mark is an independent assurance from the British Standards Institution that an item has been manufactured to British Standards. The Gas Board strongly recommends that you buy only equipment which carries this label.

FURNITURE AND FIRE

Many materials used in upholstery are inflammable and every year fires started by furniture catching light injure and kill many people (see page 13). New regulations to reduce these risks have recently come into force and all upholstered furniture must now carry the triangular warning labels (see page 13) if tests show that it could become ignited by matches.

Permanent labels must also be attached, in such a way that makes it difficult to remove them and in a position where they can be seen if the furniture is tilted at right angles to its normal placing (e.g. on the underneath of the seat of a chair). These labels must be rectangular in shape, their dimensions (minimum) 75 mm. × 50 mm. and the wording and design specifically detailed.

New codes are constantly being drawn up and details of these can be obtained, free of charge, from local authority Trading Standards Departments, Citizens' Advice Bureaux and Consumer Advice Centres (see also page 146).

## SAFEGUARDS

The safety of the fabric and contents of the home is not only threatened by fire, however, and there are a number of general safeguards which you can make a habit of observing.

ALWAYS:

1  Lock doors and close windows when leaving premises unoccupied. Have safety locks installed if you can afford to.

2  Stop papers and milk if you are going away.

3  Destroy 'no milk for X days'-type notes which may have been left lying about by the milkman.

4  Remember that double glazing acts as a certain deterrent to intruders, reducing the ease and increasing the noise and time of entering.

5 Remove baskets below letterboxes if you are going away so that the post is not left wedged in view of passers-by.

NEVER:

1 Leave keys under mats or on strings through the letterbox.

2 Open windows on to pathways unless they are above head height, since burglars may easily climb in.

3 Open your garage doors from the inside without making sure that no one is likely to be passing on the outside.

For safety in using gas see page 214. For safety in using electricity see page 219.

## ACCIDENTS

### Preventing Accidents

Many accidents—and there are more in the home than there are on the roads—are caused by carelessness, and you have to be aware of potential dangers before you can form the good practical habits which prevent them. Statistics show that domestic accidents fall into five main categories—cuts, falls, burns and scalds, poisoning and suffocation. While these *can* happen to anyone, the elderly and the very young are particularly vulnerable. Table 7 following shows how each of the common types of accidents may happen and how they can be prevented.

### In Case of Fire

PRECAUTIONS

1 Keep a fire extinguisher handy, in the kitchen or the hall, and be sure that you know how to use it.

2 Keep a fire-smothering cloth, woven from non-inflammable glass fibre, near the cooker for use in an emergency.

3 Make sure that you know where your nearest telephone is and that you could locate the 9 digit (emergency services are summoned by a 999 call) in the dark.

4 Do not store large quantities of inflammable material in the space under your roof. This *can* become tinder dry and present a potential fire hazard.

5 Avoid the storage of large drums of inflammable liquids (e.g. paraffin, petrol) in the garage.

DEALING WITH SMALL FIRES

1 Drench with water at once (including paraffin heaters) except those caused by

a) burning fat, cooking oil;

b) electricity.

2 Smother burning deep-fat pans with a folded cloth (preferably damp), a plate or even the soil from a nearby plant pot, or sand.

TABLE 7: PREVENTING ACCIDENTS

| Type Of Accident | How It Can Happen | How To Prevent It |
|---|---|---|
| **MAIN CATEGORIES**<br>**1 Cuts** | Careless use of kitchen or garden tools. | *Do:* carry sharp tools point downwards; keep sharp knives in drawers away from children; wrap all breakages, particularly of glass, in several sheets of newspaper before placing in the dustbin; place used razor blades in a safe container before throwing away.<br>*Do not:* store sharp utensils out of your easy reach—you must be able to *see* how you are picking them up; leave sharp knives in washing-up water where they cannot be seen; allow young children to run about with glasses or cups in their hands. |
| | Insertion of easily broken glass in low windows and internal doors. | Use specially toughened glass in low level windows and internal doors. Place tubs of plants or small pieces of furniture along the bottom of floor length windows. |
| | Trailing flexes or scattered toys causing falls against doors. Putting a hand through a shut window. | Avoid trailing flexes; put toys away when finished with. Never try to open a sticking window by pressing against the glass. |
| | Cutting hands on sharp edges of opened tins. | Do not try to prise off lids with a knife or with the fingers; cut the lid right out and place it in the empty tin. |
| | Glass breaking in the hand while drying it. | Hold the glass at the top of stem so that bowl is not 'twisted' off. Dry *very* gently. |
| **2 Falls**<br>**a) General** | Slipping on wet or highly polished surfaces. | Avoid vinyl floor coverings which become slippery when wet. Wipe up spillages immediately, particularly of grease. Use non-slip floor polishes; do not polish under mats. |
| | Catching foot in worn floor coverings. | Keep floor coverings in good repair and cover worn or torn places with mats. |
| | Tripping on stairs.<br>Overbalancing off chairs or stools used for reaching up to high shelves/cupboards. | Fix a handrail if there are no banisters.<br>*Always* stand on a properly balanced stepstool or, preferably, a stepladder. |
| **b) Elderly people** | Poor sight, impaired mobility, dizziness and general low state of health causing lack of perception of steps and | Light any stairs or steps brightly. Line edges of awkward or dimly lit steps with a white edging or band of white |

| Type Of Accident | How It Can Happen | How To Prevent It |
|---|---|---|
| | stairs, loss of balance and slow reactions. | paint. Keep floors clear. Ban trailing flexes. Recess door mats into the floor to prevent tripping. |
| | Use of sloppy slippers or dressing gowns with trailing hems or belts. | Keep footwear and clothing in good repair and belts tied. |
| | Slipping in the bath. | Use a non-slip bath mat in the bath. |
| c) Children | Falling out of prams, cots, high chairs. Falling down stairs. | Use a safety harness every time the equipment is used. Fix a safety gate at the top or bottom of the stairs (or both) as appropriate and *keep it closed.* |
| | Falling out of windows. | Keep windows firmly latched. Fix bars across windows. Place books or plants on sills to discourage climbing. |
| | Falling through banisters (horizontal or vertical) which are so widely spaced that a small child can pass between them. | Fix decorative panels (not glass) or additional balusters to reduce spaces. |
| | Being carried by another person who falls. | Never carry children while wearing sloppy shoes or rickety heels. Keep floors clear. Do not bend forward while carrying a child. |
| 3.1  Burns | Falling against unprotected fires. Being hit with falling fireworks or firework carried in pocket being ignited. | Fix a BSI-approved guard. Do not allow young children to carry fireworks at all. Arrange to watch from a safe distance, preferably from indoors. *Always* have an adult at hand to supervise. *Never* let anyone throw a firework. Control bonfires and do *not* light with petrol or paraffin. |
| | Children playing with matches. | Keep matches and lighters well out of reach. Never allow a child to light a fire. |
| | Inflammable clothing catching fire, e.g. a nightdress worn by a child standing in front of a fire or reaching out to a mantelpiece. | Use a fireguard. Make or buy children's garments of non-inflammable fabrics. |
| | Using a thin cloth to remove tins from the oven. | Use properly padded oven gloves or a thick cloth. See also page 192 for a guide to the safe use of cookers. |
| | Fires caused by: a) careless use of cigarettes and matches | Check furniture and empty ashtrays before going to bed. Never throw lighted matches and cigarette ends into waste-paper baskets. Use deep or covered ashtrays. Never smoke in bed. |
| | b) ignition of inflammable liquids such as paraffin, petrol, dry cleaning fluid, paint | Store all such liquids in an outhouse or garage in tightly sealed, *labelled* cans. Do not smoke where any of these is stored. |
| | c) chimney fires | Have chimneys swept at least once a year. |

| Type of Accident | How It Can Happen | How To Prevent It |
|---|---|---|
| | d) chip-pan fire: fat overflowing on to lit jets | Never leave chip pans unattended. Do not fill more than two-thirds full. (*Do not use a fire extinguisher unless you know that it is of a type suitable for use on oil.*) |
| | e) electrical faults such as: frayed flexes | Repair all frayed flexes and do not run them under carpets. |
| | fuses of the wrong size | Check the size of fuse recommended for all appliances (see page 66). |
| | faulty wiring | Investigate any consistent crackles registering on sound equipment. Check hot plugs and switches. Unplug as well as switch off TV set and other large appliances when not in use. If in doubt, seek professional advice. |
| | f) curtains and other hangings being blown across flames or airing falling on to the fire | Do not place portable fires under curtains. Do not leave airing hanging above heat source when you go out. See page 192 for general procedure in case of fire. |
| 3.2 Scalds | Spillage of hot liquids due to tipping of saucepans, kettles, teapots or handles coming off cups. | Keep the very young and the very old out of the kitchen as much as possible. Turn all saucepan handles and kettle spouts inwards. Use the back burners of the stove whenever possible. Fix a cooker guard. Do not reach across the spout of a boiling kettle. Do not use cups with cracked handles. Keep kettle flexes out of the reach of children. Avoid overhanging tablecloths which can be pulled by a toddler, bringing down full teapots, etc. |
| | Burst hot-water bottles. | Reject hot-water bottles which have sticky or thin patches. Use a thick protective cover round them. Never leave one in a cot with a baby. |
| | Bathwater too hot. | Run cold water into the bath first and always test water to be used by a child or an elderly person before they enter it. |
| | Using a wet cloth to take hot tins from the oven. | Use thick *dry* cloths *or* oven gloves, never tea-towels. |
| 4 Poisoning a) From inhaled fumes | Gas leaks. | Keep gas appliances in good repair. Check for blockage of flues and vents. A free gas safety check on your appliances is available if a) you are 65 years old or over and live alone; b) you are a registered handicapped person of any age and you live alone. IF YOU SMELL GAS IN THE HOME: |

| Type Of Accident | How It Can Happen | How To Prevent It |
|---|---|---|
| | | 1 Put out all cigarettes and naked flames. |
| | | 2 Check that pilot jets are lit and all other taps switched off. Re-light unlit pilot jets. |
| | | 3 Open doors and windows. If smell persists: turn off main supply and call emergency service. |
| | | IF YOU SMELL GAS IN THE STREET: |
| | | Notify emergency gas service. |
| | Access to cleaning fluids. | Store all noxious cleaning fluids well out of children's reach. |
| | Car exhaust fumes overcoming enthusiastic mechanic. | Do not leave the engine running in the garage. Carry out repairs in the open air. |
| | Paraffin stoves burning inefficiently, releasing fumes. | Keep wicks in good repair. Make sure that portable fires are standing level. |
| b) From swallowing poisonous liquids and solids | Children chewing painted wood. | Use non-toxic paints on all nursery furniture and check that toys you buy are guaranteed as harmless. |
| | Children drinking poisonous liquids (e.g. bleach, paraffin, disinfectant). | *Never* pour poisonous liquids into lemonade or milk bottles for storage. *Label* every bottle if liquids are transferred from them well out of reach. Keep pesticides and weed killers, *labelled*, outside the home. |
| | Eating drug pills by mistake. | Always keep pills and tablets |
| | | a) in their original, labelled containers with special lids if children are around; |
| | | b) locked up or out of easy reach of children. |
| | | Flush unrecognized or surplus tablets down the toilet *or* return them to the chemist. Do *not* place them in the dustbin. |
| | Drinking medicine or eating tablets by mistake at night. | Never take drugs in the dark when you cannot read the label. Remember that poisonous liquids (e.g. iodine) are marketed in brown/blue *ridged* bottles. |
| | Children eating poisonous berries. | Discourage children from using attractive berries (e.g. deadly nightshade, mistletoe, holly, privet) and seeds (e.g. laburnum, lupin) as play 'food'. |
| 5 Suffocation | Babies and children are most vulnerable. Accidental suffocation may be caused by: | |
| | a) overlaying | Do not share a bed with a baby or small child. Do not allow cats or dogs to sleep in a baby's pram or cot. Use a safety net if necessary. |

| Type Of Accident | How It Can Happen | How To Prevent It |
|---|---|---|
| | b) child's position | Do not put soft pillows into prams or cots—babies tend to turn on to their faces. Buy a cot with a BSI mark. Do not let babies sleep overnight in a plastic-lined carrycot. |
| | c) feeding | Never leave a baby alone with a feeding bottle in a pram or cot. Make sure that the baby is properly 'winded' after feeding. Lay a baby on its side after feeding. |
| | d) inhaling vomit | |
| | e) playing | Do not allow children to play with plastic bags and discourage them from covering their heads. Throw away unwanted plastic bags. |
| MISCELLANEOUS | | |
| 1 Electrical accidents | Shocks received from: | |
| | a) metal objects pushed into sockets | Fit safety (masked) sockets or leave a spare plug in unused points. Have new sockets installed at waist height. |
| | b) handling plugs/switches with wet hands | Use rubber plugs in the kitchen or utility room. Use pull-on switches in the bathroom or have the switch fixed outside the room. Remember, *never* take electrical equipment (other than shavers) into the bathroom and do not install an electric power point there. |
| | c) wrongly wired electrical plugs | Make sure that you know the correct, up-to-date colour coding; keep an official coloured diagram handy (see page 83). |
| | d) electric blankets | Have them serviced regularly and use only as recommended by the manufacturers. Disconnect underblankets before going to bed. |
| 2 Bruises, bumps | Doors from wall-hung cupboards swinging open. | Make sure that all catches function properly. *Always* close doors after use. |
| | Inconvenient placing of cupboards, etc. Standing up under shelf or cupboard level. Being hit by standing on rakes, etc. Tripping in the garden. | Pad awkward corners if necessary. Fix shelves and cupboards as low as possible. Do not leave garden tools lying flat on the ground. Keep paths swept and in good condition. |
| 3 Drowning | Children falling into garden ponds. Slipping in the bath. | Enclose the pond or cover it. Supervise baths being taken by elderly and very young people. Use a non-slip bath mat *in* the bath. Use a non-slip mat on the bathroom floor. |

3 If electricity is involved, switch off the main supply or unplug the appliance and use water or a fire extinguisher as appropriate. The exception is the TV set which you should unplug before smothering flames with a rug or blanket.

DEALING WITH CHIMNEY FIRES
1 Call the fire brigade—you can rarely deal adequately with this emergency yourself.
2 Close doors and windows to reduce the draught.
3 Move rugs, furniture and ornaments from the surrounding area.

DEALING WITH LARGE FIRES
1 Evacuate the premises completely. Close as many doors and windows as possible to limit the spread of the fire.
2 Call the fire brigade. Check that all members of the family are outside.
3 *Do not* re-enter the house to salvage valuables, etc.
4 If you are trapped:
a) try to reach a room facing the street if possible;
b) open or break the window to get air to breathe and to call for help;
c) stay close to the floor;
d) if possible, block the bottom of the door to prevent smoke from entering;
e) do not either jump out, except as a last resort, or try to get through smoke-filled halls, passages or stairways; you may be overcome by fumes.

## FIRST AID

### First Aid in Case of Emergency

Remember that the most you can or are expected to do is to administer FIRST aid—you may arrest or prevent further damage and pain only. The most important thing is to keep a cool head and assess whether or not you are going to need further help; if you cannot cope or are uncontrollably frightened, call for help immediately. If you can help, ask anyone nearby to call the emergency services and give details of what has happened while you are making the patient comfortable, controlling bleeding and making sure that respiration continues. Remember:
1 A little blood (which most people react to) goes a very long way and injuries may not be as bad as you think at first.
2 An unnatural position indicates broken bones and should not be corrected.
3 Breathing is all-important—it is no good arresting bleeding from someone who has ceased to breathe!

PRELIMINARIES
1 Stop the cause of the injury or condition—e.g. move off any load which has fallen on to the victim or turn off gas which has overcome him.

2 If the victim is conscious and able to move without aggravating the condition, get him to the casualty department of the nearest hospital at once—call an ambulance or use an available car, but control bleeding first.

3 If the patient is unconscious, check that he is breathing—listen to his nose or mouth and watch the rise and fall of his chest. If he is, continue your check—for identification and for any tags which might indicate specific conditions (e.g. diabetes). Place him in the recovery position if you cannot detect the cause of the unconsciousness (see Figure 10.1).

4 If the patient is not breathing, lay him on his back and check that his tongue is not blocking his throat. If he does not begin breathing tilt the head to one side. Administer the 'kiss of life' as described below and, as soon as he is breathing, place him in the recovery position.

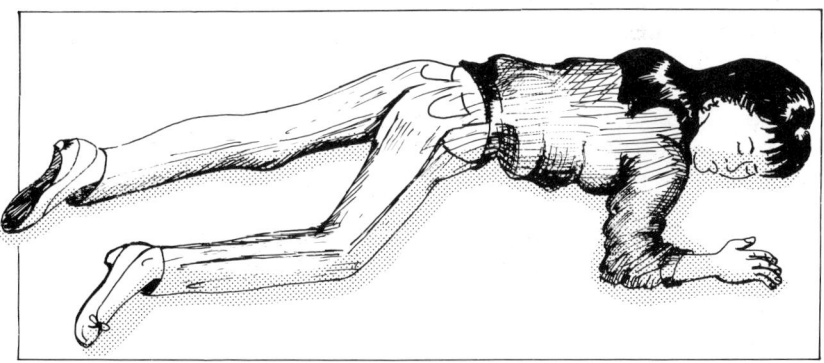

*Figure 10.1 The recovery position*

'THE KISS OF LIFE' (ARTIFICIAL RESUSCITATION)
1 Kneel at the head of the victim, place a folded coat or blanket under his shoulders and tilt the head back by pressing the forehead down with one hand and lifting the chin with the other (see Figure 10.2).

2 Remove anything such as vomit, blood or false teeth which might block their airway.

3 Pinch the nostrils together, steadying the neck and chin with the other hand.

4 Take a deep breath, open your mouth wide and place your lips tightly round the patient's mouth. Blow gently into the mouth until the chest rises. Lift your own head and watch the chest fall. Repeat this 6 times in quick succession.

5 Continue the 'kiss' at the rate of 10–15 breaths a minute (i.e. every 4–6 seconds: count slowly from 1 to 4 if in doubt). Continue until the chest begins to rise and fall of its own accord.

6 Ensure that the patient is breathing regularly and then turn him into the recovery position, i.e. the leg and arm on one side drawn up, body turned on to front and the head tilted to one side.

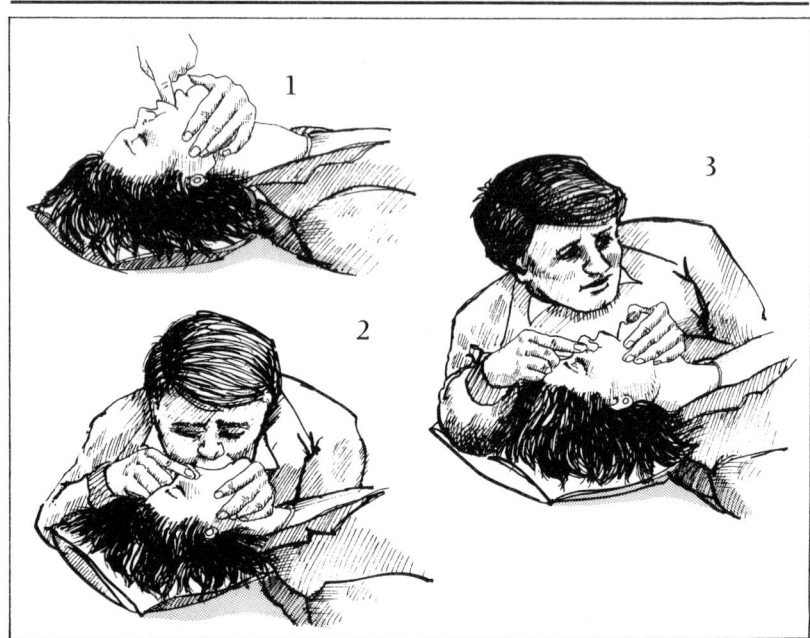

*Figure 10.2 Artificial resuscitation*

CONTROLLING BLEEDING

This is of importance secondary only to efficient respiration. Profuse bleeding must be stopped as quickly as possible and a doctor or ambulance summoned.

To control bleeding while you are waiting, grasp the sides of the wound and squeeze them firmly together; or apply a large pad of the cleanest material available. If there is embedded glass or other foreign body in the wound or there appears to be a fracture at the site of the bleeding, do not press; cover the wound with a pad and renew it as it becomes soaked. If the bleeding is from an arm or leg which does not appear to be fractured, raise it and support it in this position to diminish the flow.

If none of the above steps is possible or effective, try to locate the nearest 'pressure point' (i.e. where large vessels are close to the skin and a pulse can be felt). These are located below the armpit for the arm and below the groin for the leg. Apply pressure to these points for a few seconds and release it gently, repeating the process until the bleeding is reduced. Do not attempt to apply a tourniquet unless you are a trained 'first-aider'.

When bleeding has been controlled, treat the patient for shock (see page 204), keep him at rest and covered lightly, but give nothing at all to drink or to eat. Wipe the face over the mouth area gently with a moist cloth.

## First Aid Box/Medicine Chest

Equipment needed for the treatment of minor injuries should always be available and the best way of ensuring this is to keep a special box or cupboard, clearly recognizable, for these items and for storing currently prescribed medicine and standard remedies. It should have a lock and key and be easily accessible to adults but completely out of reach of children, even with the help of a chair or stool. The name and telephone number of your doctor should be written on the lid or inside the cupboard door. The contents should include:

| *Item* | *Use* |
|---|---|
| A pair of round-ended scissors | For cutting dressings |
| A pair of spade-ended tweezers | For removing splinters and picking up sterile dressings |
| A clinical thermometer | For taking temperatures |
| An eye bath | For bathing inflamed eyes |
| Several safety pins | For securing bandages or slings |
| Packet of paper tissues | For wiping or for disposing of dirty dressings |
| Cotton wool | To pad dressings, clean injuries |
| Sterilized absorbent gauze | To dress minor wounds |
| Unbleached triangular bandage | To form a sling for supporting arm/hand injuries |
| Crêpe bandage: 75 mm. (3″) wide | For bandaging sprained joints |
| Open weave bandages (assorted widths) | To protect wounds from dirt and chafing |
| Adhesive plaster dressings | To cover minor wounds |
| Tablets: | |
| a) soluble aspirin | To relieve pain and lower temperature |
| b) junior aspirin | For children |
| c) paracetamol | Similar to aspirin, with no risk of stomach irritation |
| d) travel sickness | To be taken, if necessary, before a journey |
| Cream: | |
| a) antiseptic | For cuts and bruises |
| b) antihistamine | For bites, stings, sunburn |
| Liquids: | |
| a) oil of cloves | For toothache |
| b) calamine lotion | To relieve sunburn, irritation, bites, stings |
| c) kaolin and morphine mixture | To relieve diarrhoea and intestinal discomfort |
| d) antiseptic solution | For adding to water when bathing wounds |

## First Aid Treatment

The following list includes the most common situations in which first aid is required, but it is not exhaustive. It is a very useful step for at least one member of the family or of the household to take a St John's Ambulance Brigade or British Red Cross Society course in First Aid, if only to familiarize them with possible occurrences and so reduce the fear which causes people to lose their heads in emergencies.

ASPHYXIATION/SUFFOCATION
Find the cause and remove it (e.g. turn off the car engine; remove bedclothes). Open windows. Apply artificial resuscitation if necessary.

## BURNS

*Minor*
> Place the affected part under cold running water for 5 minutes to relieve pain and cool the tissues. Cover with a gauze dressing if the area is likely to be chafed.

*Severe*
> Any burns more than 3 inches square require immediate medical attention. Relieve pain by applying cold wet cloths. Cover lightly with a dry cloth and treat the patient for shock while waiting for medical help.

*Chemical burns* (caused by corrosives such as acid or caustic soda)
> Pour cold water freely over the affected part—if spattered over a large area turn on a shower over the victim. Send for medical assistance.

*Fire burns*
> Remove any *loose* charred clothing but do *not* pull any which is adhering to the skin. Keep smouldering clothing damp with cold water, applying no pressure. Remove any jewellery, socks or shoes near the burnt area if possible, before the tissues swell. Cover burns with a clean cloth. Treat patient for shock while awaiting help.

## CHOKING

If instinctive coughing does not clear the obstruction, ask the patient to bend forward and slap him sharply between the shoulder blades. If this is not effective, lay him across a chair or table with the head and chest hanging down; repeat the slap.

If the victim is a child, hold him upside down and slap his back but if this is still not effective, send for medical help at once.

## CONVULSIONS

These are usually caused by epilepsy and manifested by collapse, threshing limbs, biting of the tongue and possibly frothing at the mouth. Keep your head—it may be a distressing sight—and move furniture away from the victim to prevent him from hurting himself.

If you can, slip a knotted handkerchief or even a pencil between the teeth to prevent the tongue from being bitten through. On recovery, the patient should be kept quiet and reassured. If there is a recurrence, call a doctor immediately.

## CUTS

Hold the edges together and place a dressing plaster firmly across it, with the dressing over the open wound. If very deep, take the patient to the casualty department of the nearest hospital to have it stitched.

## DISLOCATION

A joint slips, or is forced, out of place, causing pain, distortion and swelling. Keep the affected part as still as possible, supporting it by hand or by using a sling. Call for medical help.

## ELECTRIC SHOCK

Switch off the current before touching the victim if he/she is still in contact with the electrical equipment; remove the offending item.

If you are *certain* you cannot feel the heart beating, give the chest a sharp thump in the middle. Do this only as a last resort, however, as it is very dangerous and is best left to someone who has been trained to do it. If breathing has stopped, give the kiss of life and continue to do so until help arrives. If the victim is unconscious but breathing, place him in the recovery position. Treat for burns and shock.

## EYE INJURIES

If a foreign body cannot be removed by blinking, pull down the eyelid and try to dislodge the obstruction with the corner of a clean handkerchief. If the object is embedded in the eye or cannot be seen, cover it with a clean pad kept in position with plaster and take the patient to the nearest hospital.

If acid or other noxious fluid has entered the eye, flood it with cold water for 10–15 minutes and get help as soon as possible.

## FAINTING

Sit the patient down with his head between his knees *or* lay him down with his feet higher than his head. If he is already unconscious, loosen any tight clothing, open windows and, if outside, keep other people away. On recovery, let the patient rest until feeling better.

## FRACTURES

Characterized by pain, swelling, distortion of the limb and tenderness at the lightest touch. Do not move the victim or try to straighten the limb. Treat for shock and keep the patient reassured until help arrives.

## NOSE BLEED

Sit the patient down with his head over a bowl or sink. Pinch the nostrils together while applying a cold pad or cube to the bridge of the nose. Encourage the patient to breathe through his mouth and not to sniff.

If bleeding does not stop within 15 minutes, take him to the nearest hospital or send for the doctor.

## POISONING

Telephone a doctor *immediately* you have discovered that someone has swallowed any type of poison, including overdoses of drugs. If the lips are burned or stained and the patient is not breathing, use the mouth-to-nose method of resuscitation instead of mouth-to-mouth.

## SCALDS

Remove any hot clothing from the area and bathe it freely with copious cold water. Do *not* break blisters. Cover lightly with gauze held in place with small strips of plaster well away from the tender area if it is likely to be chafed.

SHOCK

This manifests itself in low blood pressure and a weak heart beat—usually following an accident. Make the patient as comfortable as possible and reassure him. Cover him with a light blanket. Let him rest full length with the feet higher than the head if possible; if there is a chest or abdominal injury, support the shoulders in a slightly raised position.

## HOME NURSING

There are many occasions when a member of the family is too poorly to get up but not sufficiently ill to be in hospital—even the common cold can be treated successfully with a few days in bed. In the case of serious illness the doctor's treatment can be considerably enhanced by good nursing at home. Any skilled dressings required will be carried out by the district nurse if you apply for help, but general day-to-day care can be satisfactorily administered with the help of imagination, patience, observation and goodwill as long as you are free to do it.

### Arranging the Sick Room

1 Place the bed so that the patient has a view out of the window.
2 Position the bed so that there is room to move at both sides of it.
3 Put a small table or cupboard beside the bed for drinks and foods to be placed and for the patient's personal possessions, including tissues and a 'waste-bag' (this can be fastened to the side of the cupboard or table with a piece of plaster or adhesive tape). Add a covered jug of water or fruit juice, a glass and a small bell.
4 Make sure that there are comfortable chairs for visitors.
5 Place a screen across the window so that it can be opened without subjecting the patient to draughts.
6 Clear a drawer or chest-top to hold the equipment required.
7 Make sure that there are books or magazines within reach.
8 Provide a bedside lamp within easy reach of the patient.
9 Provide a portable radio.
10 Brighten the room with attractive pictures and flowers.
11 Use an ironing board or cantilevered table pushed across the bed for serving meals on.

THE BED
1 A single bed is more convenient to deal with than a double bed if this can be arranged.
2 A backrest can be used to help the patient to sit upright if stacked pillows arranged like an armchair are not satisfactory.
3 A bedcradle will help to keep the weight of the clothes off injured feet or legs. It can be improvised from a stool or cardboard box.
4 A 'sheepskin' is useful for an immobile patient to lie on, preventing friction on heels, elbows and buttocks which can cause bedsores. (If this

is not available, small foam pads covered in pillowcases may be used under tender areas.)

5 If the patient is incontinent (i.e. not in control of his bladder or/and rectal functions), the bed should be protected by a rubber or plastic sheet with a draw-sheet made from old folded sheeting placed over it.

Backrests, bedcradles, sheepskins and rubber sheets may be borrowed by courtesy of the district nurse, health visitor or the Red Cross; bedpans or urinals may also be borrowed if the patient is not able to get up.

6. If the patient cannot get out of bed while it is changed follow this procedure:

a) Remove the pillows and turn the patient on to his side.

b) Roll the bottom sheet from the side up against his back.

c) Tuck in the clean sheet at the side and roll the patient on to it.

d) Remove the dirty sheet from the other side.

e) Unroll the clean sheet and pull it tight before tucking it in.

f) Change the top sheet if necessary and replace the rest of the blankets, etc. while the patient is lying down.

g) Change the pillowcases and replace the pillows.

## Nursing Routine

1 Carry out the doctor's orders implicitly. If observations are required (e.g. amount of sleep, temperature changes), write them down so that you do not forget; make a note of the times at which the observations were made.

2 Serve meals punctually—see page 131 for details of serving. Remove used trays, crockery, etc. as soon as they are finished with.

3 Adjust the pillows and help the patient to move at frequent intervals throughout the day.

4 Assist the patient to the toilet whenever necessary, keeping a good standard of hygiene for him, yourself and any equipment used.

5 Keep the patient well supplied with fluids.

6 Keep the patient's skin clean, dry and fresh. If he cannot get to the bathroom give him a daily bedbath after attending to his toilet needs.

a) Collect two large towels and one smaller towel, two flannels, warm water, soap, talcum powder and teeth cleaning necessities.

b) Remove the patient's pyjamas.

c) Having folded back the bedclothes, place one large towel or thin blanket under the patient and cover him with the other.

d) Wash and dry the face, using one flannel and the smaller towel.

e) Wash each part of the rest of the body in sequence, using the second flannel, covering up the lower part while washing the upper and vice versa. Let the patient wash as much of himself as he can.

f) Dry each part thoroughly and dust the limbs with talcum powder.

g) Turn the patient on his side and wash his back. Dry and powder it thoroughly.

h) Let him clean his teeth and rinse his mouth if he can.
i) Redress him in clean pyjamas. Comb his hair.
j) Attend to nails if necessary.
k) Make the bed and make the patient comfortable.
7 Keep an air-freshener block or wick in the room to ensure a pleasant atmosphere. Change flower water daily.
8 Provide a night-light if the patient is nervous in the dark.
9 Keep yourself clean and tidy, dressed suitably and as cheerful as possible.
10 Try to arrange some relief for yourself every day. When a patient is in bed, constant attention is required and this can tax your vitality and patience if you have no break. Even hospital nurses have time off!

## Taking Temperature, Pulse and Respiration

TEMPERATURE
Use a clinical thermometer and place it under the patient's tongue. Warn him not to bite it and not to talk. If this is not possible, e.g. with a child, place the bulb in the armpit and lower the arm firmly. Make sure that the mercury is well shaken down before using it. Keep it in place for 2 minutes while the patient lies still and quiet. You can be counting the pulse and respiration during this time. It is important that you do not take the temperature less than 20 minutes after a meal, drink or bath.

Remove the thermometer, take the reading and note it if necessary (normal: 98.4° F, 37° C). Shake the mercury down. Rinse the thermometer in cold water and place it in a small jar of antiseptic solution until next required—wipe it with a piece of cotton wool before next use.

PULSE
The most convenient place to count the pulse is at the wrist. Place 3 of your fingers over the throbbing artery (do *not* use your thumb—it has its own pulse) and, using the second hand of a watch or clock to measure the time, count the number of beats you feel in 1 minute. The average rate for an adult is 70–80 beats per minute, for a child 120–140, but a slight deviation is not usually significant.

RESPIRATION
Take the rate of this after counting the pulse so that the patient is unaware of your doing so. Consciousness of breathing being counted often accelerates it. An adult normally breathes 16–20 times a minute, a baby 30–50 times.

## Contagious Illness

If the patient is suffering from an infectious illness or one which is contagious (infection may be picked up without actually being in contact with another person who is suffering from the illness; contagion implies actual contact with the sufferer), special nursing precautions have to be taken:

1 Try to isolate the patient in a room of his own.
2 Restrict visitors, especially if the illness is of a contagious nature.
3 Nurse the patient in bed until his temperature falls.
4 Keep the room clean, well ventilated and free from flies.
5 Give a light diet and plenty of fluids.
6 After doing anything for him wash your hands thoroughly to prevent the spread of infection.
7 Keep separate drinking and eating utensils for the patient, wash them separately and sterilize them in Milton solution or place them in cold water, bring to the boil and keep them boiling for 10 minutes.
8 Burn or bury left-over food.
9 Wash bed linen in hot water and dry out of doors.
10 Return library books in a plastic bag with an explanatory note to the Librarian: burn magazines and papers used by the patient. Let infectious children play with washable toys only—inexpensive ones are best burnt.

● Remember the importance of early immunization against diphtheria, whooping cough, tetanus, smallpox, tuberculosis, measles and poliomyelitis.

## ———————————— FURTHER STUDY ————————————

### Things to Do

1 Look around the room in which you are sitting and identify the danger areas. What precautions do you think you could take to make it accident proof?
2 Practise mouth-to-mouth resuscitation. Use a tissue between your mouth and that of your 'patient' if you cannot use a model.
3 Make a list of the various rooms in your home. Tabulate the items in each room which could cause accidents and the steps you would take to prevent them from happening.
4 Collect as many examples of safety guarantees and consumer protection signs as you can; look around the area in which you live to see which retail shops display association membership.
5 Find out how to apply a sling to be used to support:
   a) a sprained wrist;
   b) a hand bitten by a dog.

### Questions to Answer

1 Write out and complete each of the following statements with the correct term chosen from the list in the right-hand column.

a) In dealing with accidents it is more important to restore breathing than it is to control _____ .

respiration

b) _____ are caused by contact with extreme dry heat such as fire or very hot cooking vessels.

inhaled

c) Certain liquids such as nitric acid or strong alkalis can cause burns because they are _____ .

dislocation

d) The injuries caused by extremely hot liquids and by steam are known as _____ .

shock

e) Playing games with plastic bags and other 'helmets' can cause _____ owing to lack of available air.

burns

f) Toxic fumes can be fatal if they are _____ , the lungs being unable to obtain sufficient oxygen.

scalds

g) A bad fall can cause a person to try to save himself by putting out his hands, resulting in the _____ of the wrist bone.

suffocation

h) A sudden jerky movement could cause a shoulder to become swollen, painful and immobile because of the _____ of the joint.

bleeding

i) Nearly every accident victim requires the same final treatment of warmth and reassurance because he is suffering from _____ .

fracture

j) While counting a patient's pulse and taking his temperature, you can also count his _____ rate.

corrosive

2 What do you understand by 'a state of shock'? How would you recognize this condition and how would you treat it?

3 What precautions can you take to make your premises as burglar-proof as possible while you are away from home on holiday?

4 What accidents would you be on guard against in
  a) your bedroom;
  b) the garden;
  c) the garage?

5 How would you keep a child of 7 comfortable and contented while he has to stay in bed for a week?

## GAS

Although the householder is responsible for the *use* of gas, the Regional Gas Authority bears the responsibility for actually *supplying* it. When you first move into new premises make a note of
a)  where the main supply enters and can be switched off.
b)  the telephone number of the local emergency service,
c)  the telephone number of the local Gas Workshop,
so that it is always possible to summon help quickly.

Until recent years all gas supplied to the home was produced from coal—indeed, it was referred to as 'coal gas'. Today all domestic gas is natural gas, a supply having been discovered beneath the North Sea which is distributed throughout the United Kingdom. Unlike coal gas, natural gas is not poisonous but it can still cause explosions if mixed with air and ignited—in other words, if carelessly used. It is also odourless but the characteristic smell is deliberately introduced in order to indicate the fact that it is leaking. For the safety precautions to be observed in dealing with gas leaks, see pages 195–6.

### Installation of Gas Supply

All pipes used in carrying gas to the street main and then to the domestic premises, including the meter, are the responsibility of the gas industry: all those from the meter and all appliances used are the responsibility of the user, although any installation of equipment must be approved by the Gas Board.

Because of the potential explosive danger of gas it is very important that equipment should be installed by skilled fitters and repaired by trained specialists. No appliance is approved by the Gas Board unless it carries the BSI safety mark (see page 191). The pipe connecting the gas main to the consumer's meter is called a service pipe. The meter may be fixed inside or outside the premises, the present policy being to place it in a specially designed box outside.

If installed indoors it should be placed:
a)  in a well-ventilated position;
b)  somewhere where it cannot become damp;
c)  away from heating or cooling appliances.

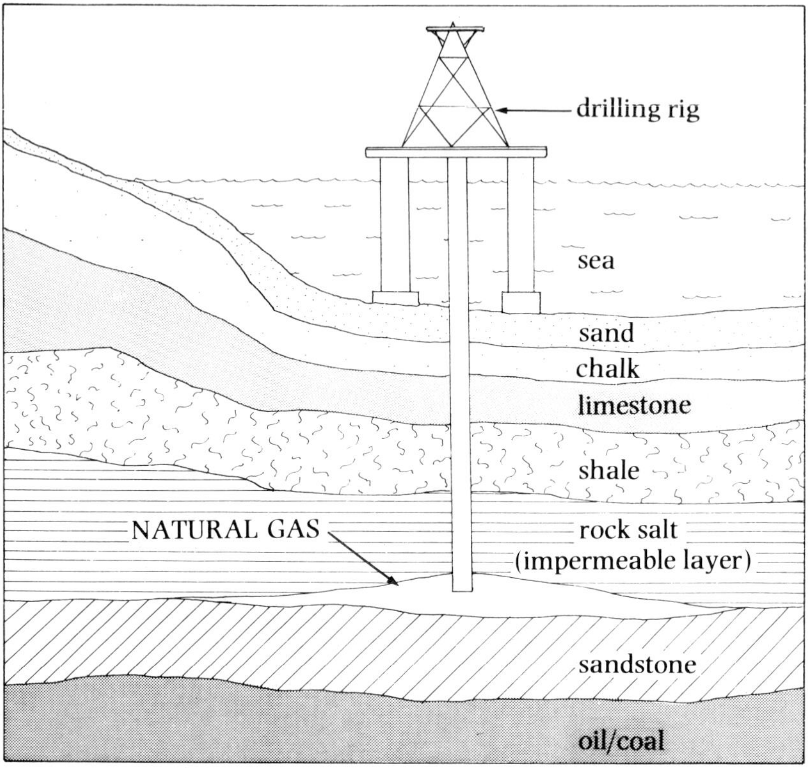

*Figure 11.1  Obtaining natural gas from beneath the sea*

drilling rig

sea

sand
chalk
limestone

shale

NATURAL GAS

rock salt
(impermeable layer)

sandstone

oil/coal

Methane 90%
Ethane 4%
Propane 3%
Butane 2%
Nitrogen 1%

Calorific Value 37 MJ/m³
Air required for combustion 9.5m³/m³ gas
No sulphur so does not corrode appliances
Contains no carbon monoxide and is therefore non-poisonous.

*Figure 11.2  The approximate composition of natural gas*

*Figure 11.3  The characteristics of natural gas*

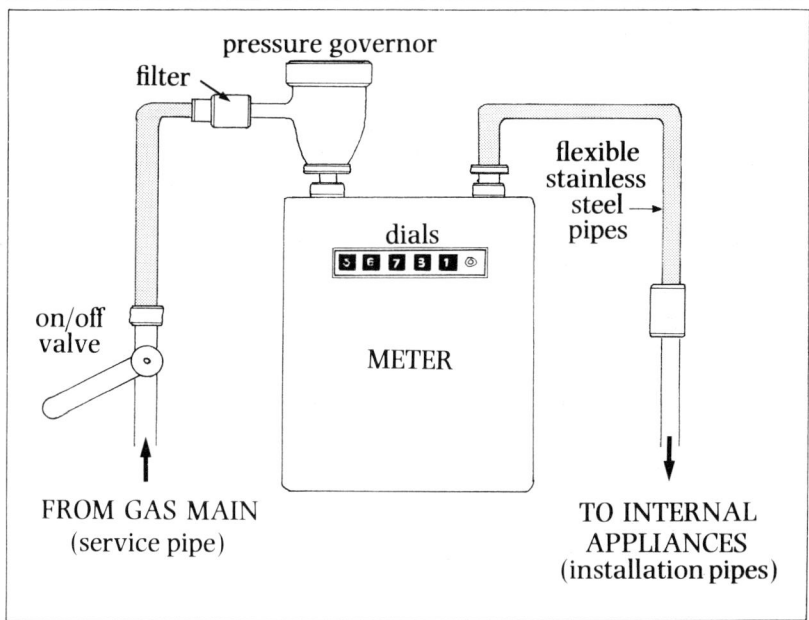

*Figure 11.4  The passage of gas from the main to domestic appliances*

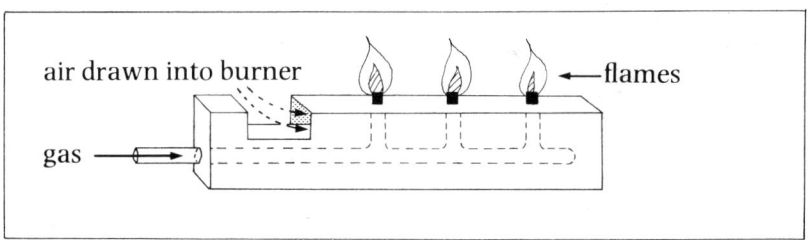

*Figure 11.5  The mixing of gas and air to produce combustion at the burner*

If placed outside it:
a) is installed in a lockable 'cupboard';
b) allows the meter to be read in the absence of the householder, without the inconvenience of making special arrangements;
c) avoids the necessity of estimated accounts.

The gas flowing through the meter, the amount being registered as it does so, is carried to various rooms in the premises through installation pipes. Each gas outlet point is separately controlled by a gas 'tap'. For correct combustion the gas piped to internal appliances must be supplied at the correct pressure (note the 'pressure governor' shown in Figure 11.4 which, incidentally, should *never* be interfered with by the consumer). The correct amount of air required for combustion is mixed with the gas at the burner (see Figure 11.5).

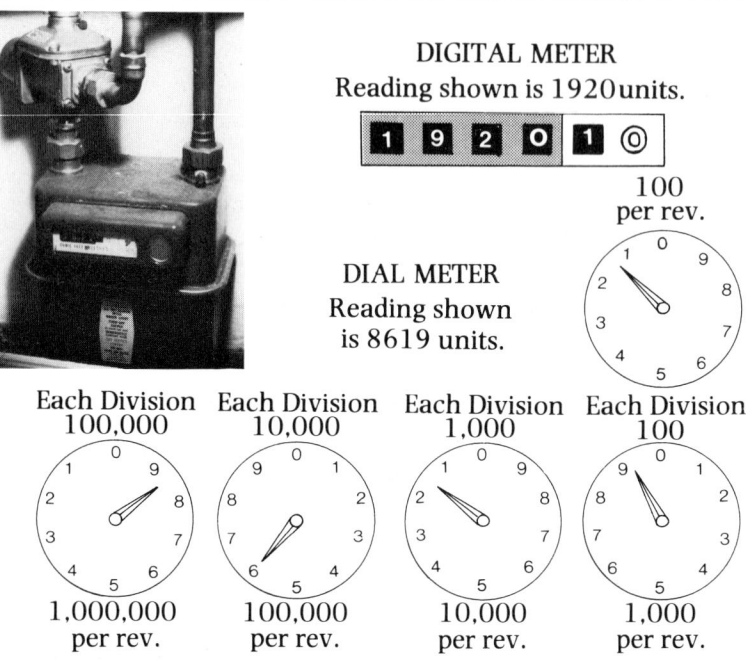

Figure 11.6  *Reading the gas meter (photo Robert Rowat)*

**Reading the Meter** (now referred to as the Consumer Unit)

There are two types of meter (see Figure 11.6):
a) a direct reading index where gas consumption is displayed as a row of digits which is easily read (first 4 figures only);
b) a dial meter where the figures are shown on a series of dials, 4 with black hands, 2 with red.
When reading the digital meter, read from left to right, the 4 black figures only. When reading the dial meter, copy down the figures indicated by the hands, using the lower one if the hand is between two figures (except if it is between 9 and 0, when you read 9).

Gas is measured in cubic feet, calculated in units of 100. The reading you have just made will tell you how many hundreds of cubic feet you have used since the last reading if you deduct the previous number from the present one. You can then, if you wish, calculate your gas bill. Normally an official meter reader will do this at 3-monthly intervals, but you may read it at any time for your own information. Although measured in units of 100 cubic feet you are charged for your gas by the 'therm'. (A therm is 100,000 British Thermal Units (Btu), a Btu being the amount of heat required to raise the temperature of one gram of water one degree Centigrade: approximately 600 Btus are required to heat a pint of water to boiling point.)

To convert cubic feet into therms you need to know the calorific value (CV) of the gas (i.e. its heating capacity). This is shown on your gas bills, together with the cost of a therm. The formula you use is:

$$\frac{\text{calorific value (CV)} \times \text{hundreds of cubic feet}}{1000} = \text{therms}$$

For example, if it is stated that your gas has a calorific value (CV) of 1035 and you have used 2,800 cubic feet, your calculation will be:

$$\frac{1035 \times 28}{1000} = \text{approximately 29 therms}$$

The cost of what you have consumed, therefore, will be:

$$29 \times \text{the current price per therm}$$

If the current price per therm is 28p (you will get an idea from your previous bill) the amount shown on your bill will be:

$$29 \times 28p = \underline{£8.12}$$

## Paying the Bill

Many premises have a coin slot meter attached to the gas meter and you pay for the gas as you use it. At regular intervals, quarterly or more (if necessary), the meter is emptied by an official, who is the only person who should have access to the money.

Bills for gas are normally sent out each quarter and these include a standing charge plus the cost of the therms used. There are actually two different tariffs, a standard one and a cheaper one which levies a higher standing charge but a lower rate per therm. Conditions vary from region to region but if you have gas central heating or a number of other gas-fired appliances you may qualify for the cheaper tariff.

*A gas bill*

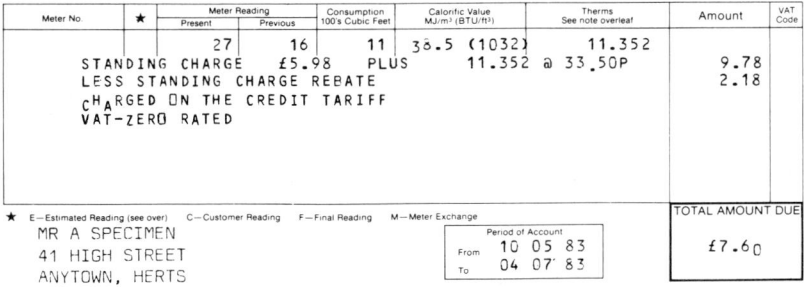

| Meter No. | ★ | Meter Reading | | Consumption | Calorific Value | Therms | Amount | VAT |
| | | Present | Previous | 100's Cubic Feet | MJ/m³ (BTU/ft³) | See note overleaf | | Code |
|---|---|---|---|---|---|---|---|---|
| | | 27 | 16 | 11 | 38.5 (1032) | 11.352 | | |
| STANDING CHARGE £5.98 PLUS | | | | | | 11.352 @ 33.50P | 9.78 | |
| LESS STANDING CHARGE REBATE | | | | | | | 2.18 | |
| CHARGED ON THE CREDIT TARIFF | | | | | | | | |
| VAT–ZERO RATED | | | | | | | | |

★ E—Estimated Reading (see over)   C—Customer Reading   F—Final Reading   M—Meter Exchange

MR A SPECIMEN
41 HIGH STREET
ANYTOWN, HERTS

Period of Account
From 10 05 83
To 04 07 83

TOTAL AMOUNT DUE
£7.60

112 231 5473

Date of Account (Tax Point)
06 07 83

Premises supplied if other than account address

To ease payment of gas bills you may choose to make a regular monthly payment instead of a quarterly settlement. An estimate of the cost of your year's consumption is calculated and divided by twelve. Providing this figure exceeds £4 you may then pay a fixed sum each month and this is adjusted periodically if necessary. This amount can be paid through your bank, by direct debit (see page 150), or through the National Giro. You can also ease the shock of paying out large sums at 3-monthly intervals by buying 'stamps' at the Gas Showrooms and saving up weekly amounts.

**Using Gas**

1 Make sure that your main gas tap is fully turned on so that your gas pressure is correct. The groove in the head of the valve should be in line with the middle of the pipe when it is turned on and at right angles to it when it is off (see Figure 11.7). Ask a fitter to loosen it for you if you find it difficult to turn.

2 If you leave your premises for any length of time (and providing that your refrigerator is not gas-operated) turn off all taps to gas appliances, including pilot lights, and then turn off the main tap. When you are ready to re-use the gas, check first that all the taps are turned off, turn on the main tap and re-light the pilots.

If your meter is coin operated and the supply runs out, check that all taps are turned off before inserting further coins.

3 The safety precautions you should observe are as follows:

a) Never cover the ventilators installed for gas appliances—these allow the poisonous fumes to escape (i.e. the fumes resulting from combustion).

b) If you smell gas, it is more than likely that a pilot light or other burner in use has gone out. Put out any cigarettes and check whether or not this has happened. Do not use any matches. If you find a gas tap turned on but not alight:

turn it off;

if there is an electric fire in the room, switch it off;

*Figure 11.7  A gas valve tap*

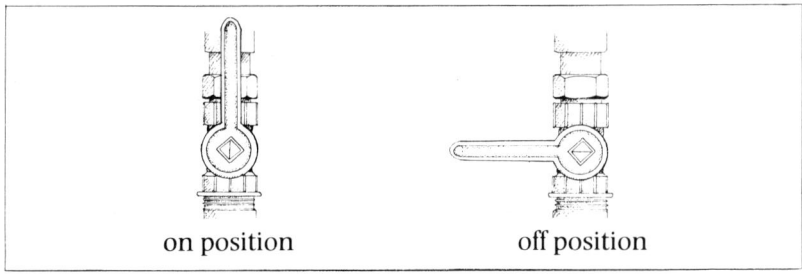

on position                    off position

open doors and windows and wait for the smell of gas to disappear before re-lighting any burner or using any naked flames;
if the smell does not disperse with airing, turn off the main supply and contact the emergency service at once.

4 If you are aware of an unusual smell from a gas fire or water heater, or if there is brown discoloration round the edges, turn off the appliance and call the emergency service at once. They are danger signals, indicating that flues are either blocked, damaged or inefficient and allowing poisonous gases to escape into the room.

5 Do not attempt to carry out your own servicing. There is a good maintenance service for gas central heating installations (see page 47) and the emergency repair service is always available.

● Note that special provision can be made at little or no cost for the use of a meter by disabled or aged people. Specially adapted gas taps and slot meters are available and meters can be moved to more convenient positions. The Home Service Adviser will call, if requested, and discuss possibilities.

BOTTLED GAS ('CALOR')
If you wish to use gas in your home but there is no main supply available, you may hire 'bottles' (large cylinders) of butane gas. The most convenient procedure is to start with two so that you have a spare to use when one runs out; the empty one is then returned to the distributors for refilling.

Specially adapted portable heaters, fires and convectors are available as well as cookers, and this gas works as efficiently as natural gas. (See also page 43.)

Adequate ventilation in rooms heated by this type of gas is essential.


## ELECTRICITY

Electricity is a mystery to many people and, because they do not understand it, they are frightened of it. It should, indeed, be treated with respect, but its circulation becomes rather more comprehensible if you compare it with water—flowing through wires instead of pipes and issuing at outlet sockets instead of taps. Whereas water will make you wet and cause flooding if not properly controlled, electricity will give you a shock and cause fire if mismanaged. The difference is that electricity will not flow at all if there is an interruption in the circuit, whereas water will leak through a break. As with water, it is difficult to imagine our lives without electricity.


### Production

When a coil of wire is rotated between magnets, an electric current is induced in the coil—this is the basic principle of generating electricity

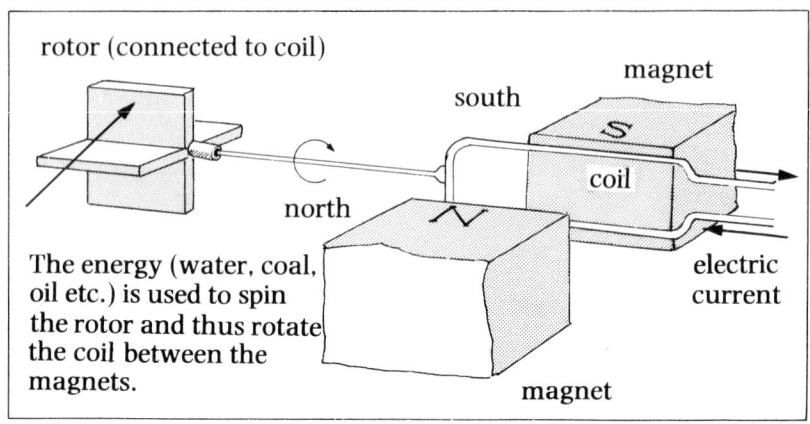

rotor (connected to coil)

magnet

south

coil

north

The energy (water, coal, oil etc.) is used to spin the rotor and thus rotate the coil between the magnets.

electric current

magnet

*Figure 11.8  A simplified model showing how electricity is produced*

in power stations (see Figure 11.8). The energy required to turn the rotor which spins the coil can be supplied from a number of sources:
a) a high velocity jet of steam, produced from water heated by coal, oil, gas or nuclear power;
b) a jet of water (hydro-electric);
c) wind (wind turbine).
   In isolated dwellings an ordinary internal combustion engine can be used to rotate the generator.

## Distribution

Domestic electricity is distributed throughout the country from power stations by the National Grid System. From the power station it is carried across the land by overhead transmission lines at very high voltage (33,000 volts, for reasons of economy); 'volt' (V) indicates the force or pressure at which the electricity is being transmitted through the cables. These lines are the ones carried by the familiar pylons which raise them well above the height of the largest vehicle. The cables are carried to transformers near our homes where the voltage is reduced ('transformed') to 240 V, which is more suitable for domestic use; and then transported to our premises by means of an underground cable. This cable consists of two wires, one 'live' and one 'neutral'. It goes first to a sealed fuse box and then to the household meter (see Figure 11.9).
   After the meter the two conductors pass into the household main fuse box or 'Consumer Unit', which can be opened by the householder and contains a switch which controls the household supply (ON and OFF). The current flows through this unit, and is registered as it is used, to supply power to the required outlets via wires passing through walls and under floors. From the consumer unit at least three circuits are supplied:

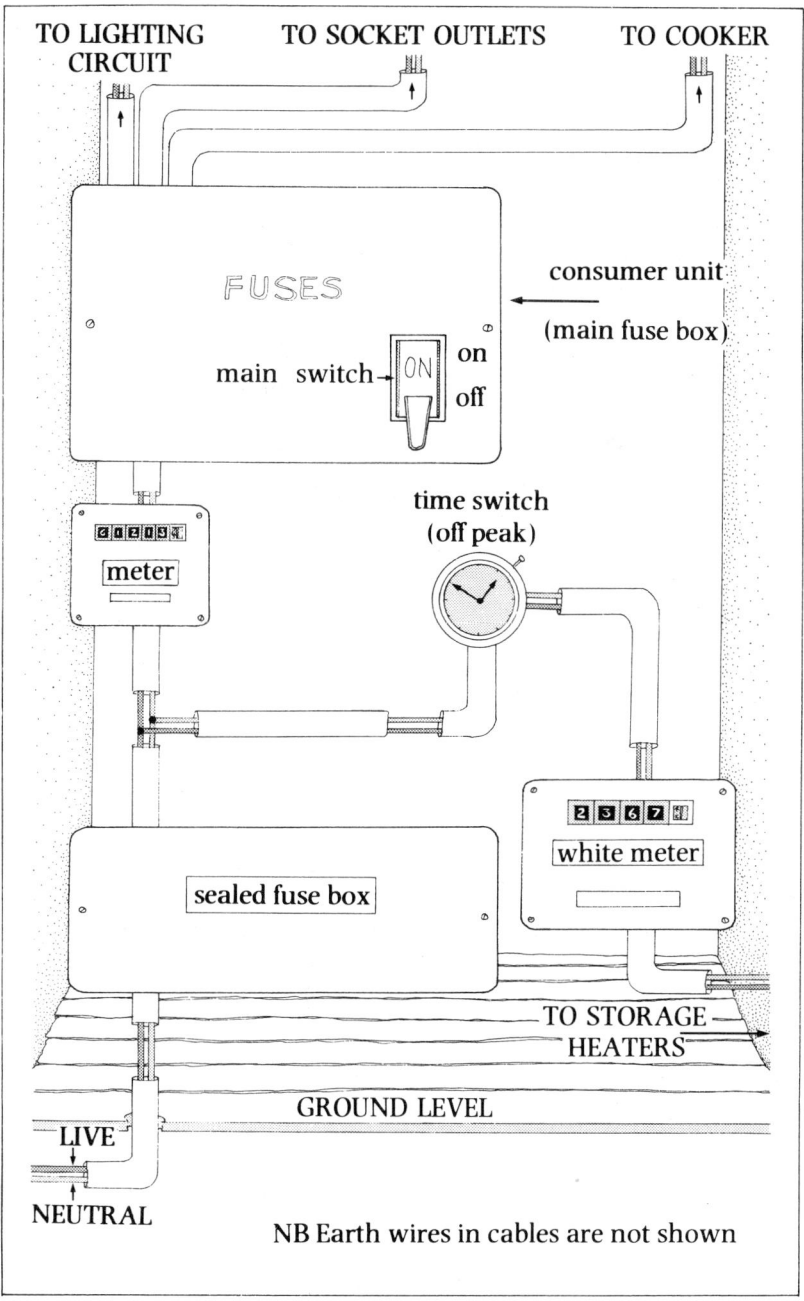

TO LIGHTING CIRCUIT

TO SOCKET OUTLETS

TO COOKER

FUSES

consumer unit (main fuse box)

main switch → | ON | on / off

meter

time switch (off peak)

sealed fuse box

white meter

TO STORAGE HEATERS

GROUND LEVEL

LIVE

NEUTRAL

NB Earth wires in cables are not shown

*Figure 11.9 A simplified model showing the distribution and metering of domestic electricity*

*A Consumer Unit (Delta*
*Accessories and Domestic Switchgear)*

a) lighting;
b) socket outlets;
c) cooker.

Each circuit has its own fuse so if one circuit fails the others should not be affected. It is very helpful if the fuse holders are labelled for easy repair (see page 82). In addition to those mentioned above, an additional cheap rate circuit may operate from a time switch at off-peak periods, passing through a 'white meter' (see page 47).

Some of the newer wiring systems include small circuit breakers which are substitutes for removable fuses—see page 65.

### Fuses/Flexes/Plugs

For use, colour coding and wiring see pages 65, 82–4.

### Reading the Meter

As for gas meters, there are two types (see Figure 11.10):
a) the digital meter;
b) the dial meter.

Both of these record the amount of electricity used, measured in units. A unit is one kilowatt hour (kWh), that is, 1,000 watts used for one hour.

White meters have two digital indicators, one recording the electricity used during the day and one for that used during 'off peak' or lower priced periods.

When reading the digital meter, read the figures from left to right, ignoring the last one (this is similar to the milometer in a car). When reading the dial meter, read the figures indicated on the dials from left to right, ignoring the lower one marked $\frac{1}{10}$. If the pointer rests between two figures, record the lower one unless it is between 9 and 0, when you use the figure 9.

To calculate your bill, subtract the number of consumed units recorded on your previous bill from the present reading and multiply it by the cost of each unit (which will be shown on your old bill). To this

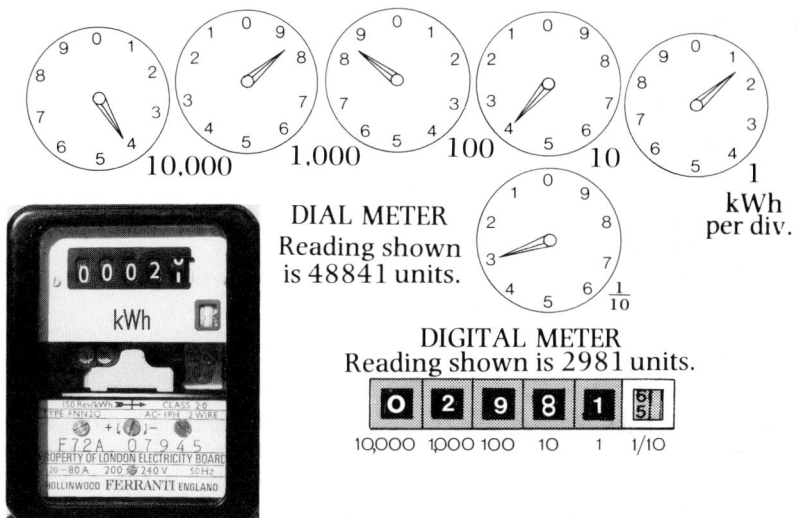

*Figure 11.10  Reading the electricity meter (photo Electricity Council)*

must be added a standing charge which covers the cost of making the supply available and which will be made whether or not any electricity is used. This charge is sometimes made separately and the units charged at a standard rate; sometimes it is spread over the first 100 or so units used and the rest are charged at a lower rate. You may also have a surcharge which covers fluctuating basic fuel prices.

## Paying the Bill

The electricity meter is read, like the gas one, by an official reader every quarter, but you may arrange to have your bill estimated for a year and pay for it in monthly instalments. You can request that your bank pays a direct debit (see page 150), you can pay through the National Giro, or you can buy 'stamps' for small amounts whenever you can to save up for the large demand.

See page 47 for use of night-storage heaters, etc.

## Safety Precautions

1 Two safety devices are normally incorporated into each electrical circuit.

a) fuses—these are the weak links which melt and break the electrical circuit if the current is excessive (see page 65);

b) an earth wire—for reasons of safety, an earth wire is incorporated in each of the circuits leaving the consumer unit (or main fuse box). The earth wire is a 'protective conductor' used to carry escaping electric currents to earth, thereby reducing the risk of the user of an appliance receiving an electric shock. (Note that plastic-covered equipment, e.g. hair-driers, does not need an earth wire.)

2  Power cuts happen, often without warning, and it is as well to be prepared at all times with substitute heating, lighting and cooking facilities such as:

a large torch—check at intervals that the battery has not become inactive;

candles and matches—with satisfactory holders;

a camping gas appliance—to use for cooking (also available as a lighting appliance);

a hot water bottle—to replace an electric blanket (water can be heated on the camping stove);

a paraffin heater—to replace heating power (check that there is paraffin in the container).

3  In the event of power cuts:

a)  Turn off all electrical appliances and remove the plug of the TV set—the sudden surge when the power is restored may cause accidents.

b)  Open the refrigerator door as little as possible so that cold air is not lost.

c)  Keep the freezer lid or door closed—food will be quite safe for at least 10 hours and it is seldom that a power cut lasts longer.

Reduced voltage may be recognized by the dimming of lights, reduction in heat, slow cooking and reduced TV picture. This sometimes precedes a full power cut or may be a temporary economy measure at the distribution centre, but be on guard. In times of extreme difficulty, notice is usually given in advance of the times of cuts to be expected.

4  The marks shown below indicate two safety guarantees:

a)  that the appliance is double insulated and does not require an earth wire (as in hair-driers, portable TV sets, etc. which are plastic covered. Plastic is an electrical insulator.);

b)  that a specimen of the appliance has passed the tests set by the British Standards Institution for electrical safety (BEAB—British Electro-technical Approvals Board).

*The double insulated symbol (BSI) and the mark of safety (BEAB)*

## THE TELEPHONE

The telephone operates in isolation from the household electrical supply, power being supplied in separate circuits by British Telecom. Power was always carried by overhead wires supported by telegraph poles but it is now becoming more usual for them to be buried underground.

### Charges

Installation costs have to be met by the consumer but most repairs are carried out free of charge. A quarterly rental is charged and to this is added the cost of the calls made. These are monitored on a computer and the cost varies according to the distance over which the calls are made. The small letters shown beside the Code Number in the booklet supplied indicate the rate at which the call is charged: x pence per y number of seconds. Local calls are charged at a standard rate.

At present, calls made after 1 p.m. are charged at a lower rate than those made during peak morning periods, and after 6 o'clock in the evening the charge is lower still. At weekends the cheap rate operates all day.

If calls have to be made through the operator (i.e. if STD is not possible) the cost of the call will be notified immediately if a previous arrangement has been made with the operator (ADC). Person-to-person calls may only be charged for if the designated person is contacted.

### Instruments

The designs of the actual telephones are becoming more attractive and there is a choice of several colours. Instruments may be free-standing or wall-mounted as convenient.

The normal ringing tone can be modified to a buzz or a trill; for partially deaf users an amplified bell or hooter may be substituted and for the completely deaf a flashing neon bulb may be used. Extension bells may be installed so that calls may be heard in remote rooms or in the garden.

Extra-long flexes can be attached (by the technician) to allow instruments to be carried from room to room; inlet sockets may be fixed so that the instrument may be plugged into different parts of the house as required.

For those who are not able or do not wish to have their own telephones, public call boxes are installed at occasional distances in the countryside and at much shorter intervals in built-up areas. Calls are normally 'bought' by inserting coins into the box, but long-distance calls can be made, by special arrangement, with the charges reversed (the operator asks for the consent of the receiver).

H

## Services Offered

Normal dialled or operator-serviced calls—local, national, international
Directory enquiries
Time checks ('Speaking Clock')
Alarm calls at specified times
Reversed-charge calls
Tele-messages (replacing the former Telegrams)
Weather reports
Road condition reports
Business/financial news
Cricket scores
Recipes
Stories, etc.

SAFETY STEPS
1 It is a good idea to learn how to dial 999 without looking at the instrument, in case you need to do so in the dark in the case of emergency. (Learn the positions of the digits of your doctor's number, too.)
2 If you live alone, it may be reassuring to you to have an extension telephone beside your bed in case you are taken ill; alternatively, a long flex may enable you to carry the main instrument through to your room.

## WATER

As you travel about the country you will find, besides lakes and rivers, large stretches of water known as reservoirs. These are man-made lakes which augment the natural resources which are used to make our domestic water available. Sometimes, pumping stations are employed to raise the water in underground reservoirs (fed by rainwater) to the surface (see Figure 11.11).

Water is carried by large underground pipes to local 'water works' where it is tested for purity and made fit to drink—some premises receive two qualities of water, one for general purposes, one for drinking.

### Hard and Soft Water

We have already mentioned hard and soft water (see Chapter 9) and the reason for different areas receiving different types of water now becomes apparent. Rainwater is very soft water but as it soaks through the earth and underground rocks it absorbs salts (calcium bicarbonate, calcium and magnesium sulphates). This water then collects in reservoirs or underground lakes from where it is pumped to a water station and piped

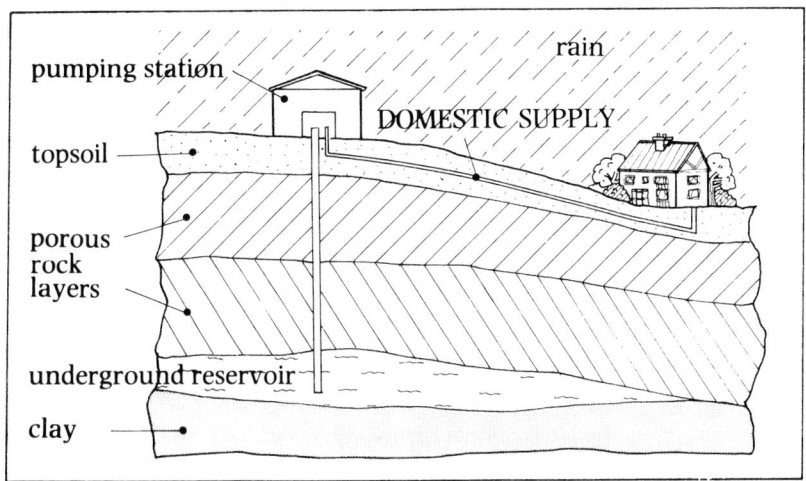

*Figure 11.11 Supplying water from an underground reservoir to our homes*

to our homes (see above). The greater proportion of water supplied to homes in the United Kingdom is, in fact, hard water. (The areas in which soft water supplies are found are mainly in Scotland, Wales, Ireland and, in England, the Lake District.)

The amount and type of salts which are absorbed by the water depends on the nature of the rocks in the area in which the rain falls. The rocks in one area might be granite, in another limestone or chalk. The amount of salts is measured in parts per million (ppm) and this gives an indication of the hardness of the water, e.g. very soft water has 0–55 ppm while very hard water has 450–500 ppm.

DRINKING WATER

Most people find that hard water is more palatable than soft water and for this reason it is used in the manufacture of beers and mineral waters. It is also beneficial for the growth and maintenance of healthy bones and teeth (see page 128).

SOFTENING HARD WATER

1 Heating alone softens hard water to a certain degree. When heated above 60° C (140° F), water which is hardened by calcium bicarbonate salts deposits a white powdery 'chalk' (calcium carbonate) on the inside of its container. This can easily be seen on the electric kettle element or the inside of an ordinary kettle. It can be a nuisance, particularly in the pipes of non-independent central heating systems, where its presence can completely block the flow of water (a section of heating pipe removed from an old building has been observed where even the finest of needles could not be passed through the rock-hard deposit). In most areas the water remains hard (permanent hardness) even at this elevated temperature, so that it will not lather easily.

2 Hard water can be softened after it has entered the house by installing a water softener in the pipeline. This device contains a harmless chemical (sodium carbonate) which must be renewed at regular intervals (this is the same substance as is used in bath crystals). Usually the tap in the kitchen is not connected to the water softener.

3 The alternative and most common way of coping with hard water supply is to add detergents or bath salts to the water used for washing clothes/dishes or for bathing. The problem caused by the 'fur' formed in domestic boilers and hot water pipes is overcome by the installation of an 'indirect heating system' (see page 44) and by restricting the temperature of domestic hot water to 60° C (140° F) by means of a thermostatic control.

## The Main Supply

Until the water enters your premises the responsibility for the efficiency of the water supply belongs to the Water Board Authority. A valve (known as the 'stop-cock') isolates the main water supply from your domestic supply, situated as close to the inside of the house/garden bounds as possible and at least 750 mm. (2′ 6″) below the ground. It is usually protected with a hinged, cast-iron cover. (Make sure that you know where this is and you are able to turn it off—use a purpose-made tool or a piece of wood 50 mm. × 25 mm. (2″ × 1″) with a V-shaped cut in the end.) From here a service pipe (usually known as the *rising main*) enters the premises through a floor close to the sink. There should be a further stop-valve in this pipe so that the water flow can be halted from inside the house (particularly useful in bad weather when a pipe has burst). A drain-cock is attached (see Figure 11.12) so that the pipes can be emptied.

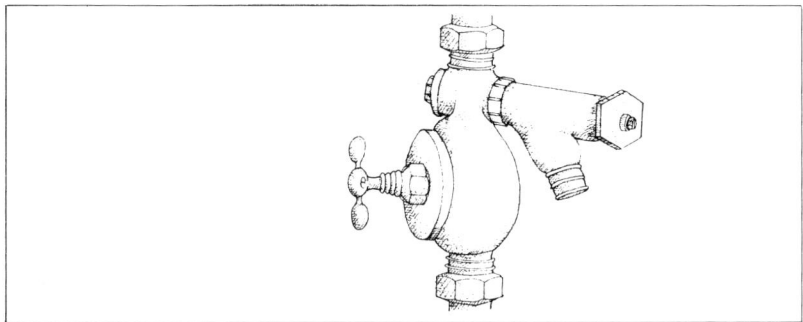

*Figure 11.12 A stop-valve (left) and a drain-cock*

## The Internal Supply

There are two ways in which water may be distributed:
1 By direct supply—the main pipe feeds all taps, cisterns and some types of water heater.

2 By indirect supply—the main pipe feeds one tap at the kitchen sink and a tank of 50 gallons minimum capacity which in turn feeds through two pipes:

a) the hot-water cylinder;

b) lavatory cisterns, basins and bath.

When moving into new premises make sure that you understand the supply system. Identify and label all the stop-valves so that the correct one can be turned off in case of emergency.

## Equipment

If you intend to have any *new* facilities installed which depend on the water supply, e.g. a shower or an extra lavatory, you must notify the water authority at least a week in advance. This does not apply to the repair of existing equipment and a competent plumber (preferably a member of the Institute of Plumbing) will advise you about the local by-laws relating to repairs and installations.

If work is carried out without the required approval, the local water authority can insist on appliances being removed at the householder's expense.

## Emergencies

1 Except in the circumstances of extreme drought (not frequent) the use of water is rarely restricted and our chief difficulties are experienced during very cold weather, when unlagged pipes and cisterns can freeze. This danger can be alleviated when severe frosts are forecast by:

a) lagging all water pipes in the loft and any exposed outside pipes;

b) checking that the stop-cock is working easily;

c) sprinkling cooking salt over the stop-cock to prevent it from icing-up;

d) putting in all waste outlet plugs (bath, basins, sinks);

e) making sure that there are no dripping taps;

f) checking that ball-valves in cisterns are working efficiently so that overflow leaks do not freeze and block the pipe;

g) emptying any outside lavatory cisterns and tying up the ball-valve;

h) keeping the inside temperature above freezing point (usually one centrally placed small heater will be sufficient);

i) draining the systems (cold and hot) if the house is to be left unoccupied (remember to switch off the heating system and leave a note near the switch to remind yourself that the water must be fully circulating before it is switched on again).

2 A pipe bursts because frozen water has a greater capacity than liquid water (remember milk bottles with the caps lifted as the milk freezes!) and, in expanding, cracks the pipe. So long as the water remains frozen there is no indication of trouble, but once it begins to thaw leaks become apparent. When this happens:

a) Turn off the main stop-cock at once and drain all the water in the pipes from the taps.
b) Send for a plumber.
c) While waiting, tie up the ball-valves of cisterns.

## Minor Repairs

DRIPPING OVERFLOW PIPE
This is usually due to the ball-valve of the cistern becoming jammed or faulty; or a hole in the ball-float.
1 Cut off the water flow by lifting the ball-valve arm and tying it to a stick placed across the tank.
2 Replace the ball-valve washer.
3 Bend the ball-float arm slightly. If the ball does not float it may be punctured in which case a new ball must be fitted.
   If in doubt, consult a plumber.

CLEARING AIR-LOCKS
1 A knocking noise when the tap is turned on or an interrupted flow from a hot water tap usually means that there is an air-lock; this usually happens when some plumbing work has been carried out and the main water supply has been temporarily cut off. The pressure of the main supply will usually correct this—attach a short length of hose between the cold and hot water taps in the kitchen, turn on the hot water taps in the bathroom and then both taps in the kitchen. If this is unsuccessful, call a plumber.
2 An air-lock in the central heating water supply may result in a radiator remaining cold all over or in parts. In this case it is necessary to 'bleed' the radiator, causing the flow of hot water to push out the unwanted air.
a) Fit the tap (square bored, usually) which is supplied with the radiator to the valve at the top of the panel.
b) Hold a bucket or bowl underneath the valve and, very gently, turn the tap until a slight hissing sound is heard.
c) Continue turning *very* slowly until the hissing stops and water begins to seep.
d) Close the valve immediately.

## SEWAGE DISPOSAL

This service is very closely associated with the provision of water and is normally charged for on the same bill as the water rate.

## Soil Pipe System

Pipes which carry human excreta from lavatories to the public sewer are called soil pipes. Waste, flushed down with clean water from the

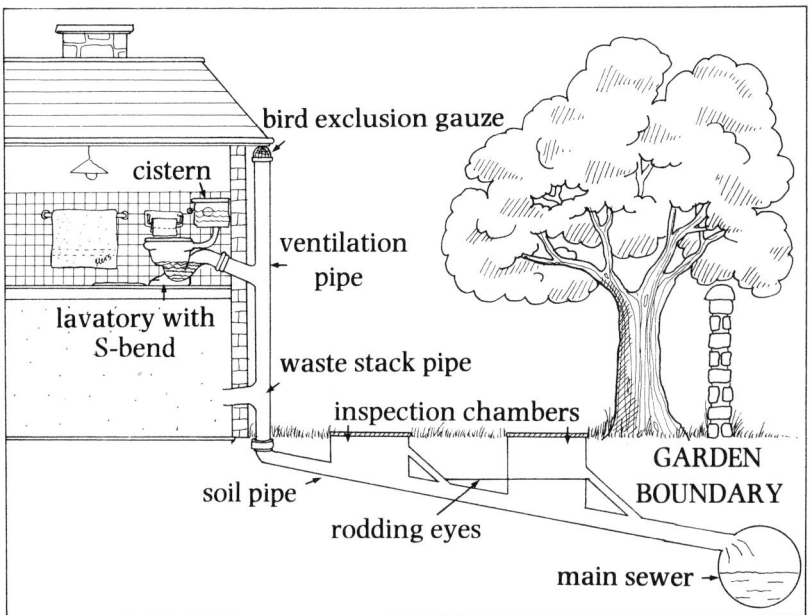

*Figure 11.13  A soil pipe system*

cistern, is carried from the lavatory into a stack pipe connected to the soil pipe. The upper end of the stack pipe is ventilated at roof level, the lower end disappears at ground level (see Figure 11.13). The ventilator pipe, together with the S-bend at the lavatory pan, prevents smells from entering the house. Two inspection chambers with cast-iron covers are usually provided—one adjacent to the house and the other near a boundary wall. These inspection chambers have 'rodding eyes' through which clearing rods may be inserted to dislodge any blockage in the drain which may occur. The soil pipe drains into the main sewer which runs under the roadway and this is connected to the sewage works.

## Cesspool Drainage

Very few premises nowadays are not connected with main drainage but some remote areas still rely on cesspools or septic tanks or soak-aways for the disposal of their sewage. In most cases, these are large chambers, sometimes bricked, into which sewage refuse is drained and which have to be emptied at intervals. Generally, there is no unpleasant smell present except, perhaps, while the chamber is being emptied, and from inside the premises no difference from main drainage is apparent. The council is responsible for emptying the tank, either regularly or by appointment, and this is done by inserting a large suction pipe into the top of the chamber and sucking the contents in a sealed tanker.

## Earth Closets

These are very rare nowadays except in very remote areas. A bucket with a seat fixed over it serves as a lavatory and after each use a quantity of soil (mixed with or augmented by a disinfectant powder if desired) is sprinkled into it. At frequent intervals the bucket is emptied, either by the owner into a 'compost' pit well away from the dwelling or, very seldom nowadays, by the local authority 'night-soil' operators who collect from a community and make a communal 'tip'. The bacterial activity of soil breaks down the waste matter and reduces the bulk (and the smell) into valuable compost.

## Chemical Toilets (e.g. 'Elsan')

The portable type of chemical lavatory is well-known to campers and caravanners. A chemical liquid is added to the container which cancels sewage odours and breaks down the contents. These drop into the body of the container which is almost completely separated from the top 'pan'; the contents are regularly deposited in a purpose-dug trench or pit and are eventually decomposed by bacterial activity.

## WASTE WATER DISPOSAL

Water from sinks, wash basins and baths is carried by waste pipes which are also connected to the stack pipe, assisting in the dispersal of solid sewage and joining the main sewer. Surface water from roofs and roads may be:
a) drained via the soil pipes into the main sewer;
b) carried away by a separate drainage system ('storm water' pipes) to discharge into rivers;
c) carried into soak-aways adjacent to the house and allowed to soak into the ground (usually only where the soil is permeable, well-drained and at high level).

## DRY REFUSE DISPOSAL

Kitchen hygiene is dealt with elsewhere in this book (see page 234) and this is augmented by the council's responsibility to collect and dispose of our refuse regularly. This service, like road-sweeping, verge cutting and personal services such as education, fire and police services, is paid for through the rates.

## Dustbins

The provision of dustbins or their equivalents is the responsibility of the local authority, as is their emptying. It is the householder's responsibility:

a) to use them as efficiently and hygienically as possible (see below);
b) to make refuse containers accessible for emptying or collection.

TYPES
1 Galvanized iron—becoming less general in use; noisy.
2 Rubber/plastic—less noisy, lighter but cannot be used for hot ashes.
3 Plastic/paper sacks—these may be placed inside loose-based bins *or* suspended from lidded metal rings at waist height (if the latter, a wire 'cage' is advised, to be fixed to the ring and surround the bag so that stray cats and dogs cannot scratch at the contents). These are light and hygienic but paper bags cannot be used for damp rubbish and neither paper nor plastic ones for hot ashes.
    All 3 types must have well-fitting lids.

USE
1 Unless lined with a paper or plastic sack which will be collected, the bottom of the bin should be lined with clean newspaper. A sprinkling of specially produced dustbin powder will prevent bad smells from arising.
2 Wrap all rottable refuse, such as peelings, meat scraps, stale food of any kind, before placing in the bin. Empty tins and packets make good receptacles for vegetable peelings and other scraps.
3 Allow hot ashes to cool before placing in the bin, whatever its nature.
4 Wrap broken glass, crockery and discarded razor blades very well, or place in boxes or tins before placing them in the bin.
5 Wrap soiled dressings of any kind before placing in the bin if they cannot be burned.
6 Keep the lid firmly in place.
7 Stack newspapers or magazines separately, tied into bundles.
8 *Never* put unwanted medicines or tablets into the bin—empty the bottles before discarding them; burn tablets before throwing away the containers, or flush them down the lavatory.
9 Do not place garden refuse, masonry rubbish or old car batteries in the bin—take them to the appropriate skip at the local tip.
10 Ask the council refuse collectors to call specially if you have large quantities of rubbish to dispose of, e.g. if you are moving house. A polite telephone call and an appreciative tip, if you wish, will procure you good service.

### Refuse Lorries

These tour every street to collect household rubbish. Bins are emptied or bags collected and thrown into the interior, where they are crushed and 'minced' by means of hydraulic equipment.

### Methods of Disposal

These vary from district to district, but invariably one of the following methods is used:

J

a) incineration—this is effective but expensive;
b) tipping—the cheapest, most widely used method but there are some health hazards;
c) tipping at sea—coastal towns sometimes use this method but it is not encouraged owing to the cumulative pollution effects.

RE-CYCLING
In this country alone we throw 18 million tons of rubbish a year into our dustbins, costing the country, at present, a staggering £500 million annually for collection. Local authorities are fast running out of sites to dump the mass of rubbish that the householder throws away and more coastal based councils are resorting to tipping at sea. Some authorities have started schemes to recover and re-use waste products, e.g. Bottle Banks, newsprint pulping. By throwing away much of our 'waste' we create the necessity for importing replacements, so increasing the price.

## THE POST OFFICE (See also The Telephone)

The service of delivering and collecting letters and parcels is one with which we have become so familiar that we take it for granted. This is only a very small part of the wide range of services offered by the Post Office, however, and the following is a list of additional activities connected with the work of this establishment:
Sale of postage stamps, stamped envelopes, air-letters
Provision of application forms for:
licences for TV, dogs, shooting, dealing with or keeping game, holding a firearm, driving a car, etc.; renewal of vehicle licence; British Passport; British Visitor's Pass
Sale of stamps other than postage:
National Insurance; contracts; legal forms
Sale of money orders, National Savings Certificates, Premium Bonds
SAYE (Save As You Earn) service
National Savings Bank
Cheap banking account and money-transfer service (Giro)
Distribution of:
retirement and widows' pensions; sickness and invalidity benefit; supplementary pension; refunds on National Health prescriptions; child benefit
Sale of Thomas Cook Travellers' Cheques
Registration and insurance of letters, parcels
Messenger service
Poste-restante service
Delivery of tele-messages
Free postal service for:
blind people (item must be marked 'Article for the Blind'); petitions to the Queen; letters to Parliament via an MP

Provision for inspection of:
the electoral roll; Post Office Guide; list of useful addresses (e.g. CAB); classified telephone directories

## SPECIAL SERVICES

Local authorities offer 3 main categories of special services apart from those mentioned on pages 2, 226–30.

### Protective Services

These include assistance to the public by the police, the ambulance service, the fire brigade and the coastguard (each summoned by dialling 999). Most local authorities co-operate with each other in providing these services, so that in the case of emergency there is additional help to call on.

Consumer protection is also provided by local authorities; although the offices are often manned by volunteers, the council will pay the rent and rates of the premises. Free advice is given in confidence on personal matters of all kinds—the law, jobs, shopping, etc.

### Personal Services

These facilities are provided to keep the quality of life at an acceptable level; they include museums, libraries, schools, street lighting, bus services, airports, homes for children and the elderly (see pages 100–101).

### Environmental Health

This service ensures that the environment in which we live is healthy and safe and includes the maintenance of the refuse disposal, drainage and sewage services already mentioned. The standards of hygiene practised in abattoirs, restaurants, cafés, hotels and shops are supervised; the provision and maintenance of parks, gardens, roadside planting and grass verges are also responsibilities of this department of the council.

_____ **FURTHER STUDY** _____

### Things to Do

1   Find out the connection between coal, oil and natural gas.
2   Look at any excavations being made in the roads in your district and try to identify which service is being repaired or installed.

3 Find out the cost of a telephone call *both* during a normal day *and* during the weekend to:
 a) any city you choose in Scotland or England;
 b) any town you know in Wales;
 c) Adelaide, Australia;
 d) Paris, France;
 e) Washington, USA.
4 Trace the history of the postal service, identifying the part played by Sir Rowland Hill.
5 Find as many stamps as you can which reflect historical events. Discover the date of each event.
6 Find out the real meaning of 'pylon' and the significance of the letters STD.
7 Pour 250 ml. ($\frac{1}{2}$ pt.) of good quality soapless washing-up liquid into a measuring jug. Take 4 tall glasses of exactly the same size and pour into each one 125 ml. ($\frac{1}{4}$ pt.) of one of the following:
 a) cold tap water;
 b) hot tap water;
 c) cold distilled water; ⎱
 d) hot distilled water; ⎰ or rain water.
Add the liquid detergent a little at a time, shaking the glass as vigorously as possible, until $2\frac{1}{2}$ cm. (1″) of lather forms on the top of the water. Compare the amounts of detergent required in each case to make a lather.
 Repeat the demonstration using liquid soap instead of washing-up liquid.
8 Find out the difference between temporary and permanent hardness of water.

## Questions to Answer

1 Write out and complete each of the following statements with the correct term chosen from the list in the right-hand column.

| | | |
|---|---|---|
| a) Some of the newer electrical wiring systems incorporate ——————— instead of fuses. | butane |
| b) The consumption of electricity is measured by a meter which registers the number of ——————— which have been used. | generator |
| c) The force with which electricity is pushed through wires is measured in ———————. | magnesium sulphate |
| d) The amount of electricity which passes into an appliance is measured in ———————. | hydro-electric |
| e) A piece of machinery which rotates a wire coil between two magnets is called a ———————. | sodium carbonate |

**f)** Gas which is produced from under the sea and known as 'natural' gas consists mainly of _____ .

circuit breakers

**g)** The gas which is liquified under pressure and stored in 'bottles' ready for use is _____ .

kilowatt hours

**h)** Hard water contains dissolved salts, mainly calcium bicarbonate, calcium sulphate and _____ according to the area from which it comes.

volts

**i)** Commercial water softeners contain _____ which is the same chemical as that used in bath salts.

methane

**j)** Because there are many waterfalls in Scotland to provide power, electricity is mainly supplied by a _____ system.

amperes

**2** What do you understand by 're-cycling'? Give some examples. What arguments can you make to recommend it *or* to discourage it?

**3** The postal service and the telephone are our main means of communication today. How did people receive news of each other before the Post Office came into being?

**4** Which of the two modern methods of communication between two people mentioned above do you consider to be the more satisfactory? Give your reasons.

# Healthy Living 12

The preceding chapters have focused on different aspects of the mechanics of living and have touched only lightly on the fact that life (hopefully) lasts for a long time and should be *enjoyed*. Much attention has been given to the material possessions which we need and desire, but at the end of the day the most important priority is good health. Without this, money is useless and, although good treatment can be purchased, good health cannot be bought. The quality of life is very significant and we need to set ourselves good standards in order to enhance it, but the most salient factor of all is the well-being to make the most of it.

The original word to describe health is 'whole' and the Greeks coined a phrase 'a healthy mind in a healthy body'—a *whole* person in our present use of the word, meaning complete. Permanent peace of mind is too much to expect in the modern world of strain, stress and problem areas but at least within the home there can be an attempt to keep a positive standard of tolerance, optimism, security and relaxation. Emotions must have outlets, of course, and, indeed, modern medicine appears to subscribe to the theory that pent-up unexpressed reactions may cause much otherwise inexplicable illness; but anger, resentment, excitement and frustration *can* be talked about, understood, respected and kept within acceptable bounds.

Serious illness and deplorable results of accidents cannot always be avoided but attitudes of mind can be developed to cope with them without despair, and at least we can take some measures to ensure that unnecessary ailments are avoided.

1 Make sure that you have protected yourself and anyone dependent upon you from whooping cough, etc. by taking advantage of immunization and inoculation provided by the Health Service.

2 Practise good hygiene, for yourself and for those around you.

## HYGIENE

### In the Kitchen

1 Bacteria live around us, in the water we drink, the air we breathe, the soil we walk upon and in our bodies, and, fortunately, they are not all harmful (e.g. those which convert lactose—milk sugar—into lactic

acid during the manufacture of cheese). However, there are a number which have undesirable effects and the most common ones are transmitted as shown below; many are carried on our hands in the ways indicated, and so to the food which we prepare with them. The conclusion is obvious:

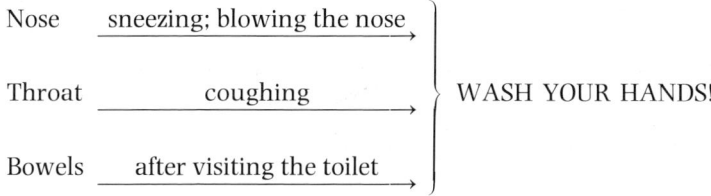

2 Cuts and sore places on your hands may also carry harmful bacteria, so cover them with waterproof dressings.

3 Your hair is exposed constantly to the air and cannot be washed as often as your hands; some dead hair will become loose and fall out, so if your hair is long, tie it back while you are preparing food.

4 Pets may bring all sorts of contamination in from outside, even if they never leave the garden, so always wash your hands after dealing with them. As far as possible, keep your pets out of the kitchen.

5 Wash up in hot, soapy water so that plates, cups, glasses and cutlery are really clean when next used. Avoid using cracked crockery (germs lurk in the stale traces of food which you cannot prevent from collecting in the cracks) and be particularly careful to wash between the prongs of forks.

6 Use clean tea-towels as often as possible (preferably every day). Do not dry off used ones over a radiator—bacteria love warm wet conditions.

7 Use a clean hand-towel or fresh paper towel to dry your hands on, *not* a tea-towel.

8 Wear a clean apron so that dust from your clothing does not fall into the food you are preparing.

9 Do not smoke while you are cooking—ash is not poisonous but it is not a desirable ingredient of any dish!

10 Remove food scraps as soon as possible after they are rejected so that flies are not attracted (see page 236). They do not necessarily have to be thrown away—they may be placed in the refrigerator or larder, put out for the birds or merely covered over. (If put in the garden, spread them on a high bird-table if possible; if they have to be thrown on to the lawn or soil, avoid doing so at night, otherwise stray animals and unwanted vermin may be attracted.) If they *are* thrown away, wrap them first.

FOOD POISONING
The effect of harmful bacteria ingested with food may manifest itself in anything from a mild stomach ache to a fatal combination of several distressing symptoms. The most common causes are:

a) salmonella—usually resulting from bacterial contamination from human or animal excreta;

b) staphylococci infection—often originating in prepared food products.

*Salmonella*

This causes infectious bowel disease, in varying degrees of severity; in extreme cases it can be fatal. Animals can be affected by the organism and indirectly transmit the infection through meat, milk and eggs. There is a particular hazard in using frozen poultry when it is only partially thawed, or in eating it before it is completely cooked. There is no danger if meat is well cooked through, as salmonella bacteria are destroyed by high temperatures.

*Staphylococci*

This type of bacteria is present in the throat, the mouth, the nose and in superficial injuries. It only becomes harmful if kept warm for several hours, so the most reliable ways of preventing infection are:

a) to cook food as soon as it is prepared;

b) to cool food rapidly if it is not to be eaten immediately and refrigerate it until required;

c) to reheat (réchauffer) cooked foods thoroughly and once only.

The symptoms of staphylococci infection are less severe than those of salmonella but still include distressing pain, sickness, dizziness and weakness.

Remember that bacteria are destroyed by high temperatures but only retarded by low ones, so:

1 Do not re-freeze deep frozen foods once they have been thawed.

2 Do not partly cook any food.

3 Observe the 'Sell By' dates on packaged goods and do not take any risks.

Fortunately, much deterioration of food is indicated by the obnoxious smell it produces as the bacteria break it down and release unpleasant gases. *Never* use food which does smell bad, or is discoloured.

Tinned food occasionally deteriorates with the same results and the gases given off cause the can to bulge. Look carefully when buying 'reduced for quick sale' items to check that the tins are not 'blown'. If in doubt about the wholesomeness of any food, destroy it rather than put the health of the family at risk. If you buy food which you suspect is not safe for eating when you get it home, take it to your Environmental Health Officer at once—you may well save other people from an unpleasant experience.

PESTS

Food left uncovered, either in the kitchen or in a bin, is vulnerable to the attention of flies and cockroaches, neither of which is desirable.

*Flies*

Think of a rotting compost heap or of a pile of manure on a hot day and consider where the flies have been which are hovering over your table! Flies have some very unpleasant habits, including discharging their excreta and vomit wherever they may land; food may well become a carrier of some of the diseases present in their deposits.

Unless you keep every door and window shut it is impossible to keep flies out, but at least they can be discouraged. Besides the precautions already described, fly deterrents (aerosol sprays, etc.) may be used, but the instructions should be read carefully before use.

*Cockroaches*

These are the large black beetles which emerge at night and are almost a hallmark of unhygienic premises. They seek food but will also eat fabric and paper; like flies they spread bacteria from their bodies and infect food with their excreta. They can also be dealt with by using an aerosol insecticide—read the can to make sure that it is effective against cockroaches and follow the instructions carefully.

Any severe infestation of pests inside the premises or outside in the garden can be referred to the Environmental Health Officer. 'Super' strains of fleas, flies and rats have already been identified, immune from what, until recently, has been effective treatment, and special procedures may be required.

## In the Living Room

1 Keep the room well ventilated as well as warm. Fresh air is always a good counter-agent to infection.
2 Do not leave handkerchiefs lying about.
3 Observe the general rules of cleaning.
4 Cover dishes of sweets or fruit when not actually being offered (to dissuade the attentions of flies).

## In the Bedroom

1 Keep the room well ventilated.
2 Place soiled clothing in a dirty-linen box or basket while awaiting laundering.
3 Never put dirty clothing away in drawers.
4 Brush outer garments before storing.
5 Clean mud and stains off shoes before putting them into the wardrobe or cupboard.
6 Observe the general rules of cleaning.

## In the Bathroom

1 Keep the bath, basin and toilet clean, giving *daily* attention.
2 Hang up damp towels as soon as they are used. Launder frequently.

3  Spread face flannels out so that they dry. Launder frequently.
4  Keep 'sponges' cleaned regularly—dry by draining after use.
5  Keep toothbrushes clean and drained in a special rack. Never use someone else's toothbrush.
6  Flush disinfectant down the lavatory pan regularly or hang a solid block over the rim or in the cistern.
7  Keep the lavatory seat clean—wipe over daily with cloth wrung out in hot, disinfected water. Keep a special towel (laundered frequently) beside the pan for individual users to wipe over the seat with.
8  Make sure that there is always a reserve pack or roll of toilet tissue at hand.
9  Keep a roll or pack of paper towelling at hand for use in case of necessity or for visitors.
10  Provide a waste-bin (preferably not a basket) for everyday use. Empty daily or as necessary.
11  Keep the room well ventilated but not cold.
12  Observe the general rules for cleaning.
   ●  In the event of a situation calling for intensive home nursing (see Chapter 10) make the hygiene of the bathroom a high priority, equal only to that of the kitchen. The remaining rooms can wait until the emergency is over.

## Outside

1  Keep drains clean and disinfect them weekly.
2  Keep paths and passages swept.
3  Collect any blown-about rubbish and place it in the dustbin.
4  Wash any injuries (grazes, cuts) incurred out-of-doors with warm water containing antiseptic and cover with an aerated dressing.

## LOOKING GOOD AND FEELING GOOD

Most of us *look* a great deal better when we *feel* good, and vice versa, but good looks should not be regarded as limited to 'Miss World' or 'Mr Universe' attributes. The sheer beauty of a healthy body, well-cared-for skin and hair and an obvious *joie de vivre* is not to be underestimated; there is absolutely no substitute.

## Your Figure

An attractive figure is of little value if there is no vitality to animate it, just as beautiful make-up is no lasting alternative to the glow of health.
   Eating habits have already been discussed (Chapter 6) but it is worthwhile remembering that between one-third and one-half of the population of Britain is overweight; obesity in schoolchildren is a deplorable but unfortunately all too common sight. The current habit

of travelling everywhere by car instead of walking; of sitting and watching television instead of *doing* things; of automatically equating entertainment with eating, e.g. eating sweets while watching a film; of 'keeping them quiet' by providing endless supplies of crisps, chocolates, etc., all contribute to this situation. Being overweight is a condition to be avoided because not only is it aesthetically unpleasing, but it can lead to:

disorders of the heart;
respiratory problems;
strain on joints and ligaments;
possibly diabetes.

However, it is equally undesirable to be too thin. An obsessional desire to be ultra-slim can lead to a psychological disturbance called anorexia nervosa. Taken to extremes this can be fatal, and even in moderate stages it causes much distress to the subject and anxiety to her/his family and associates.

The following lists will help you to sort out the amount of food which you can and should consume to stay fit and free from flab.

Eat generous amounts of:

| | |
|---|---|
| Chicken | Root vegetables |
| White fish | Green vegetables |
| Eggs | Salads |
| Cottage cheese | Fresh fruit |
| Milk (dried, skimmed milk is low in fat and high in protein) | Yoghurt |

Eat moderate amounts of:

| | |
|---|---|
| Red meat, lamb | Potatoes |
| Ham | Pasta |
| Bacon (grilled) | Rice |
| Smoked fish | Margarine (low calorie) |
| Bread | Tinned fruit in natural juice |

Avoid (generally—an *occasional* 'treat' is allowed)

| | |
|---|---|
| Sugar | Cakes |
| Chocolate | Biscuits |
| Sweets | Fried foods |
| Butter | Crisps |
| Margarine | Dried fruit |
| Fizzy drinks | Tinned fruit in syrup |

The figure which you would like and that which Nature intended for you may not be the same—as always, a compromise can be the answer. Nature endows you with your skeletal frame, your metabolic rate (i.e. the efficiency with which the chemical reactions of your system change food into living matter with the release of energy) and your appetite. Everybody's metabolism is slightly different from everyone else's and, whereas some people can eat very fattening foods and gain no weight, others have to control their food intake extremely carefully. Generally, putting it very simply, the intake of food is like the investment of money—if you put a great deal in and do not use much up you will gain considerably. But money and superfluous tissue are not equally desirable—the 'profit' of over-eating is unwanted fat, only dissipated by 'spending' it, in this case, on physical activity. Moreover, your requirements vary with your age, your occupation and whether you are male or female.

You need to find for yourself the most favourable level of eating and exercise which allows you to maintain a weight which pleases you and is becoming to you. 'Crash diets' can be dangerous and are usually effective only on a short-term basis. It is much more sensible to eat smaller quantities of all the foods your body requires and discipline yourself to a programme of exercise which keeps your muscles firm, your posture good and your vitality high, all of which will help your figure to remain trim and well proportioned. 'Exercise' *does* include activities you can enjoy, such as swimming, dancing and yoga.

## Your Skin

Your skin is the protective layer which covers your entire body—it is flexible, waterproof and porous, and its nature varies from part to part of your body, e.g. the skin on your inner wrist is much more sensitive than that on the soles of your feet. Overall, it has to stand up to a great deal of wear and tear—pressure which bruises it, friction which chafes it, heat which scorches it and cold which chaps it are normal hazards. At the same time it regulates our body temperature by excreting perspiration, wards off infection by producing acid secretion (this can be broken down by detergents, which results in an allergy) and is continually renewing itself. (You will see some of the dead skin particles which are constantly shed if you turn your dark socks or tights inside out as you take them off.)

*Figure 12.1  Hair follicles in the skin*

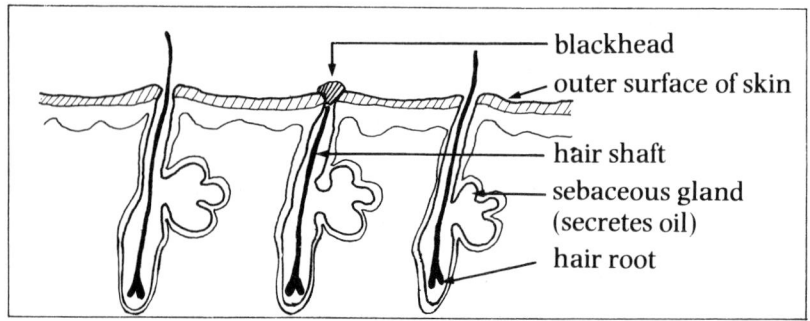

blackhead
outer surface of skin
hair shaft
sebaceous gland
(secretes oil)
hair root

Most people who refer to their 'skin' are talking about that on their faces. Facial skin is always exposed and is rather different in structure from that on the rest of the body. It contains many tiny hair follicles, sweat glands and oil glands, making it more 'open' than body skin and so easier to moisturize, but at the same time presenting many more problems in caring for it.

## SKIN TYPES
### Dry
As you grow older your skin naturally tends to become drier, and requires a moisturizer at the beginning and end of the day. There is no need to purchase expensive cosmetics—baby lotion or a thin film of petroleum jelly will suffice. Young men with dry skin will know the tender feeling of their faces after shaving; the use of a shaving cream which contains a moisturizer and a baby powder which is patted on afterwards will help to alleviate this.

*Diet* should include oily fish, dairy foods, liver, fresh vegetables and fruit, plenty of fluid. (Dry skin requires good supplies of vitamin A.)

### Oily
An oily skin is a problem shared by boys and girls alike, particularly during their teens; those with dark hair and olive complexions seem to suffer most. The skin needs to be kept very clean, using a mild soap and warm water 3 times a day. The suds should be completely rinsed away afterwards. A moisturizer used in the morning and at night (a medicated one if necessary) will help, and boys will find that an alcohol-based after-shave lotion will reduce the oiliness of the skin.

*Diet* should include plenty of high protein foods, fresh fruit and vegetables and plenty of fluids, but exclude fatty foods.

### Normal
So-called 'normality' means that the skin type is a combination of dry and oily characteristics, dry on the cheeks, slightly oily on the forehead, nose and chin. A mild soap can be used, well rinsed off and followed with a moisturizer night and morning.

*Diet* should be generally well-balanced, containing a minimum of fatty foods and plenty of fresh fruit, vegetables and fluids.

● Note that hygiene is important to every type of skin. Face flannels should be kept separately from others, towels should be clean and powder puffs should be changed often (they can be washed!).

## ACNE
This skin condition is at once the most common and the most distressing of all teenagers' problems. Ironically, cleanliness and spots, and lack of cleanliness and lack of spots *can* go together. The term 'acne' covers a wide range of degrees of severity, from scattered spots and pimples to serious disfigurement with pustules and boils.

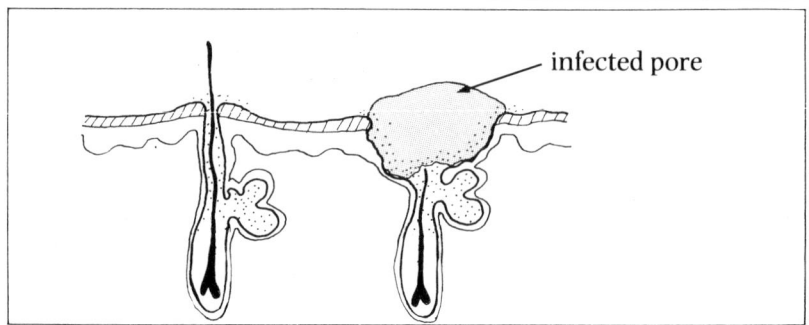

*Figure 12.2 The formation of a pustule*

It is caused by a disorder of the sex glands set up by the rapid production of sex hormones during puberty. Some of these hormones speed up the production of body secretions, causing a general imbalance; this in turn stimulates other glands to secrete superfluous oil and it is this excess which is the base of the trouble. The surface of the skin becomes excessively greasy and this lowers the efficiency of the acid layer, allowing bacteria settling on the skin to be absorbed. The pores of the skin become blocked with dead skin cells and a blackhead is formed. If infection develops, pus forms and the characteristic yellowish 'head' becomes apparent (see Figure 12.2).

Severe cases of acne require medical attention and any boy or girl distressed by the condition should consult a doctor for advice. Normally the occasional spot or pimple will respond to good hygiene (*not* squeezing, which only forces the infection into the surrounding tissues), a minimum of fat in the diet, and time—you *do* grow out of it!

Although body skin is different from facial skin, it does need attention. After bathing or showering, rub a little oil over your body, particularly into elbows, knees and feet, to replace the natural oils lost in the water and make the skin soft and supple. (This prevents cracks, pads of hard skin and discoloration.)

Special care must be given to the armpits, where perspiration takes place more freely than anywhere else. If perspiration cannot dry easily it gives off an unpleasant smell (BO—body odour) which does little to make you 'nice to know'. The amount of perspiration secreted varies from person to person but everyone needs to practise daily washing and use of a deodorant. An anti-perspirant may become necessary in some cases—this closes the pores but it is debatable whether or not this is advisable.

Other areas of the body also need daily bathing, particularly for girls. Body secretions which dry on to clothing give off very distasteful odours which can usually be completely avoided by good hygiene and by changing underclothes every day. Expensive 'feminine' toilet preparations are not essential—soap and water is all that is required.

## Your Hair

The state of your hair reflects that of your general health. The colour, texture and curl of your hair is determined by your own heredity and you cannot do a great deal about changing it. However, you can always keep it looking as attractive as possible and the easiest way is to brush it for about 3 minutes a day, providing it is not naturally greasy. Always brush it thoroughly before washing it to remove dust, fluff, lacquer and tangles.

HAIR TYPES
*Dry*

If you compare the soft sheen of a child's hair with your own you will see that, like your skin, it tends to become drier as you get older; sometimes looking lifeless and with ends becoming brittle and tending to split. Regular washing with a gentle shampoo or cream suitable for dry hair will improve it and it can be revitalized with a hair conditioner applied after each shampoo. Once a month, massage the conditioner well in and leave it on for 20–30 minutes before washing your hair. If your hair becomes very dry, comb warm olive oil or baby oil in and leave for 10–15 minutes. Scalp massage between shampoos will encourage the sebaceous glands to produce more oil. The use of harsh dyes, too much lacquer and over-bleaching can produce effects similar to those of ageing.

*Greasy*

If you have oily skin you will probably have greasy hair as well. Shampoo it as frequently as is convenient, using warm, not hot water and avoiding vigorous rubbing which stimulates the activity of the oil-producing glands. Sometimes a 'body perm' will assist in drying out greasy hair but, like the use of bleaches, etc., this should not be more than an occasional resort.

*Normal*

Lucky you! Use the shampoo of your choice, preferably one with a built-in conditioner. The regular visit to the hairdresser for a skilled cut, together with a good daily brush, should suffice to keep your hair looking at its best.

GENERAL HAIR CARE
1 Care of the hair should become a habit very early in life, so shampoo-time should be made a pleasant experience. Special mild shampoos are available for using on children's hair, so that they do not connect hair-washing with eye-smarting.
2 Choose brushes made from either natural bristle or a mixture of bristle and nylon. Wash them frequently, at least every time you wash your hair.
3 Do not share your brush with anyone else. Dandruff, which is caused by dead cells of skin accumulating around the hair roots (depending on

how much oil the sebaceous glands of your scalp produce) is contagious and easily spread by using a brush, or comb, belonging to a sufferer.

4 Buy combs which have rounded ends to the teeth, otherwise your scalp may be scratched by sharp points.

5 Do not use metal combs for the same reason.

6 Use only the recommended amount of shampoo. Too liberal a use may cause difficulty in rinsing out completely and the hair may be left looking dull instead of glossy. (As you squeeze the water out, your hair should 'squeak' if it is thoroughly rinsed.)

7 Do not use hot combs and heated rollers too often or at too high a temperature, as they can scorch and weaken the hair.

8 If you use a hairdrier, do not turn up the heat too high; this can cause the hair to become brittle.

9 Unless you are having a blow-dry do not brush your hair when it is wet—comb it through gently and give it a good brushing when it is dry.

10 Choose a hairstyle which you can manage yourself. Frequent visits to hairdressers are expensive items.

11 Do not use too much lacquer or practise too much back-combing which makes the hair dull, lifeless and brittle.

12 Let the wind blow through your hair occasionally—like the rest of your body, your scalp benefits from fresh air.

## Your Teeth

One of the things which even your best friend will hesitate to tell you is that you have bad breath. Providing that your general health is good, the most likely cause is your teeth. The use of toothpaste will sweeten your breath for an hour or so but, to ensure that you are not unpleasant to be near, you must do much more:

1 Choose your toothbrush with care. Bristle brushes are no longer recommended by dentists because they do not dry quickly and can harbour bacteria. The bristles also have sharp points which may tear the gums and open a field for infection. Brushes favoured by dental experts now are flexible, multi-tufted nylon ones with rounded ends and soft or medium tufts.

2 Cut down your consumption of sugary foods. Sugar is the main culprit in the formation of plaque, a 'plating' substance which builds up on the surface of teeth. It contains harmful bacteria which produce toxins causing tooth decay and gum disease. Children should be trained as soon as they produce teeth not to expect anything but a drink of water after they go to bed. 'A sweetie to go to bed with', or a sweetened drink, means that all through the night the teeth will be bathed in a weak sugary solution and the bacteria will have all they need to flourish.

3 Establish good dental hygiene as early as possible. Teeth *should* be cleaned after every meal, but at least first thing in the morning (or after

breakfast) and just before you go to bed. Brush them with a gentle up and down movement to dislodge the shreds of food which collect between the teeth. Side to side brushing does not do this and may tear the gums. If you need to eat between meals choose apples or raw carrots rather than biscuits or cakes.

Another way of making sure that the spaces between the teeth are completely cleared and plaque discouraged is to use dental floss. This is a fine thread of nylon which you slide between your teeth to remove debris and, properly used, it is very effective. You do need to be shown by your dentist or dental hygienist how to use it, however, as you can damage your gums and encourage infection if it is not employed correctly.

4 Let children see that you take care of your teeth and encourage them to copy you. Pay regular 'check-up' visits to the dentist and take them with you from an early age so that there is no fear associated with the occasion.

5 Use a toothpaste containing fluoride—it has been proved that it helps teeth to resist plaque and, if you are one of the people who feel strongly about taking 'additives' into the system, remember that you do not actually swallow the paste.

## Your Hands

We cannot hide our hands and nails and other people do notice them, whether we are shaking them in greeting, filling in forms or just sitting and chatting over a cup of tea. Not everyone is blessed with graceful hands and well-shaped nails but we can all take care of what we have and make them presentable at all times. After we have removed the natural oils in hot detergent water, dug them into soil or dust, frozen them while hanging out washing in the winter and, perhaps, alas, nibbled the nails, it is not surprising that they are not always beautiful.

1 Wash up in rubber gloves. Buy a size larger than your normal glove size so that a little air can enter to prevent sweating; or wear thin cotton gloves under the rubber ones.

2 Keep your hands out of water as much as you can and, if you cannot wear gloves, use a barrier cream. Keep a bottle/tube of non-greasy hand cream by the sink so that you can rub in a little after every time you have put your hands in water for any length of time.

3 Your nails, like your teeth and hair, are very much a matter of heredity and their health depends on your diet—as in your pre-natal state, good supplies of mineral elements (from fresh fruit and vegetables) and protein (from animal products) are valuable.

a) Keep your nails filed to follow the shape of your fingers and do not let them become too long (they trap dirt and can easily be torn). Use an emery board rather than a metal file as this gives a smoother finish and does not split the layers of nail tissue.

b) Push back your cuticles every time you dry your hands. If they become neglected use cotton wool wrapped round an orange stick and soaked in a commercial cuticle remover.

c) Use a soft buffer to produce a natural sheen. If you wish to wear clear or coloured varnish, renew it immediately it becomes cracked or chipped.

d) If you bite your nails find some way of disciplining yourself to stop doing so. There are various 'cures' on the market, but the best way is to set yourself a target of reward and 'do it your way'.

## Your Feet

You can only be as active as your feet will allow you to be and if you have painful toes, heels or soles the discomfort does tend to be reflected throughout your body. Your posture suffers and your expression betrays you. Early care, however, can ensure comfortable years ahead.

1 Give your feet as much freedom as possible; walk about the house without shoes (providing that you have observed all the safety precautions previously mentioned regarding floor surfaces) and exercise your toes by alternately spreading them out and relaxing them and curling and relaxing them. Rotate your feet to improve the circulation and slim the ankles. These exercises can easily be carried out unobtrusively while you are sitting and reading or watching television.

2 Buy properly fitting shoes. Most of us are fortunate enough to be born with a pair of perfect feet, but a glance at those belonging to older people will often show you how they can be disfigured and distorted. Corns, bunions and hammer toes are commonplace and nearly all of them are caused by unsuitable footwear. Fashion can certainly be followed, but remember that:

a) Loosely-fitting shoes, sandals or slippers which give no support, force your feet to be tensed and your toes to be curled in order to keep them on.

b) Shoes which are too narrow crush your toes and make them overlap each other.

c) Very high heels cause your body weight to be thrown forward on to the delicate foot bones, causing them to become distorted by bunions.

d) Shoes which are too short will have a similar effect and cause corns on the top of curled-under toes.

e) Leather is better for the hygiene of the feet because it 'breathes'; plastic soles and uppers can cause the feet to sweat.

f) Socks and tights which are too small can do almost as much damage as tight shoes.

g) Rubber or plastic 'wellies' should be worn only as protection against bad weather conditions—they do not allow sufficient air to reach the feet.

h) Sloppy slippers worn about the house are a safety hazard and do nothing for your posture; it is better to go barefoot.

i) Reputable footwear retailers will measure your feet when you buy shoes and advise you as to your correct fitting (see page 190).

3 Wash your feet every day with soapy, not detergent, water and use a pumice stone to remove any thickened skin. Dry them thoroughly, especially between the toes.

4 Wear clean socks or tights every day.

5 Cut the toenails straight across, just trimming off the sharp corners. Bad cutting may result in in-growing nails which are very painful and may eventually require surgery.

6 If you have any problems with your feet, treat yourself to a visit to a chiropodist occasionally.

## Your Personality

Having achieved your objectives of glossy hair, glowing complexion, sweet breath, well-kept hands and a trim figure, put it all together and what have you got? Nothing, unless your personality is as attractive as your appearance. There is a very old adage which states that 'handsome is as handsome does' and, if you look critically at your friends and neighbours, you will see that it has stood the test of time. *You* are happy to know people because of what they are, not for what they look like, and you will be considered by others in the same way. The combination of a pleasant smile, a welcoming manner, a sense of humour, lively interest and thoughtful consideration are worth every aspect of classical beauty or contemporary glamour.

## SOCIAL HABITS

### Smoking

The risks of regular smoking have been spelt out so many times that it is almost superfluous to repeat them—potential lung cancer, bronchitis and heart problems alone should be sufficient deterrents. Even if these are fortunately avoided, the efficiency of your taste buds is impaired, your appetite is accordingly diminished, your breath and your clothes may smell of stale tobacco. Need more be said?

### Drinking

More women drink alcohol nowadays than ever before and the incidence of alcohol abuse among them is growing steadily. Social drinking is acceptable to most people but it becomes a serious matter when addiction develops in either sex. Apart from the financial stress and being unable to carry out normal functions efficiently (such as holding a job or running a home), excess alcohol reduces the appetite, coarsens the skin and may have disastrous long-term effects upon the liver. See page 104 for helpful organizations.

## Sleep

Although perhaps, an *unsocial* habit rather than a social one, it is something which everyone must do. Our sleep pattern changes as our lives progress—the very young baby sleeps most of the day and night, adults need at least 8 hours of undisturbed sleep and the elderly often manage quite happily on a few hours, although they do tend to indulge in odd naps throughout the day. Problems are usually associated with schoolchildren and adolescents, who view early nights with horror. During periods of growth and great activity, however, regular hours of sleep are important—mental functions are improved when the nervous system is rested, and looks deteriorate when eyes are dark-rimmed.

Good habits of rest should be encouraged; reading in bed, a bedroom radio or even a nightlight may all be successful.

## HEALTH FOODS

There is reason to believe that modern techniques of farming, using chemical fertilizers and pesticides, may, if used indiscriminately, destroy Nature's delicate balance. Moreover, the amount of refined and pre-packaged food available today is slowly but surely changing our eating patterns. These are two of the reasons why the 'health food' industry is booming. Supermarket chains are extending their range of natural products and now offer not only basic items such as wholewheat flour but more adventurous ones like unpolished brown rice, wholewheat spaghetti, black-eye beans, unrefined sugar, soya granules, etc. These are unfamiliar to many of us and can present problems in cooking. There are also on the market, however, a number of excellent books containing interesting information and recipes. Advice can be obtained from the smaller 'health food' shops, too, where the assistants are usually very knowledgeable about the food and have time to talk.

Otherwise, of course, many fruit and vegetables can be grown in your own garden, window box or in pots on your sills. You will know then exactly what treatment has been given to them. Garlic, parsley and chives can be grown in or out of doors, mushrooms, bean sprouts, French beans, courgettes, tomatoes, peppers and aubergines can all be grown on sunny window sills, quite apart from the root, fruit and leaf crops which can be produced on larger areas of soil.

## GENERAL ECONOMIES

Although not essential for healthy living, the practice of thrift and avoidance of waste are parts of a well-balanced attitude to life, and many small economies can not only save pennies which accumulate into pounds but are a good insurance against difficulty in coping with leaner years. Below are some of the everyday ways in which savings can be made without deprivation.

## Heating

1 Buy solid fuel at summer prices.
2 Keep outer doors closed when central heating is switched on.
3 Turn off radiators in unused rooms except when they require airing.
4 Fit thermostats to boilers and radiators.
5 Have a white meter installed (see page 47).
6 Insulate the premises (see page 50).
7 Boil only the amount of water you are actually going to use from a kettle.
8 Do not allow gas flames to lick round the outside of pans—the heat is in the tip of the flame.
9 Make use of steamers and pressure cookers wherein several items may be cooked at once; use the oven for as many dishes as possible at one time.
10 Avoid the use of open fires—much heat is lost up the chimney.

## Lighting

1 Turn off lights in unoccupied rooms, providing that safety is not impaired.
2 Use dimmer switches to match the amount of light being used to the amount required.
3 Use spotlights for localized illumination if a bright overhead one is not necessary.
4 Avoid dark shades which reduce the amount of light available.
5 Use low wattage lamps in bedrooms.
6 Use fluorescent lights in kitchens where constant lighting is required (see page 64).

## Clothing/Household Goods

1 Buy dry-cleaning fluid in jars or bottles rather than aerosol cans—two-thirds of the cost is for the container.
2 Read detergent packets carefully and use only the suggested amounts.
3 Attend evening classes to learn how to make your own clothes.
4 Re-use long tacking threads. Wind them back on the reel as you remove them.
5 Cut down adults' skirts and trousers to make children's garments.
6 Unpick and re-make unsatisfactory hand-knitted garments.
7 Make waistcoats from cardigans with worn elbows.

8 Keep belts, buttons, zips and fasteners from any garment which is being completely discarded.

9 Make face flannels from the best parts of worn towels.

10 Make cushions from unwanted bolsters and eiderdowns.

Other economies

1 Monitor telephone calls (see page 144).

2 Remove torn areas of gift-wrapping paper, iron it and save it for re-use.

3 Untie knots in string instead of cutting them, wind it up and store for re-use.

———————————————— **FURTHER STUDY** ————————————————

## Things to Do

1 Find out the difference between the bacilli of staphylococcus and streptococcus, the symptoms of infection and the curative treatment.

2 Discover what 'botulism' is and how it can be avoided.

3 'Useful bacteria' have been mentioned on page 234. Find out as many examples of these as you can and discover how they are useful.

4 Borrow a skeleton model of a leg and foot, if possible. Place the foot into shoes of various types and note the resulting position of the bones.

5 Find out the meaning of the word 'réchauffé' and discuss the benefits and dangers of the practice.

6 Find a picture of a grain of rice and discover the difference between brown and white rice.

7 Find out the average price of similar amounts of
6 different deodorants;
6  ,,  shampoos;
6  ,,  moisturizers;
6  ,,  toilet soaps.

## Questions to Answer

1 Write out and complete each of the following statements with the correct term chosen from the list in the right-hand column.

a) Varying in number in different parts of the body ——————— glands in the skin secrete oil.

anti-perspirants

b) The covering on the root of hair on the skin is known as a ———————.

plaque

| | | |
|---|---|---|
| **c)** | Dead skin particles which collect on the scalp shed on to the shoulders as a white powder which is referred to as _____ . | bunion |
| **d)** | If skin pores become blocked with infected dead cells a condition of _____ is likely to result. | polished |
| **e)** | The daily use of a _____ will prevent the development of unpleasant odours given off by certain parts of the body. | taste buds |
| **f)** | _____ contain a metallic component which closes the pores and inhibits the natural secretions. | dandruff |
| **g)** | If teeth are not efficiently cleaned a layer of _____ builds up which discolours them and can lead to gum disease. | sebaceous |
| **h)** | When the outside layers of rice grains are removed the grain is said to have been _____ . | follicle |
| **i)** | Shoes which are too short can cause the foot to develop a _____ because the joint of the big toe becomes bent as the foot is pushed into the shoe. | deodorant |
| **j)** | Flavours are registered by the _____ in the tongue; these can be partially destroyed by constant smoking. | acne |

**2** Describe exactly what steps you would take to prevent the spread of a common cold through a household. Explain your decisions.

**3** What do you understand by the term 'well groomed'? Describe what you would look for if you were interviewing a candidate for a hotel receptionist's position.

**4** How would you differentiate between thrift and parsimony? Give as many examples as possible.

**5** If your pocket-money is very limited, how could you ensure that:
    **a)** your teeth are kept in good condition;
    **b)** your hair is shiny and attractive;
    **c)** you smell agreeable?

## METRIC WEIGHTS AND MEASURES
### Solids

Most pre-packed foodstuffs are now sold in metric quantities. Most metric recipes are based on a weight unit of 25 grams (g.) which is slightly less than an ounce. When following recipes, *never* mix the two systems—use either metric or imperial measures.

Kitchen scales are available which are marked in both metric and imperial weights or in metric units only.

*Gram (g.)*
>    28 g. is an approximate equivalent to 1 ounce (oz.)
>    (but for convenience we use 25 g.)
>    225 g. is an approximate equivalent to 8 ounces
>    1000 g. equals 1 kilogram

*Kilogram (kg.)*
>    1 kilogram is an approximate equivalent to 2 lb. 4 oz.
>    (often marked as 1 kg. (2.2 lb.) as on bags of sugar)

### Liquids

*Millilitre (ml.)*
>    568 ml. is an approximate equivalent to 1 pint (pt.)
>    1000 ml. equals 1 litre

*Litre (l.)*
>    1 l. is an approximate equivalent to $1\frac{3}{4}$ pt.
>    (often marked as 1 l. (35.2 fluid oz.))

MEASURING JUGS

Most measuring jugs are marked to the following round measures:

$$125 \text{ ml.} = \tfrac{1}{4} \text{ pt.}$$
$$250 \text{ ml.} = \tfrac{1}{2} \text{ pt.}$$
$$500 \text{ ml.} = 1 \text{ pt.}$$

SPOON MEASURES

These work out, approximately, as follows:

$$2.5 \text{ ml.} = \tfrac{1}{2} \text{ teaspoon}$$
$$5 \text{ ml.} = 1 \text{ teaspoon}$$
$$10 \text{ ml.} = 1 \text{ dessertspoon}$$
$$15 \text{ ml.} = 1 \text{ tablespoon}$$

# Length

*Centimetre (cm.)*
    2.5 cm. is an approximate equivalent to 1 inch
    15 cm. is an approximate equivalent to 6 inches
    20 cm. is an approximate equivalent to 8 inches
    100 cm. equals 1 metre
*Metre (m.)*
    1 m. is an approximate equivalent to 3 feet 4 inches

## OVEN TEMPERATURE SCALES

| Electric: Celsius (° C) | Electric: Fahrenheit (° F) | Gas: Oven Mark |
|:---:|:---:|:---:|
| 110 | 225 | $\frac{1}{4}$ |
| 130 | 250 | $\frac{1}{2}$ |
| 140 | 275 | 1 |
| 150 | 300 | 2 |
| 170 | 325 | 3 |
| 180 | 350 | 4 |
| 190 | 375 | 5 |
| 200 | 400 | 6 |
| 220 | 425 | 7 |
| 230 | 450 | 8 |
| 240 | 475 | 9 |

# Index

abrasive(s) 76, 119, 120
absorbent(s) 182, 183, 186
accident(s) 190, 192, 193–7, 204, 220, 234
account(s) 154–7, 158, 159, 161, 211;
 budget 156–7; current 154–6; deposit
 157
acetate 14, 169, 183
acetone 182, 183, 184, 185, 186
acne 241–2
acrylic(s) 23, 169
additives 127, 138, 147, 245
adhesive(s) 184, 201
adoption 90, 104
advertisements 2, 12, 145, 146
advertising 145
after-care 92, 94
agitation 168
air 30, 181, 226, 237, 246; bricks 30;
 freshener 206
airing 178, 195, 215, 249
alcohol/alcoholism 104, 130, 241, 247–8
allowance(s) 99, 100, 102, 141, 142
aluminium 35, 71, 76, 117, 119; foil 50,
 116
amino acids 126, 131
amyl acetate 183, 184, 185, 186
animal(s) 14, 105, 184, 236
anorexia nervosa 239
anthracite 41
anti-perspirant 242
antiseptic 201, 206, 238
artificial resuscitation 199, 200, 201
ash(es) 41, 229, 235
ashtrays 194

baby/babies 89–90, 94, 95, 206, 248
bacteria 228, 234, 236, 237, 242, 244
bags plastic 178, 197, 207; refuse 229
ball float 226; valve(s) 225, 226
bamboo 19, 35
banking 154–9
bank(s) 154, 155, 156, 157, 158, 159,
 161, 214
banisters 193, 194
bath(s) 75, 76, 194, 195, 197, 225, 228,
 237; eye 201
bathroom 197, 205, 226, 237, 238
bed(s) 244, 248; clothes 204; cradle(s) 204,
 205; linen 170, 174, 207; pan 205;
 sick 204, 206; sizes 15; sores 204;
 types 15

bedroom(s) 237, 248, 249; lighting 64
beech 18, 19
benefits 69, 92, 99, 100, 230
'Best Before' mark 147
bicarbonate calcium 223; of soda 113
blanket(s) 17, 198, 199, 204, 205; dry
 cleaning 181; electric 197, 220
bleach(ing) 75, 171, 173, 183, 196;
 chlorine 169, 174, 186; hair 243;
 hydrogen peroxide 174; hypochlorite
 174; instructions 169
bleeding 198, 199, 200, 203; controlling 200
blinds 37
British Standards Institution 118, 121,
 191, 194, 197, 209, 220
budget(ing) 136, 143–5
building society(ies) 4, 5, 6, 161
bulk buying 116, 148
burns 192, 194–5, 202

calcium carbonate 223
calories 129, 130; empty 130
calorific value 213
cane 19
carbohydrates 126, 127, 128
carbon tetrachloride 182
carpet(s) 11, 54, 77, 80, 183, 195; buying
 25; classes 25; classification 28;
 cleaner 184; shampoo 183, 185, 186;
 sweeper 80; types 23
casserole(s) 120, 133; electric 79
cast iron 118, 119
cedar 18, 19
central heating 223, 249; air-lock 226;
 dry 46; electric storage 46; gas 213;
 maintenance 81; plants 106; servicing
 144; solid fuel 60; wet 44
ceramic glass 119; tiles 22, 24
cesspool 227
chair(s) 13, 77, 191, 193, 194, 201, 204
charge(s) bank 156, 157, 159; maintenance
 3; reversed 221; service 3; telephone 221
cheese 132, 133, 235, 239
cheque(s) 155–7; book 154, 155, 157,
 161; cards 156, 158, 161
chemical toilets 228
child benefit 100, 230; minders 101
children('s) 11, 43, 90, 93, 96, 100,
 105, 138, 194, 196, 201, 202, 206,
 207, 244; garments 249; growth 128;
 homes 231; meals 129; shampoo 243

chimney 194, 198, 249
china 124, 171; *bone* 122; *patterned* 136
chiropodist(s) 94, 247
chocolate(s) 239; *stain* 184
cigarettes 194, 196, 214
cistern(s) *lavatory* 224, 225, 226, 227
Citizen's Advice Bureau 103, 146, 180,
    191; *family needs* 89; *mortgages* 5;
    *property purchase* 7; *tenancies* 2
clinics *chiropody, well-women* 94; *audio,*
    *baby, diabetic, family planning,*
    *ophthalmic, orthopaedic, psychology, VD*
    95
clothing 194, 202, 203, 235, 237, 242,
    249; *expenditure* 144
cloths 195, 202; *fire smothering* 192;
    *table* 124, 125, 133, 177, 195; *tray,*
    *trolley* 125; *oven* 194
coal 41, 209, 216
cockroaches 236, 237
cocoa *stain* 184
code 190; *colour* 197; *International*
    *Textile Care Label* 168, 169, 180;
    *number* 141, 156; *stock control* 150,
    151; *telephone* 221
Code of Practice 190; *advertising* 145, 148;
    *broadcasting* 145; *dry cleaning* 180;
    *footwear* 190, 191
coffee *stain* 132, 184
coke 41
college(s) 17, 92; *community* 97; *education*
    98; *further education* 96, 97; *higher*
    *education* 97; *mono/polytechnics* 98;
    *sixth form* 97; *tertiary* 97
colour(s) 32, 172, 183; *carpets* 25; *fast*
    172, 175; *hair* 242; *loose* 182; *paint*
    31
colourings 147
commodity labels 150
community *centres* 96, 102, 103; *colleges*
    97; *Health Council* 93; *relations* 92
condensation 53, 60
conditioner(s) *fabric* 173; *hair* 243
conduction 118
consumer *advice centre* 180, 191; *protection*
    231; *rights* 146; *unit* 212, 216, 217,
    218, 219
convection 48
convector(s) *electric* 42; *fan* 48; *fireplace*
    41; *gas* 42; *natural* 48; *portable* 215;
    *radiant* 43
cooker(s) 76, 109, 119, 192, 195, 217,
    218; *choosing* 54; *electric* 55, 57, 118;
    *fuses* 82; *gas* 57, 58–60; *hoods* 61;
    *microwave* 54, 57, 117; *multi-* 79;
    *portable* 215; *pressure* 54, 74, 249;
    *slow* 54, 79; *solid fuel* 60; *table-top* 79
copper 117, 118, 119, 121; *care* 76
cork *sheets* 22; *tiles* 22, 24, 52
cot(s) 194, 196, 197, 202, 238
cotton 14, 175, 177, 180, 186; *bedclothes*
    17; *carpets* 23; *curtains* 36; *starching*
    173; *tablecloths* 124; *washing* 169

cream(s) 74, 243; *barrier* 245; *hand* 245;
    *shaving* 241; *stain* 184
credit 157, 159, 161; *buying* 148; *cards*
    158–9; *facilities* 145; *note* 147; *sales*
    149
crockery 73, 205; *broken* 229
cupboard(s) 109, 114, 193, 197, 204,
    237; *airing* 178; *freezer* 114, 115;
    *medicine* 201; *meter* 211
current 65, 203, 216, 220
curtains 32, 77, 195; *dry cleaning* 181;
    *fittings* 34; *headings* 35; *heavy* 179;
    *measuring* 37; *net* 173
cushions 250; *fastenings* 38; *fillings*
    38; *foam* 15
cutlery 71, 72, 76, 117, 120, 124, 133,
    235
cuts 192, 193, 201, 234

damp(ness) 60; *course* 30; *effects* 29;
    *proofing* 30; *rising* 30; *survey* 7
date marks 147, 150
decorating 25; *materials* 148; *preparations*
    30; *responsibility* 3
dental *care* 94, 244; *floss* 245; *hygiene*
    244–5
deodorant 242; *stain* 185
department *casualty* 199, 202; *Education*
    *& Science, Employment, Environment,*
    *Health & Social Security, Home Office,*
    *Treasury* 92; *Inland Revenue* 141;
    *Trading Standards Consumer Protection*
    146
detergents 71, 73, 75, 76, 77, 84, 124,
    169, 170–2, 179, 182, 183, 184,
    185, 186, 224, 240, 245, 247, 249;
    *dishwasher* 117
diabetes 199, 239; *diabetic* 93, 95
digestion 130, 136; *digestive system* 127
direct debit 150, 157, 214
discount trading 148
disposal *dry refuse* 228–30; *methods* 229;
    *sewage* 226, 231; *waste water* 228
doctor(s) 90, 93, 94, 95, 104, 129–31,
    200–205, 222
doors 77, 191, 193, 197, 198, 215, 237,
    249; *care* 75; *lighting* 64; *maintenance*
    81; *sliding* 110
double glazing 52, 191
down *duvets* 17; *pillows* 16
drain 109, 226, 238; *cock* 224
drainage 7, 231; *cesspool* 227
draught(s) 53, 61, 198, 204; *excluders* 54;
    *prevention* 48; *production* 43
dressings 201, 204, 229, 235, 238
drier(s) 165, 166, 167, 176; *hair* 244;
    *tumble* 109
drugs 196, 203
dry cleaning 179–81, 249; *expenses* 144;
    *fluid* 183, 184, 185, 186, 194;
    *instructions* 195; *laundrette* 181
dustbin(s) 228, 230, 238; *powder* 229;
    *types* 229

duvet(s) 16, 32, 179

earnings 142; *gross* 141; *limits (lower,*
   *upper)* 142; *net* 141
earth(ing) 65, 179; *closets* 228; *wire*
   84, 217, 219, 220
earthenware 122, 124, 188
education 8, 98, 104, 228; *adult* 97, 99;
   *department* 96, 102 (& *Science*) 92,
   98; *further* 96; *health* 95; *service* 96
eggs 171, 236, 239; *stain* 185
elderly, the 11, 13, 41, 43, 51, 89, 91,
   101, 130, 137, 148, 192, 193, 195,
   197, 231, 248
electricity 20, 157, 166, 198, 215;
   *accidents* 197; *board* 65; *charges* 145;
   *cookers* 54, 55, 119; *direct debit*
   *payment* 150; *distribution* 217; *faults*
   195; *fires* 43, 192, 214; *generator* 215;
   *goods* 148; *heating* 47; *hot water supply*
   49; *inlet* 81; *mains* 58, 64, 81, 82, 83,
   198, 217, 219; *meter* 216; *points* 61;
   *static* 173; *token stamps* 150
emergency(ies) 143, 198, 225, 238;
   *services* 192, 196, 215, 231
energy 126, 128, 129, 130, 239
entertaining 132
entertainment 144, 239
enzymes 172, 183, 184, 185, 186
equipment 110, 204, 205; *kitchen* 109;
   *labour saving* 74; *laundry* 109; *small*
   117, 125; *water* 225
estate agent(s) 5
estimating *curtains* 37; *electricity* 219;
   *gas* 214; *wallpaper* 32
eye(s) 243, 248; *bath* 201; *injuries* 203;
   *rodding* 227

fabric(s) 237; *bonded* 36; *conditioners,*
   *softeners* 173; *curtain* 35; *wall*
   *coverings* 34; *upholstery* 77
faeces *stain* 185
fainting 203
falls 192, 193
fan(s) *extractor* 43, 61; *heater* 43; *oven*
   56, 59
fat(s) 240, 242; *burning* 192, 195;
   *nutrients* 126, 127, 128
feather *cushions* 38; *duvets* 17; *pillow*
   16
feet 240, 246, 247
fibre *content* 168, 180, 181; *food* 127;
   *glass* 36, 50, 75, 192
fire(s) 191, 192, 194, 195, 196, 198,
   215, 249; *brigade* 198, 231; *burns*
   202; *electric* 43, 214; *extinguisher* 192,
   195, 198; *gas* 43, 215; *guard* 194;
   *log* 41; *oil* 146; *portable* 215; *service*
   288
first aid 198–204; *box* 201
fish 116, 239, 241
flex(es) 66, 193, 194, 195, 218, 221,
   222; *clamp* 83, 84; *iron* 179

flies 207, 235, 236, 237
flooring 19, 198, 246; *brick* 21; *boards*
   22; *care* 75; *cork* 22; *parquet* 21, 22,
   24; *quarry tiles* 21; *tiles* 22; *types*
   22; *linoleum* 22; *woodblock* 22
floor *covering(s)* 76, 193, 194, 197;
   *choosing* 20
flock 14
flue(s) 47, 195, 215; *balanced* 48
fluid(s) 131, 205, 207; *dry cleaning*
   181, 182, 183, 184, 185, 186, 194,
   196, 241, 249; *noxious* 203
fluorescent 61, 63, 64, 249
fluorescers 172
foam *carpet backing* 23; *chips* 38;
   *insulation* 51; *latex* 15; *mattresses* 16;
   *pillows* 16
food 125–32, 148, 239, 240, 241; *buying*
   136; *containers* 76; *convenience* 138;
   *expenditure* 144; *frozen* 113; *functions*
   126; *health* 248; *labelling regulations*
   146; *left-over* 113, 207; *play* 196;
   *poisoning* 235–7; *pre-packed* 146;
   *processor* 78, 79; *scraps* 229, 235;
   *shreds* 245; *storage area* 109; *sugary*
   244
freezers 76, 114–16, 115, 220
fruit 127, 129, 237, 239, 241, 245, 248;
   *juice* 185; *stains* 183
fuel 157; *coal* 41; *lighter* 183, 184;
   *savings stamps* 149; *solid* 41, 249;
   *wood* 41
fumes 48, 51, 60, 106, 195, 196, 198, 214
furniture 12, 148, 191, 193, 194, 198,
   202; *care* 75; *dining/living room* 13;
   *fitted* 18, 20; *nursery* 196; *polishes*
   74; *self-assembly* 20
fuse(s) 65–6, 84, 195, 218, 219; *box* 216;
   *mending* 82

garage 3, 4, 109, 114, 156, 166, 192,
   194, 196
garden(s) 193, 197, 221, 231, 235,
   248; *refuse* 229
gas 166, 195, 196, 198, 209, 216;
   *bill* 213; *board* 209; *boiler* 44;
   *calor* 43, 58, 215; *composition* 210;
   *cookers* 54, 57, 58, 119; *direct*
   *debit payment* 150; *fires* 43, 215;
   *heating* 47; *inlet* 81; *mains* 43, 81,
   209, 211, 214, 215; *meter* 209;
   *natural* 47; *refrigerator* 112; *supply*
   209, 211
girobank 5, 157, 158, 230
glands 240, 241, 242, 243, 244
glass(es) 117, 118, 124, 193, 200,
   204, 235; *broken* 229; *care* 73, 75;
   *casseroles* 120; *ceramic* 119; *drinking*
   71, 72, 122, 123, 133; *heat resistant*
   122; *ware* 122–4
government 159; *grants* 98; *legislation*
   190; *local* 93, 98; *purchase schemes* 5;
   *services* 92; *sponsored mortgages* 6

grant(s) *death* 142; *education* 98;
 *home improvement* 7; *insulation* 51;
 *training* 98
grass *stains* 183, 185; *verges* 231
gravy 171; *stain* 185
grease 171; *pans* 71; *stains* 182, 183,
 185
grill(s) 56, 58; *contact* 78; *gas* 59;
 *infra-red* 54; *level* 55
guarantee(s) 150; *building* 7; *carpets* 25;
 *electrical appliances* 220; *sealed*
 *windows* 53; *small equipment* 118

hair 206, 235, 238, 243–4, 245, 247;
 *driers* 220, 244; *follicles* 240, 241
handicapped, the 99, 104, 195; *clubs*
 95; *registered* 94
hand(s) 235, 245, 247; *cream* 245
health 234, 243, 244, 245; *centres* 95;
 *education* 95; *environmental* 231; *foods*
 248; *& safety at work* 96; *& Social*
 *Security* 92, 101; *visitor* 93–4, 95,
 101, 129, 130, 205
heat *economy* 240, 249; *loss* 52; *marks*
 185; *water* 223
heaters 225; *circulator* 49; *fuses* 82;
 *paraffin* 220; *portable* 215; *storage*
 47, 217; *water* 224
heating *central* 44; *council property*
 4; *domestic* 45, 225; *flat* 3; *gas* 49;
 *immersion* 49; *methods* 45; *over-sink*
 49; *skirting* 48, 49; *sources* 41;
 *storage* 49
hire purchase 148, 149, 161; *avoidance*
 11; *payments* 144
hob(s) 54, 76, 119; *ceramic* 55;
 *fittings* 55, 59; *magnetic induction*
 55; *portable* 58
hobby(ies) 97, 144; *clubs* 102, 103
home *helps* 91, 101; *Laundering*
 *Consultative Council* 168; *nursing* 204,
 238
hospital(s) 93, 95, 96, 103, 199, 203,
 204
hydrogen peroxide 174
hygiene 205, 231, 234, 238, 241, 242,
 244, 246; *dustbins* 229; *knives* 120;
 *kitchen* 228, 234; *shop* 95

immunization 95, 207, 234
income 4, 5, 142, 143, 156; *net* 154;
 *tax* 141, 157
infection 206, 207, 236, 237, 240, 242,
 244, 245
ink 184; *stains* 183
inoculation 234
inspection chamber(s) 227
instalments 149, 150, 161
instructions *double glazing* 53; *dry*
 *cleaning* 181; *fly deterrents* 237;
 *laundering* 169; *manufacturers'* 76, 77;
 *slow cooker* 79; *washing machine* 168

insulation 249; *cavity walls* 50, 51;
 *curtains* 53; *curtain linings* 35;
 *electrical appliances* 220; *floors* 53;
 *materials* 50; *polyester* 17; *tank* 49,
 50; *underlays* 23; *wall* 52; *window,*
 *door frames* 54
insurance 249; *freezers* 116; *garage* 3;
 *home* 144; *mortgage* 4, 5, 6; *national*
 92, 93, 99, 141; *pets* 105; *policy loan*
 161; *tenancy* 2
interest 159, 160, 161, 162; bank account
 157; *credit buying* 149; *mortgages* 6;
 *overdraft* 156
iron(s) 176, 177, 178, 179, 184, 185;
 *care* 179; *electric* 80; *mineral* 128, 129,
 130, 131; *mould* 185; *setting* 168
ironing 70, 176–8; *board* 81, 176, 204

joules 129
juice 183, 239; *fruit* 183, 185, 204
juicer 78
'junk' foods 130

kapok 14, 38
kettle(s) 195; *electric* 80, 223
key(s) 192, 201
kilowatt hours 218
'kiss of life' 199, 203
kitchen 192, 193, 197, 224, 235, 236,
 238, 249; *equipment* 109, 190;
 *furniture* 75; *hygiene* 228, 234; *lighting*
 64; *planning* 109; *small equipment* 125;
 *taps* 226; *water* 225
knives 71, 72, 190, 193; *electric*
 *carving* 80; *kitchen* 121

labels 181, 182, 194, 196; *blankets*
 17; *care* 168, 174; *commodity* 150;
 *'dry clean only'* 180; *foods* 138;
 *furniture safety* 13; *upholstered furniture*
 191
lactovegetarians 131
lamps *bedside* 204; *candle* 62; *filament*
 62, 63; *mushroom* 63; *reflector* 63;
 *special* 63; *standard* 62, 63; *table* 62
larch 18, 19
latex foam 15
laundrette 164, 166; *dry cleaning* 181
laundry 164, 166; *aids* 173; *bills* 144;
 *procedure* 174
lavatory(ies) 226, 227, 228, 229, 238;
 *cistern* 225; *extra* 225
leaks 208; *gas* 195–6; *water* 215, 225
leisure 89, 97; *services* 102
libraries 231
licences 230; *pets* 144; *stamps* 149;
 *television* 144, 149
lighting 20, 64, 218, 249; *artificial*
 61; *automatic* 62; *bills* 144; *circuits*
 217; *fuses* 82; *types* 62
lights 249; *dimming* 220; *fluorescent*
 249; *indicator* 115, 117; *spot* 62, 64,
 249

linen 14, 177; *bed* 170, 174; *curtains*
    36; *starching* 173; *table* 124, 173, 174
linings 120; *curtains* 53; *drawers* 178;
    *inter* 36, 181; *non-stick* 118; *oven* 56,
    60
linoleum *sheets, tiles* 22, 54
loans *availability* 5; *bank, insurance
    policy* 161; *property* 4; *recovery* 7
local authority *accommodation* 2; *approval*
    51; *children* 101; *children's dept* 90;
    *colleges* 97; *dustbins* 228; *earth
    closets* 228; *education* 96; *housing* 8;
    *mortgages* 45; *refuse disposal* 230;
    *repairs & maintenance* 14; *schools* 96;
    *special services* 231; *universities* 98
locks 191, 210; *maintenance* 81

magazines 11, 144, 145, 148, 190, 204,
    207, 229
mahogany 18, 19
main(s) *drainage* 227; *electricity* 58,
    64, 81, 82, 83, 198, 217, 219; *gas*
    43, 81, 209, 211, 214, 215; *sewer*
    227, 228; *water* 81, 224, 226
maintenance *availability* 4; *charges* 3;
    *council property* 4; *expenses* 144; *home*
    81; *responsibility for* 3
meals 205, 244, 245; *invalids'* 204; *on
    wheels* 91, 101; *ordinary* 127; *planning*
    127; *serving* 136; *special* 129
measuring *carpets* 29; *curtains* 37
metabolic rate 239
metal 73; *goblets* 124; *objects* 197;
    *pans* 119; *polish* 121
meter 209, 215; *coin slot* 213, 214;
    *dial* 212, 216, 218, 219; *digital* 212,
    218, 219; *electricity* 18, 216; *gas*
    211, 212; *reading* 212, 218; *white* 47,
    217, 218, 249
methylated spirits 182, 183, 184, 185,
    186
milk 186, 191, 236, 239; *mother's* 129;
    *stains* 183; *sugar* 234
mineral elements 127, 128, 131, 245
mirrors 34; *care* 75; *lighting* 64
modacrylic 23
mortgage(s) 1, 3, 5, 142, 144, 157,
    161; *availability* 4; *elegibility* 7;
    *types* 6
moving house 8

nail(s) 206, 245–6, 247; *varnish* 184, 185
national *girobank* 5, 214; *grid* 216, 219;
    *Health Service* 92, 93–6, 142; *Insurance*
    92, 93, 99, 141, 142, 230; *Savings
    Bank* 5, 230; *savings certificates* 160,
    230
natural gas 47, 58, 209, 210
newspapers 144, 145, 146, 148, 193, 229
non-stick finishes 118, 179
nurse(s) *district* 90, 94, 204, 205; *night*
    101; *state registered* 93, 94, 101

nursery(ies) *day, private* 101; *furniture*
    196; *nurses* 101; *schools* 96
nursing *home* 204; *precautions* 207;
    *routine* 205
nylon 173, 244, 245; *bags* 178; *bristle*
    243; *carpets* 23, 25; *curtains* 36;
    *pillowcases, sheets* 17; *washing* 169

oak 18, 19
oil 195, 216, 240, 242, 243, 244, 245;
    *boiler* 44; *of cloves* 201; *cooking* 192;
    *fires* 43, 146; *heating* 47; *polish* 74;
    *stains* 182, 183, 185, 186
oven(s) 54, 55, 195, 249; *electric* 56;
    *gas* 59; *gloves* 194, 195; *table-top* 58;
    *temperatures* 253
overflow *leaks* 225; *pipes* 226

paint 31, 186, 194; *bills* 144; *maintenance*
    81; *remover* 183, 186
pan(s) 249; *deep-fat* 192; *frying* 118;
    *milk* 118
paper(s) 178, 191, 207, 235, 237; *gift
    wrapping* 250; *sacks* 229; *tissues* 201;
    *towelling* 238
paraffin 43, 192, 194, 196, 220
PAYE 141
pension(s) *contributions* 141; *distribution*
    230; *retirement* 99, 142; *schemes* 142,
    143; *supplementary* 230; *war* 99
personal services 93, 228, 231
pests 236
phosphorus 126, 128, 129, 130
Piezo system 60
pillow(s) 16, 197, 204, 205
pine 18, 19
pipe(s) 30, 215; *heating* 223, 224;
    *maintenance* 81; *service* 209, 211; *sink
    outlet* 84; *soil* 226, 228; *stack* 227;
    *storm water* 228; *unlagged* 225
planning 92; *family* 95; *kitchen* 109; *meals*
    127
plastic 14, 73, 197; *adhesive* 178; *bags*
    178, 207; *blinds* 37; *containers* 116;
    *curtains* 36; *curtain fittings* 35;
    *dustbins* 229; *foam* 51; *insulator* 220;
    *laminated* 75, 110; *sacks* 229; *sheets*
    205; *shoes* 246; *spatulas* 118; *tray-
    cloths* 124–5; *veneers* 18; *ventilation
    discs* 60; *'wellies'* 246
pleats 176, 178, 179
plugs 65, 179, 195, 218; *re-wiring* 83;
    *wall* 85; *waste outlet* 225
plumbing 7, 109, 226; *dishwashers* 116;
    *washing machines* 164–8
plumbline 33
plunger *sink* 84
poison(s) 196, 203
poisoning 192, 195, 203, 215
police 231; *force* 8; *service* 228
polishes 73–5, 193
pollution 230
polyester 17, 23, 169, 175

polyether 15
polypropylene 23
polystyrene 15, 50
polythene 116, 117
polyurethene 15, 22
Post Office 93, 150, 157, 158, 230; *guide*
    231; *savings bank* 159
powder *baby* 241; *biological* 171; *puffs*
    241; *soap* 171; *starch* 183; *talcum*
    183, 185, 205; *washing* 167, 168, 170,
    184
power *cuts* 229; *stations* 216
prescriptions 93; *refunds* 230
pre-school playgroups 96, 97
pressing 179, 181
pressure 240; *blood* 204; *cooker* 54, 74,
    249; *gas* 214; *governor* 211; *point* 200;
    *water* 226
protective services 93, 231
protein(s) 126, 127, 130–2, 172, 241,
    245; *stain* 183
pulse 206

quilts *continental, sleeping* 16

radiator(s) 44, 48, 226, 235, 249
radio 98, 145, 204, 248
rateable value 8
rates 1, 2, 7–8, 144, 228, 231; *council*
    4; *direct debit* 150; *rebate* 102; *water*
    8, 144
recovery position *199*
re-cycling 230
refrigerator(s) 76, 110–13, 114, 116, 133,
    214, 220, 235; *absorption* 111, 112;
    *care* 113; *compression* 110, *111*
refuse *collection* 8, 229; *containers* 229;
    *disposal* 228, 231; *garden* 229; *lorries*
    229
rent(s) 144, 231; *act* 2; *basic* 1; *book* 2;
    *council* 4; *ground* 3; *rebates* 102
repairs 157; *bills* 144; *council property* 4;
    *leasehold property* 3; *telephone* 221;
    *water* 225–6
reservoir(s) 222, *223*
respiration 200, 206; *disorders* 239
resuscitation 203; *artificial* 199–*200*, 201
rubber *dustbins* 229; *gloves* 245; *plugs*
    65; *sheet* 205; *'wellies'* 246
rubbish 229, 230, 238
rust 119, 120, 186

safeguards 190–1
safety 195, 230, 246, 247; *BSI standards*
    191; *electricity* 219; *food* 95; *gas* 214;
    *gate* 194; *heaters* 43, 249; *home* 106;
    *irons* 81; *net* 196; *sockets* 64; *standards*
    146; *switches* 64; *upholstery* 13;
    *windows* 53
salary 1, 141, 154
salt(s) 184, 185, 222, 233; *bath* 224;
    *container* 133; *cooking* 225; *dishwasher*
    117

saucepans 72, 118–20, 132, 196; *soaking*
    71
savings 1, 5, 143, 144, 157, 159–61,
    249; *SAYE* 160, 230; *schemes* 141;
    *stamps* 149
scalds 192, 195, 203
school(s) 92, 96, 101, 231; *children* 90,
    238, 248; *comprehensive* 96; *halls* 102,
    103; *lower* 96; *meals* 130; *medical
    services* 95; *middle* 96; *nursery* 96;
    *special* 99; *upper* 96, 97
scorch 183, 186, 244
screw(s) 81, 84, *85*
screwdriver 81, 85
'Sell By' mark 147, 236
septic tanks 227
services *bus* 231; *careers* 98; *education*
    96; *environmental health* 231; *family,
    community* 92; *government* 92; *health*
    93, 235; *home* 209; *leisure* 102;
    *messenger* 230; *National Health* 92;
    *personal* 93, 231; *pipes* 209, 211;
    *police* 228; *protective* 93; *school medical*
    95; *sewage disposal* 226; *social, welfare*
    92, 99; *special* 231; *telephone* 222
servicing 197; *central heating* 47;
    *contracts* 144; *washing machines* 166
sewage 228; *disposal* 226; *works* 227
sheet(s) 17, 205; *draw* 205; *ironing* 177;
    *plastic, rubber* 205
shock 200, 202–4, 215; *electric* 197, 203,
    220
shopping 11, 12, 16, 25, 70, 117, 136,
    137, 146, 148, 231; *methods* 147
shops 25, 35, 36, 137, 147, 149, 156, 231
sick room 204
silk 180; *stains* 182; *washing* 169
silver *care* 76; *plate* 121
sink(s) 76, 86, 109, 110, 225, 228;
    *blocked* 84; *care* 75; *plunger* 84
skin 128, 205, 238, 240–2, 245, 247, 248
smoke 41, 198
smoking 145, 194, 235, 247
soap 77, 241, 242, 247; *laundry* 170, 171;
    *manufacture* 171; *powder* 170, 171;
    *toilet* 178, 205; *yellow* 186
social *clubs* 141; *habits* 247–8; *security*
    92, 99, 142; *services* 8, 99–102, 104;
    *work* 95; *worker* 101
socket(s) 64, 65, 82, 109, 179, 197, 215,
    217, 218
soda 171; *caustic* 202; *lime* 122
sodium carbonate 224
soft woods 18
solid fuel 249; *boiler* 44; *cookers* 54, 60;
    *fires* 41, 42; *heating* 47
spotlight 62, 64, 249
solicitor(s) 5
stain(s) 174, 175, 180, 181; *removal*
    181–6; *removers* 183; *types* 171
sting(s) 201
stop-cock(s) 81, 86, 224, 225, 226; *valve*
    224, 225

storage *cleaned items* 11, 181; *clothes*
    178; *drawers* 15, 178; *food* 109;
    *garments* 237; *heaters* 47, 217, 219;
    *household items* 178; *over, under sink
    heater* 49; *silver* 121
suffocation 192, 196, 201
sulphate *calcium, magnesium* 222
supermarket(s) 136–7, 147, 150, 159, 248
surveyor(s) 5
switch(es) 64, 82, 195, 197; *central
    heating* 225; *dimmer* 62, 249;
    *fast-freeze* 115
symbols *dry cleaning* 180; *insulation* 220;
    *laundering* 168, 169
synthetic(s) 146; *detergents* 171, 172

table(s) 204, 237; *cloths* 124, 125, 133,
    177, 195; *cooker* 79; *laying* 133; *linen*
    125; *manners* 133; *mats* 124, 125,
    133; *mixer* 78; *settings* 134; *types* 13;
    *ware* 122, 133
tank(s) *maintenance* 81; *septic* 227
tap(s) 215; *components* 86; *gas* 211; *water*
    224, 226
tax(es) *car* 144; *income* 141; *rebate* 6;
    *return* 160, 161; *policy* 92
teak 18, 19
teeth 128, 129, 223, 244–5; *cleaning* 205;
    *false* 199
telephone 192, 221; *bills* 144; *calls* 221,
    222; *directories* 231
television (TV) 98, 144, 145, 195, 198,
    220, 239, 246; *licence* 230; *stamps*
    149–50
temperature 201, 205–7, 212, 223, 225,
    236, 240, 244; *oven* 253
thermometer 201, 206
thermostatic control 249; *boiler* 46; *hob*
    59; *hot water* 224; *iron* 176; *radiator*
    46; *room* 46
tiles 54; *floor, linoleum, vinyl* 22;
    *brick, ceramic, cork* 24; *carpet* 26;
    *glazed/unglazed* 76; *insulating* 52;
    *mirror* 34
tin(s) 193, 194, 195, 236; *alloy* 121;
    *baking* 118; *empty* 229; *lining* 119
tog rating 17
toilet 205, 235, 237; *chemical* 228;
    *preparations* 242
tooth *ache* 201; *brush* 238, 244; *paste* 248
towel(s) 36, 174, 205, 237, 238, 241,
    250; *hand, paper* 235, 238
trading checks 149
tray(s) 125, 136, 205; *cloths* 124, 125;
    *settings* 135

underblanket 197
underclothes 242
underlays 23
underwear 178
unit pricing 150
upholstery 183, 191; *fabric* 77; *fillings*
    14; *leather* 77; *materials* 14; *safety
    labels* 13; *vinyl* 77

valve 211, 214, 224, 226
vegans 131
vegetables 239, 241, 245, 248
vegetarians 131
veneer 18, 19
vent 61, 195
ventilation 30, 60, 215, 227, 237, 238
ventilator 214; *pipe* 227
vinyl 193; *care* 76; *flooring* 22; *upholstery*
    14; *wall coverings* 11; *wallpaper* 31, 77
vitamins 127, 129, 130–2; *A* 241; *D* 126;
    *functions, sources, types* 128
voltage 216, 220
voluntary *contributions* 141; *helpers* 96,
    104, 231; *organizations* 103, 105;
    *work* 89

wage(s) 1, 141, 154
wall(s) *cavity insulation* 51; *insulation*
    52; *treatment* 29
wallpaper 11, 29, 31–4, 178; *estimating*
    32; *hanging* 33
walnut 18, 19
Warnock Report 99
washbasins 76, 86, 225, 228, 237
washing 70, 175; *clothes* 224, 242; *dishes*
    245; *hair* 243; *hand* 166; *instructions*
    169; *loads* 170; *machines* 166–9, 170;
    *powder* 167, 168, 170, 171–2, 184;
    *temperature* 168, 169
washing machines 76, 109, 144, 164,
    165, 166; *choosing* 168; *loads* 170;
    *powder* 171
washing up 71, 193
waste *bag* 204; *bin* 238; *basket* 194, 238;
    *water disposal* 228
water 170, 198, 204, 205, 212, 215, 220,
    226, 235, 241, 244, 245; *authority* 8;
    *board* 117, 224; *content* 147; *distilled*
    179; *drinking* 223; *hard* 171; *heater*
    224; *diet* 127; *inlet* 81; *marks* 185;
    *rates* 8, 14; *soft* 171; *softeners* 117,
    224; *storm* 228; *supply* 222; *waste
    disposal* 228
wattage 65, 66, 218, 249
white meter 47, 217, 218, 249
white spirit 180, 183, 185, 186
window(s) 77, 109, 191, 192, 193, 194,
    198, 201, 203, 204, 215, 237; *boxes*
    248; *care* 75; *insulation* 52; *sills* 248
wire(s) 215, 216; *cutters* 82; *earth* 217;
    *stripper* 83; *telephone* 221; *wool* 79
wiring 65, 195, 218; *survey* 7
wood(s) 73; *care* 75; *classes* 18; *fuel* 41;
    *insulating panels* 52; *pole* 35; *wall
    covering* 34
wool 14, 173; *blankets* 17; *carpets* 23, 25;
    *mineral* 51; *mineral fibre* 50; *stains* 182

yew 18, 19
youth clubs 102

zip fasteners 38, 175, 250